IMPOSSIBLE VICTORIES

IMPOSSIBLE VICTORIES

TEN UNLIKELY BATTLEFIELD SUCCESSES

BRYAN PERRETT

Pen & Sword
MILITARY

First published in 1996 by Arms and Armour, then by
Cassell Military Paperbacks in 2000 and reprinted in 2000, 2001, 2002

Republished in this format in 2015 by
PEN & SWORD MILITARY
An imprint of
Pen & Sword Books Ltd
47 Church Street, Barnsley
South Yorkshire
S70 2AS

By CPI Group (UK) Ltd, Croydon, CR0 4YY

Pen & Sword Books Ltd incorporates the Imprints of Pen & Sword Aviation,
Pen & Sword Family History, Pen & Sword Maritime, Pen & Sword Military,
Pen & Sword Discovery, Pen & Sword Politics, Pen & Sword Atlas,
Pen & Sword Archaeology, Wharncliffe Local History, Leo Cooper,
Wharncliffe True Crime, Wharncliffe Transport, Pen & Sword Select,
Pen & Sword Military Classics, The Praetorian Press, Claymore Press,
Remember When, Seaforth Publishing and Frontline Publishing

For a complete list of Pen & Sword titles please contact
PEN & SWORD BOOKS LIMITED
47 Church Street, Barnsley, South Yorkshire, S70 2AS, England
E-mail: enquiries@pen-and-sword.co.uk
Website: www.pen-and-sword.co.uk

Contents

Acknowledgements

I should like to express my sincere thanks to the following for their kind advice, assistance and encouragement, without which it would have been impossible for me to start, let alone finish, this book: Louise Arnold-Friend, Reference Historian, US Army Military History Institute, Carlisle, Pennsylvania; Lieutenant-Colonel John Bullen MSc, ARMIT, Weston Creek ACT, Australia; Major John Carroll, Curator, The Keep Military Museum, Dorchester; Mr T. J. Clement, Librarian, The Kippenberger Military Archive and Library, Waiouru, New Zealand; Lieutenant-Colonel P. A. Crocker, Curator, The Royal Welch Fusiliers Regimental Museum, Caernarfon Castle; Lieutenant-Colonel C. D. Darroch DL, Honorary Archivist, The Royal Hampshire Regiment Museum, Winchester; Mr S. A. Eastwood BA AMA, Curator, The Regimental Museum of the Border Regiment, Carlisle Castle; Colonel A. Fender TD DL, The Queen's Own Warwickshire and Worcestershire Yeomanry Charitable Trust; Brigadier A. I. H. Fyfe DL, The Light Infantry Office, Taunton; Mr Donald E. Graves of Almonte, Ontario, Canada; Captain Colin Harrison, Regimental Headquarters The Highlanders (Seaforth, Gordons and Camerons), Aberdeen; Mr Ian Hook, Keeper, The Essex Regiment Museum, Chelmsford; Mrs Penelope James, Curator, The Queen's Royal Surrey Regiment Museum, Guildford; Mr J. P. Kelleher, Chief Clerk and Archivist, City of London Headquarters, The Royal Regiment of Fusiliers, HM Tower of London; Colonel H. J. Lowles CBE, Curator, and Lieutenant-Colonel C. P. Love, Honorary Archivist, The Worcestershire Regiment Museum Trust; Mr William McKale, US Cavalry Museum, Fort Riley, Kansas; Mr John Montgomery, Librarian, Royal United Services Institute for Defence Studies; Major J. H. Peters MBE, Curator, and Major P. J. Ball, The Royal Gloucestershire, Berkshire and Wiltshire Regiment (Salisbury) Museum; Mr Kenneth Reedie MA AMA MILAM, Curator, The Royal Museum & Art Gallery, Canterbury; Major John C. Rogerson and Major C. J. D. Haswell, respectively Curator and Honorary Historian, The Princess of Wales's Royal Regiment and Queen's Regimental Museum, Dover Castle; Katie Talbot, Librarian, The Patton Museum of Cavalry & Armor, Fort Knox, Kentucky; Colonel J. P. Wetherall, Curator, The Museum of the Northamptonshire Regiment; Colonel D. E. Whatmore, Regiments of Gloucestershire Museum, Gloucester; and W. H. White, formerly Curator of The Regimental Museum of the Duke of Cornwall's Light Infantry, Bodmin.

Bryan Perrett

Introduction

In his book *At Duty's Call*, dealing with the motivation leading to the huge expansion of the British Army's strength in 1914, the late Dr W. J. Reader made the interesting point that while every town and village has its own war memorial dedicated to those who made the ultimate sacrifice in both World Wars, there were actually very few memorials erected to those who fell in earlier conflicts, and that most of these honoured well-known local figures. In one respect this is surprising, for throughout the nineteenth century the wars against Revolutionary and Napoleonic France, lasting over twenty years, were regarded as being the United Kingdom's greatest-ever military undertaking. In another, it is not, for while his officers were considered to be socially acceptable, the Victorian soldier and his predecessors were regarded as despised figures by the public at large. The apparently sudden change of heart, of course, was the consequence of men from every walk of life serving together during the World Wars in a truly national effort. Again, collective grief following the terrible loss of life produced an understandable desire to perpetuate the memory of those who had fallen. The dead of the First World War, in particular, became known as the Lost Generation, of whom it was said they were lions led by donkeys.

If there is one thing that the study of military history teaches us, it is that not all soldiers are lions and not all generals are donkeys. Nevertheless, in this study of the motivations which led to the snatching of victories from the jaws of apparently inevitable defeats, there are a surprisingly large number of incidents in which it was the troops who won their generals' battles for them.

At Albuera, the bloodiest battle of the Peninsular War, the Allied army was commanded by Wellington's deputy, Lieutenant-General Sir William Beresford, an excellent administrator and second-in-command, but an indifferent field commander. His opponent, Marshal Nicolas Soult, had him out-manoeuvred from the beginning and by all the rules should have won a stunning victory. In the end, he was driven off the field by a determined counter-attack in which several British regiments were all but destroyed. This was the more remarkable since the French were, as always, at their most formidable when victory lay just within their grasp. In the final analysis, it was the unbelievably stubborn refusal of the British infantry to give their hereditary enemies best that won the battle.

Three years later, during the War of 1812, two equally stubborn battles were fought between small British and American armies along the Niagara river. Until then, the Americans had not fared well against the British regulars. It took Brigadier-General Winfield Scott to knock such disciplined drill and musketry into his brigade that at Chippewa it was the British who withdrew from the field. Shortly after, at Lundy's Lane, the Americans, despite heavy losses, persisted in their attack and actually succeeded in capturing the British artillery. They had, however, fought themselves to within an inch of destruction and, believing that his troops could not withstand another counter-attack, their commander, Major-General Jacob Brown, relinquished all his gains. In the view of many, the modern United States Army has its roots more firmly embedded in Chippewa and Lundy's Lane than in earlier events.

During the Indian Mutiny the troops detailed to relieve the besieged Residency at Lucknow were required to fight their way deep into hostile territory where they were repeatedly opposed by a disciplined, well-equipped enemy who outnumbered them many times. Their chances of getting through were, to say the least, remote, yet they did so, not once, but twice, partly because they were fighting for their own survival, and partly because they were driven by a burning desire for revenge against a merciless foe who had savagely butchered their children and womenfolk.

In 1859 a flotilla of Royal Navy gunboats attempted to fight its way past the Taku Forts at the mouth of the Pei-ho river. Despite there being no lack of courage on the part of those involved, the affair was badly bungled and ended in a humiliating reverse. The following year a further expedition was mounted against the forts, which were to be assaulted from the landward side. In the meantime, the Chinese had considerably strengthened their defences with numerous obstacles but, such was the attackers' determination, reinforced by rivalry between the British and French contingents, that all were overcome and several Victoria Crosses were won as the walls were stormed.

There were few years when trouble was not brewing somewhere along the wild North-West Frontier of India, but in 1897 the entire province exploded in revolt. Large scale and protracted operations were required before order was restored. In many areas fighting was severe, but none more so than on the dominant Dargai Heights. Having been captured from the rebel tribesmen, they were then abandoned on the orders of higher authority. They were promptly re-occupied by the tribesmen and it became necessary to take them again. Several regiments tried and failed with heavy loss. It was then the turn of the 1st Gordon Highlanders, whose commanding officer, Lieutenant-Colonel H. H. Mathias, knew just how to get the last ounce of effort out of his men. Their assault, pressed home regardless of loss, carried all before it and provides a shining example of the Scottish soldier's formidability in the attack.

In 1898 the United States found itself at war with Spain over the issue of Cuban independence. The decisive battle of the war was fought at San Juan Ridge, near Santiago de Cuba. On the American side the sketchy planning for the battle was made without adequate reconnaissance and on the day of the battle itself the army commander and his deputy were both ill, leaving the troops to fend for themselves. The Americans sustained twice the casualties of their opponents and it was thanks entirely to inspired junior leadership that the latter were driven from a strong fortified position. The dramatic charge of Lieutenant-Colonel (later President) Theodore Roosevelt and his Rough Riders up Kettle Hill became an American legend.

By the spring of 1917 it had begun to look as though the Palestine Front was locked solid along the line Gaza–Beersheba. However, General Sir Edmund Allenby, a former Inspector General of Cavalry, believed that it might be possible to turn the Beersheba end of the line, using Lieutenant-General Harry Chauvel's Desert Mounted Corps. The operation required careful planning, since it would be carried out in semidesert, and Beersheba itself would have to be secured before the Turks could destroy the town's wells, without which it would be impossible to advance further. Turkish resistance was more protracted than had been anticipated but was ultimately broken by the epic charge of the Australian 4th Light Horse Brigade, which swept over the enemy trenches and into the town before the Turks' demolition parties could do their work. A week later the 5th Mounted Brigade, a yeomanry formation, made an equally epic charge which destroyed the Turks' hope of making a stand at Huj, to the north. Together, these two actions foreshadowed Allenby's great victory at Megiddo the following year, the last occasion in history when cavalry proved to be the decisive arm on a major battlefield.

To some extent, the US Army's decision to form Ranger battalions, based on the British Commando model, was marred by field commanders using these highly trained specialist troops as conventional line infantry, with tragic consequences. However, on D-Day the Rangers were set an objective which accorded with their training – the elimination of a coast defence battery located above the towering cliffs of the Pointe du Hoe, capable of firing directly onto either Utah or Omaha Beaches. From the outset almost everything went wrong but in spite of every difficulty the Rangers stormed the cliffs and destroyed the guns, which they discovered had been moved inland from their original position.

Hill 112 was the most bitterly contested piece of ground in Normandy. Like Dargai Heights, it was captured and then abandoned, albeit for sound tactical reasons. It was then partially captured by the 43rd (Wessex) Division, the battalions of which became locked into a mutually destructive battle with several Waffen SS formations, little quarter being given or received by either side. Perhaps more than any other event during the campaign, the struggle for Hill 112 fulfilled Montgomery's intention of focusing German attention on the British sector of the Normandy beachhead while the Americans prepared for their decisive breakout to the south.

One of the communists' ambitions in South Vietnam was to trap and destroy a major American unit, not simply because of the physical loss it would cause, but, more importantly, because of the effect it would have on public opinion within the United States. A prominent feature would be occupied and when the Americans probed the defences they would be ambushed and cut off. The much larger force sent to their relief was the communists' real target, and it was this they sought to destroy. This was the scenario in which the crack 173rd Airborne Brigade found itself heavily engaged at Ngok Kom Leat and on Hill 875, The result was a bloody contest of wills which ended with the Americans not only breaking the enemy's grip but also driving the communists out of their own carefully prepared positions.

The reader will wish to draw his own conclusions regarding the motivations evident in each chapter. He will probably agree that the one factor present in all was the will to win, at all costs.

CHAPTER ONE

'That Astonishing Infantry' – The Albuera Counter-Attack, 16 May 1811

It was Napoleon himself who referred to the Peninsular War as the 'Spanish ulcer' which, for the seven years between 1807 and 1814 constantly gnawed away at the strength of his Grande Armée and absorbed thousands of French troops which he could have put to more productive use elsewhere in Europe. Recognising that Great Britain was the most implacable of his enemies, his initial intention had simply been to tighten up the Continental System by which, since 1793, France had attempted to deny mainland Europe to British trade. Because of wholesale smuggling the system leaked like a sieve, to the extent in fact, that at any one time a large part of the Grand Armée was said to march on boots manufactured in Northampton. Smuggling, however, was one thing, flagrantly flouting the system quite another. Portugal provided an open market for British goods, which were then shipped onwards to the rest of Europe, and in Napoleon's judgement Portugal must be taught a sharp lesson. In November 1807 a French army under General Andoche Junot invaded Portugal from Spain and occupied Lisbon. The Portuguese royal family escaped to Brazil, then a colony, leaving behind a Council of Regency which requested British assistance. This was promised the following year.

In March 1808 Napoleon allowed an attack of hubris to cloud his judgement. Marshal Joachim Murat was sent into Spain at the head of a large army and, having taken King Charles IV and his son prisoner, installed the emperor's brother Joseph on the Spanish throne, where he was to be kept by French bayonets. To Napoleon's surprise, the Spanish people would have none of it; corrupt and ineffective as their own monarchy was, it was preferable to the rule of foreigners, and the French occupation was a bitter blow to their pride. Risings took place in May, quickly spreading across the entire country. In July General Pierre Dupont's army was forced to capitulate at Baylen, many of its members being subsequently massacred. The following month the promised British assistance, an expeditionary force commanded by the then Sir Arthur Wellesley, later the Duke of Wellington, reached Portugal, defeating Junot at Roliça on 17 August and again at Vimeiro four days later. Following this, a convention was signed under the terms of which Junot's army was transported home in British ships.

Both sides, the British, Portuguese and Spanish on the one hand and the French with such Bonapartist support as they could muster locally, progressively escalated the scale of operations in the Iberian Peninsula. After its success at Baylen the Spanish regular army, badly led, under-equipped and ill-supplied, was of dubious value to its allies. Sometimes the half-starved Spaniards would desert to the enemy for the sake of a square meal, sometimes they would happily leave all the fighting to the British and Portuguese, sometimes they would give way at the first shock, and sometimes they would fight with exemplary courage. There was no way of telling in advance how they would perform; the prickly sensitivity of their officers, on the other hand, could be relied upon when it came to matters concerning the 'punto de honor', that is, questions of personal standing, prestige and honour. After a series of unfortunate experiences Wellington learned to place no reliance on them whatever, giving full vent to his feelings in a letter to Lord Liverpool when the latter suggested a joint amphibious raiding venture into the Bay of Biscay:

'It is vain to hope for any assistance, much less military assistance, from the Spaniards; the first thing they would require uniformly would be money; then arms, ammunition, clothing of all descriptions, provisions, forage, horses, means of transport and everything which the expedition would have a right to require from *them*; and, after all, this extraordinary and perverse people would scarcely allow the commander of the expedition to have a voice in the plan of operations ... if indeed they should ever be ready.'[1]

The real value of the Spaniards lay in their guerrilla bands, who conducted a savage war of atrocity and reprisal with the French, causing the latter to deploy thousands of troops to protect their lines of communication.

The Portuguese Army was in little better state when the British arrived. Its organisation, pay and conditions of service were, however, quickly reformed from top to bottom under British guidance and it became a formidable force upon which Wellington could rely implicitly, despite the fact that at any one time there were never more than 200 British officers serving as advisers in its ranks.

The British element of Wellington's armies was composed entirely of regular troops. The majority of the officer corps consisted of the sons of retired or serving officers or members of the yeoman or the rising business and professional classes, who had obtained their commissions either by purchase or through the recommendation of a well-connected patron. A small number had been granted commissions because of distinguished conduct on the battlefield, and an even smaller number were gentlemen volunteers who, lacking funds or influence, elected to serve in the ranks in the hope that their own merits would gain them a place when casualties created vacancies.

The origins of the rank and file were equally varied. Within any regiment the best men were the handful who had joined because they had a genuine interest in the life, and the reinforcement drafts of militiamen who had volunteered for service abroad. Then came those who, after a bout of heavy drinking with the recruiting sergeants, had surfaced to find themselves in possession of the King's Shilling, those whom hard times had forced to enlist, those seeking escape from some problem in civilian life, and those to whom the magistrates had offered enlistment as an alternative to imprisonment. When necessary, discipline was enforced with the noose and the lash – although commanders were unwise to use either too freely – not simply because of the number of bad characters that could be found in the ranks, but because it had to be rigidly maintained in an era when battles were fought out at a range when every detail of the enemy's uniform was clearly visible, when the fighting was terrifyingly personal and the wounds inflicted always horrific. The greatest threat to British discipline was drink, which the troops would always resort to whenever it was available, especially after a particularly harrowing ordeal such as the storming of a bitterly defended fortress, when they would, despite the draconian punishments available, remain beyond the control of their officers for days at a time and commit every crime in the criminal calendar. Such occasions were comparatively rare, and it was to them that Wellington referred when he described his troops as 'the scum of the earth!' Yet, whatever their faults, there could be no denying their fierce loyalty to their regiments, their supreme confidence that they could beat the stuffing out of Johnny Crapaud on any day of the week, or their incredible stubbornness, endurance and willingness to undergo terrible privations on Wellington's behalf. It would be wrong to suggest that they held their patrician commander-in-chief in anything like affection, but they respected him, had every confidence in his abilities and were unsettled when he was not about.

The motivation of their French enemies was, perhaps, more obvious. Although generally recruited by conscription, they were mainly the sons of pre-revolutionary peasants who believed that what had been so bloodily achieved to make France a better place was worth fighting for, and they worshipped the Emperor, who had made the name of France feared and respected throughout Europe. Their discipline was less formal than that of

13

the British, but nonetheless adequate. They would respond with wild zeal to heroic rhetoric that would leave their stolid Anglo-Saxon foes totally unmoved. Generally, they preferred to attack in column behind a screen of skirmishers. Assaults such as these, delivered with weight, speed and élan, had time and again routed the armies of Austria, Prussia and Russia, demonstrating the old truth that the French were never more formidable than when they were winning. In the Peninsula, however, such tactics usually failed against the British, whose own highly trained light infantry kept the French skirmishers at bay while their main line, drawn up behind a crest in two-deep linear formation, then used its superior firepower to shoot away the head of the column when it appeared, following up with a limited bayonet charge that drove the disordered ranks down the forward slope. In the handling of their cavalry, however, the French were frequently more expert than the British and a mistake in their presence could spell disaster.

In some respects the Peninsular War can be compared to the Desert War in North Africa 1940–1943. Wellington's army took on a distinctive personality of its own and the names of its senior officers became familiar to those at home. The fighting, too, acquired a similar sort of rhythm, with Wellington advancing into Spain each campaigning season, then retiring to the Portuguese frontier or beyond to protect his bases until, finally, in 1814, the French were driven across the Pyrenees and into France itself. Despite the ferocity of the battles fought, and the activities of the Spanish guerrillas, on most occasions the armies behaved chivalrously towards each other and, as far as was possible given the primitive medical facilities of the day, looked after the enemy's wounded; there was also regular informal contact between the outposts, during which news was exchanged and bartering for food, drink and tobacco took place.

At the conclusion of the 1810 campaign Wellington, heavily outnumbered, withdrew within the impregnable Lines of Torres Vedras, constructed across the peninsula between the estuary of the Tagus and the Atlantic. The country outside the Lines had previously been stripped bare of supplies so that in November the French, commanded by Marshal André Masséna, were forced to retire to the frontier after spending a month in a state of semi-starvation. Wellington built up his strength throughout the winter and in the spring of 1811 returned to the offensive, setting the frontier fortresses of Ciudad Rodrigo and Badajoz as his primary objectives. Splitting his army, he advanced on Ciudad Rodrigo with the main portion, sending a strong detachment under General Sir William Beresford to besiege Badajoz, which had been surrendered by its Spanish garrison in March.

Beresford, tall, lacking one eye, courageous and possessed of great physical strength, was then aged 43 and had seen active service in many areas
of the world, including India, Egypt, South Africa and South America. A
fine administrator and trainer of troops, it was he who had been largely
responsible for the reform of the Portuguese Army, in which he held the
rank of marshal. Despite the fact that his abilities as a field commander
were limited, Wellington thought highly of him, indicating that if he
should ever be incapacitated Beresford was to assume command.

Beresford reached Badajoz on 4 May but he was ill-equipped to conduct
a siege and unable to mount much more than a blockade. A day or so later
he was informed that Wellington had won a very narrow victory over
Masséna at Fuentes de Oñoro. On the 13th he received intelligence that
Marshal Nicolas Soult, who had been putting down a rising in Andalusia,
was marching rapidly to the relief of Badajoz with a 25,000-strong army[2].
He therefore decided to raise the siege and, having effected a junction with
a Spanish force under General Joachim Blake, concentrated at Albuera,
which Soult would be approaching along the road from Seville.

Albuera (spelled Albuhera in some accounts and as a battle honour) was,
and remains, the same sort of dusty little town as that upon which The
Man With No Name had such a dramatic impact in the film *A Fistful of
Dollars*. Perhaps the best description of it in 1811 is that given by Captain
Moyle Sherer of the 34th (later The Border) Regiment, in his book
Recollections of the Peninsula, published fourteen years after the event:

'It is a small and inconsiderable village, uninhabited and in ruins: it is
situated on a stream from which it takes its name, and over which are two
bridges; one about two hundred yards to the right of the village, large,
handsome, and built of hewn stone; the other, close to the left of it, small,
narrow, and incommodious. This brook is not above knee-deep: its banks,
to the left of the bridge, are abrupt and uneven; and, on that side, both
artillery and cavalry would find it difficult to pass, if not impossible; but
to the right of the main bridge it is accessible to any description of force.
The enemy occupied a very large extensive wood, about three-quarters of
a mile distant, on the other side of the stream, and posted their picquets
close to us. The space between the wood and the brook was a level plain;
but on our side the ground rose considerably, though there was nothing
that could be called a height, as from Albuera to Valverde every inch of
ground is favourable to the operations of cavalry – not a tree, not a ravine
to interrupt their movements.'

In total, Beresford had a little over 35,000 men available on the morning of 16 May. Of these, 10,400 were British, 10,200 Portuguese and 14,600
Spanish. Imagining that Soult would mount a frontal attack, he had

already begun forming his line along the rising ground parallel to the Albuera the previous afternoon. This feature, though subsequently referred to as The Ridge, was nowhere higher than 150 feet above the river. Behind and parallel to it was a shallow valley through which ran a small stream, the Arroyo de Vale de Sevitta.

The right of the line was held by six Spanish brigades which had moved into position after dark. Behind Albuera village was Major-General the Honourable William Stewart's British 2nd Division, with Count von Alten's brigade of the King's German Legion, consisting mainly of Hanoverian exiles, in the village itself. Prolonging the line to the left was Hamilton's Portuguese division, three brigades strong. Beresford's cavalry, commanded by Major-General the Honourable Sir William Lumley, having maintained contact with the French throughout the day, withdrew across the Albuera and, leaving a screen along the river bank, went into reserve behind the centre. Major-General Sir Lowry Cole's British 4th Division, having remained at Badajoz to maintain the illusion of a siege until relieved by Spanish troops, was marching towards Albuera and would also go into reserve when it arrived the following morning.

There would have been nothing wrong with Beresford's dispositions had the ensuing battle, frequently described as the most murderous and sanguinary of the entire Peninsular War, developed as he had anticipated. However, his opponent, Nicolas Jean-de-Dieu Soult, Duke of Dalmatia, was not only regarded by many as the ablest of France's marshals, but had also been described by Napoleon himself as the ablest tactician in the Empire. As his troops approached Albuera during the afternoon and evening of the 15th, he kept most of them concealed within the woodland on the west bank of the river while he carried out a thorough personal reconnaissance of the Allied dispositions. It did not take him long to establish that Beresford had the larger army, and that while the latter's deployment was entirely conventional, a frontal assault against the low ridge, involving as it did a river crossing and an advance up what would become a long, bullet-swept glacis, was likely to prove an extremely expensive business. He therefore decided to deal with the Allied army by feinting at its centre and using a concealed approach march to bring his main body onto its flank. This would give him overwhelming numerical superiority at the point of contact and would result in Beresford's line being rolled up. The destruction of the Allied army would be completed by the unleashing of the French cavalry, commanded by the redoubtable Lieutenant-General Marie Latour-Maubourg, into the shallow valley behind The Ridge. The strategic consequences arising from Beresford's elimination would extend far beyond the relief of Badajoz; Wellington, still confronted by Masséna, would be forced to look to his own safety and conduct a premature withdrawal into Portugal, thereby causing British prestige throughout Spain to tumble. In fact, the consequences would have extended even further than Soult imagined, for there were those in Parliament who objected very strongly to the prodigious cost of the war and had thus far only been silenced by Wellington's succession of victories; a major reverse, therefore, would play into their hands and might even lead to the withdrawal of British troops from the Peninsula.

The battle began at about 09:00 on 16 May when a French brigade, supported by artillery and with cavalry on its flanks, emerged from the woods and began advancing in column along the Seville-Badajoz road towards the main bridge at Albuera. Commanded by Brigadier-General Godinot, this was Soult's diversion force, and to reinforce the illusion that it was the main attack it was followed at a distance by a second brigade under Brigadier-General Werlé. In the meantime, the main body of the French, consisting of Girard's and Gazan's infantry divisions and Latour-Maubourg's cavalry, was forming up under the trees and preparing to ford the Albuera at a point approximately two miles south of the bridge.

Now under fire from the British artillery on The Ridge, Godinot pressed forward and was soon heavily engaged with Alten's Germans in the village. Upstream of the bridge a unit of Polish lancers forded the stream but were counter-charged and driven back by the 3rd Dragoon Guards; downstream, where crossing was more difficult, hussar squadrons galloped flashily into position opposite the Portuguese cavalry but did not press their attack.

Two things now happened to warn Beresford as to the danger in which he stood. Major General Zayas, on the right of the Spanish line, was suddenly alerted by the glitter of massed bayonets emerging from the wood and crossing the stream to the south. Acting on his own initiative, he moved his four battalions to the right, occupying a prominent hummock at a point where The Ridge broadened out, thereby creating the first flimsy defence of the Allied right flank.

Simultaneously, from his elevated position above Albuera, Beresford noticed that Werlé, far from giving Godinot the close support that would have been necessary had the latter been leading the main attack, had merely sent forward a grenadier battalion and some cavalry and was now marching purposefully south. This, coupled with Zayas' sudden redeployment, provided the necessary warning that his right was about to be attacked in strength and that he must, therefore, change front through 90 degrees as a matter of extreme urgency or be overwhelmed. Aides were sent galloping to his major formation commanders with fresh orders:

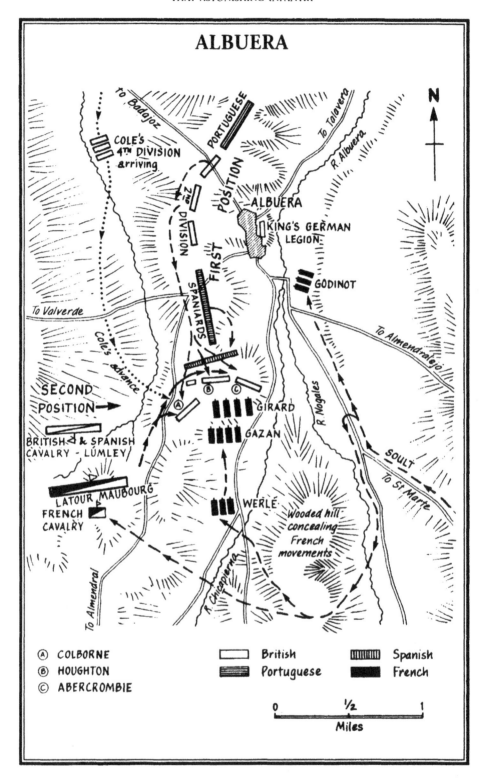

ALBUERA

COLE'S 4TH DIVISION arriving

PORTUGUESE

To Badajoz

To Talavera

R. Albuera

N

2ND DIVISION

FIRST POSITION

ALBUERA

KING'S GERMAN LEGION

To Valverde

Cole's advance

SPANIARDS

GODINOT

To Almendralejo

SECOND POSITION →

Ⓐ

Ⓑ

Ⓒ

R. Nogales

GIRARD

GAZAN

SOULT

To St Marte

BRITISH & SPANISH CAVALRY – LUMLEY

LATOUR MAUBOURG FRENCH CAVALRY

WERLE

Wooded hill concealing French movements

To Almendral

R. Chicapierna

Ⓐ COLBORNE
Ⓑ HOUGHTON
Ⓒ ABERCROMBIE

British
Portuguese

Spanish
French

0   ½   1

Miles

Blake's Spaniards were to conform to the movement already initiated by Zayas; Stewart's 2nd Division was to come up in support of the Spaniards; Hamilton's Portuguese division was to move into the position vacated by Stewart above Albuera village; and Lumley's cavalry was to protect the new Allied right flank, which now rested on the shallow valley behind The Ridge.

The plan came close to collapse almost at once. The Spaniards, as already related, had joined Beresford after dark and when dawn revealed that part of their line was in front of that of the 2nd Division, masking the latter's anticipated field of fire, they were instructed to take ground to their right. Blake was evidently still huffy about this when Beresford's ADC arrived with orders for a further redeployment, for he flatly refused to move, insisting that the French were making their real attack on the village. The truth of the matter had now become obvious, for Zayas was already in action against the columns of infantry, cavalry and artillery which, having forded the stream, had now begun to climb The Ridge. Nevertheless, even after the army commander had arrived in person to stress the urgency of the situation, Blake reacted so slowly and with such bad grace that Beresford took personal command and led the troops into position.

To everyone's surprise the Spaniards, knowing what depended upon them, fought with astonishing courage. Confronted as they were with the major part of Soult's V Corps, behind which Latour-Maubourg's cavalry were already streaming towards the head of the little valley, they succeeded in halting the French advance with their volleys despite the hail of musketry and artillery fire that was thinning their ranks minute by minute. Impressed as he was, Beresford, who had positioned himself behind them, could also see that they could not withstand such odds for long. It had now begun to rain heavily, further restricting visibility already reduced by the drifting fog of powder smoke, but with relief Beresford observed the leading element of Stewart's division, Lieutenant-Colonel Colborne's brigade, doubling forward in column of companies from Albuera village, where it had spent the first part of the morning, accompanied by an artillery battery of the King's German Legion.

Stewart was a brave and extremely popular officer, known to his men as 'Auld Grog Willie' because he was in the habit of issuing them with extra rum, for which Wellington always made him pay. Napier, who was present at the battle, comments that he was a man 'whose boiling courage overlaid his judgement.' Until his recent appointment as divisional commander he had commanded the brigade, with Colborne as his senior commanding officer; now, unfortunately, he could not resist the urge to interfere. His orders at this stage were simply to support the Spaniards, but he decided to ignore them and mount a counter-attack instead. Had Blake's troops been on the point of breaking, such a course of action might have been justified; as matters stood, they were not, although they were becoming worried by their casualties and the heavy odds to their front and were giving ground slowly.

Colborne's brigade was coming up in echelon with the 1/3rd (later The Buffs (Royal East Kent)) Regiment leading on the right, then the 2/48th (later 2nd Northamptonshire) Regiment, then the 2/66th (later Royal Berkshire) Regiment, and the 2/31st (later East Surrey) Regiment bringing up the left rear. As the brigade began to climb the hill cannon shot intended for the Spaniards but aimed too high began to whimper overhead or plough through the ranks. On approaching the crest Colborne suggested that the Buffs should either remain in column or form square to protect the brigade's right flank against cavalry attack. Stewart brushed the suggestion aside and gave orders for the four battalions to deploy into line; fortunately for the 2/31st, these did not reach them.

In succession, the Buffs, the 2/48th and 2/66th crossed the crest, the left wing of the last brushing through the right-hand files of the Spaniards. The brigade now found itself positioned obliquely on the flank of the French assault column at ranges between 60 and 100 yards. The French reacted by turning their three left-hand files towards the threat and, with the front rank kneeling, opened a spluttering fire down the length of the column. Colborne's three battalions replied with two precise volleys that sent some of the French tumbling but did not appear to affect their resolve. Stewart therefore ordered the brigade to attack with the bayonet. As the long scarlet lines began to move forward behind their deadly glittering hedges of steel, the rain became a blinding hailstorm that reduced visibility to a few yards, heralding one the greatest tragedies in the British Army's entire history.

At the head of the little valley behind the Ridge, Latour-Maubourg's cavalry found themselves confronted by Lumley's dragoons and both sides reined in to watch the other warily. Latour-Maubourg was also watching the developments on the hill to his right and, observing the attack of Colborne's brigade, took full advantage of the mistake to launch his right-hand brigade into the right-rear of the unsuspecting British infantry, the move being screened from Lumley's view by the hailstorm.

For a few moments, however, it looked as though Stewart's decision to counter-attack had been correct. The French infantry, always reluctant to face the bayonet, could be seen edging away while their officers vainly beat them with the flats of their swords to keep them in line. First to break was the 28th Légère, followed by three grenadier battalions that were driven down the slope towards the river. Colborne's brigade were within striking distance of the French supporting artillery, from which they had already begun to take casualties, when, from the right, there came a high, ringing trumpet call followed by frantic shouts of 'Cavalry!'

Suddenly, a galloping mass of horsemen, consisting of the 1st Polish Lancers and the French 2nd and 10th Hussars, some twelve hundred men in all, burst through the driving hail and smoke to the right-rear of the Buffs[3]. The three British battalions promptly faced about but did not open fire because of warning cries that the cavalry was Spanish. Before the mistake could be rectified the infantry ranks had been ridden over and fragmented into small groups of men fighting back to back against their slashing, stabbing opponents.

Having broken the brigade's formation, those Poles and the Frenchmen not engaged in cutting down the survivors vied with each other for the honour of capturing the British colours. The Buffs' colour party was quickly surrounded by a surging mass of horsemen. The colour sergeants were quickly cut down but the brief moments they gained enabled the two ensigns to escape from the press. Ensign Edward Thomas, barely sixteen years old, found temporary refuge amid the remnants of a company the commander of which had been wounded and taken prisoner. His shouts of 'Rally on me, men – I will be your pivot!' brought the remaining handful to the defence of the colour but within minutes all save two had been speared or sabred. A lancer seized the colour staff, yelling at Thomas to give it up. 'Only with my life!' he shouted, and was promptly dealt a mortal wound before the Pole galloped off with his trophy; as we shall see, he evidently did not retain it for long.

Ensign Charles Walsh was similarly seeking protection for the King's colour, the staff of which had already been broken by a cannon shot. Hemmed in by the enemy, he was wounded and would undoubtedly have been killed or captured had not Lieutenant Matthew Latham rushed and snatched the colour from him. He was in turn surrounded and set upon but fought back vigorously until a hussar's sabre slashed off his nose and part of his cheek. Despite his undoubted agony he fought on until a second sabre stroke left his sword arm hanging by a thread[4]. Still he clung to the colour with his left hand while his enemies closed in, barging each other out of the way in their eagerness to seize the prize. At length Latham, trampled and speared repeatedly, was thrown off his feet, grimly retaining his hold on the precious silk. Then, quite suddenly, there was a ringing cheer, followed by the thud of colliding bodies and the clash of steel on steel as his adversaries were swept away. His consciousness failing, he used the last of his strength to tear the colour from its staff and stuff it into his jacket.

By now the hailstorm had passed, enabling Lumley to see what was happening to the stricken brigade. He immediately despatched the 4th Dragoons (later 4th Hussars) to its relief and their counter-charge succeeded in temporarily easing the situation and even gaining a little ground, although, heavily outnumbered as they were, they were soon driven back with the loss of 29 killed. As it was, they had probably saved a larger number of lives among the infantry by enabling some of them to escape. Napier records that some Spanish cavalry under the Count de Penne Villamur was also detailed for the counter-charge but, having pulled up within a few yards of the enemy, they turned and fled.

As with the Buffs, so with 2/48th and 2/66th. Both battalions were ridden over and lost their colours in the brief, savage mêlée. The horror of what took place was subsequently recalled by Colonel Clarke of the 2/66th:

'A crowd of Polish lancers and chasseurs à cheval (sic) swept along the rear of our brigade; our men now ran into groups of six or eight to do as best they could; the officers snatched up muskets and joined them, determined to sell their lives dearly. Quarter was not asked, and rarely given. Poor Colonel Waller, of the Quartermaster-General's staff, was cut down close to me; he put up his hands asking for quarter, but the ruffian cut his fingers off. My ensign, Hay, was run through the lungs by a lance which came out of his back; he fell but got up again. The lancer delivered another thrust, the lance striking Hay's breast-bone; down he went and the Pole rolled over in the mud beside him. In the evening I went to seek my friend, and found him sitting up to his hips in mud and water. He was quite cool and collected, and said there were many worse than him. The lancers had been promised a doubloon each if they could break the British line. In the mêlée, when mixed up with the lancers, the chasseurs à cheval and the French infantry, I came into collision with a lancer, and being knocked over was taken prisoner; an officer ordered me to be conducted to the rear. Presently a charge was made by our dragoon guards, in which I liberated myself and ran to join the Fusilier Brigade at the foot of the hill.'

In less time than it has taken to read, three-quarters of Colborne's brigade had been annihilated; in fact, a mere seven minutes had elapsed since the three battalions had fired their first volleys. Now, their dead and seriously wounded strewed the slopes, the few shocked survivors were heading for the rear, and in the distance some of the lancers could be seen savagely prodding their prisoners towards captivity; so savagely that several French officers intervened forcefully to ensure the men, many of whom were wounded, received more humane treatment. In addition, the King's German Legion battery which had accompanied the brigade had also been overrun and its gunners cut down around their weapons.

The brigade's fourth battalion, the 2/31st, fared rather better. Being on the extreme left of the formation and some distance to the rear, it received just sufficient warning to prepare itself for the onset of the French cavalry. It was, moreover, an extremely well-drilled battalion and its commanding officer, Major L'Estrange, had devised a manoeuvre by which it could be got into square very quickly. This was no doubt assisted by the fact that the unit was already moving at the double in company columns at half distance[5]. Therefore, when the lancers and hussars came bearing down they were suddenly presented with a four-deep oblong of bristling bayonets, the nearest face of which belched smoke and flame that emptied saddles and sent horses crashing. Parting, the cavalry galloped past the square, taking further casualties from its other faces, and went in search of easier prey.

This was offered by Beresford and his staff, and by the Spaniards. Beresford managed to grab the shaft of a lance thrust at him then, seizing its owner by the throat, used his great strength to fling him to the ground. The staff, drawing their swords, closed round and cut their way out. The Spaniards, no longer under such intense pressure to their front, had also got themselves into some sort of order and avoided being ridden over. Nevertheless, the cavalry attack seems to have drained the last of their resources and they began to retire down the slope, their units surrounded by circling lancers and hussars, eager to close in for the kill. Just for the moment, the only unit remaining on this, the most critical sector of the Allied line, was the 2/31st's little square, only 418 men strong.

The situation now was that, on the French side, Girard's division was pulling itself together after its repulse by Colborne's brigade, its losses being more than compensated for by Werlé's arrival, and Soult was pushing Gazan's division into the lead with orders to resume the attack at once. On the Allied side, Stewart had galloped back to bring up his two remaining brigades, Houghton's and Abercrombie's. During this short pause, in which the French cavalry were still milling about the retreating Spaniards, both sides were therefore engaged in a race for possession of the crest.

Houghton's brigade, with the 29th (later the Worcestershire) Regiment on the right, the 57th (later the Middlesex) Regiment in the centre and the 1/48th (later 1st Northamptonshire) Regiment on the left, was leading. The 29th had been in the Peninsula since the war began and were one of Wellington's favourite regiments. Moyle Sherer has left us a picture of them and, given the usual rivalry between British regiments, his comments are nothing if not sincere:

'Nothing could possibly be worse than their clothing; it had become necessary to patch it; and, as red cloth could not be procured, grey, white and even brown had been used, yet, even under this striking disadvantage, they could not be viewed by a soldier without admiration. The perfect order and cleanliness of their arms and appointments, their steadiness on parade, their erect carriage and their firm marching exceeded anything I had ever seen. No corps of any army or nation which I have since had an opportunity of seeing, has come nearer to my idea of what a regiment of infantry should be than the old Twenty-Ninth.' Sherer's use of the word 'old' a decade after the event is especially poignant for the 29th, like every other British infantry regiment that fought at Albuera, was to end the day as a mere ghost of its former self.

Deploying into line for the final approach to the summit, the brigade suddenly found itself in danger of being swamped by a flood of retreating Spanish units intermingled with French cavalry. The Spaniards were shouting to be allowed through, but that would have meant creating gaps that would also have been penetrated by the enemy and, in any event, the line would almost certainly have been swept away. Houghton was therefore compelled to reach the hard decision of having to order the 29th and 57th to fire several volleys into the approaching mass, taking as much care as was possible to avoid the Spaniards. This seemed to work, for the French, recognising that there was little more to be achieved, turned away and cantered back to their own lines. Only then were the ranks opened, permitting the Spaniards to stream to the rear.

Reformed, the brigade advanced to the crest with the 2/31st conforming on its right, each battalion being played into action by its fifes and drums.

'Now is the time – let us give three cheers!' shouted Stewart, riding beside them. The men responded with a will. French skirmishers were already contesting the advance, dropping a man here and there, but Houghton forbade further firing until the line had breasted the summit. There, through gaps in the drifting smoke, could be seen the leading ranks of the enemy's huge assault column, coming on strongly and no more than 50 yards distant.

'There followed,' wrote Sir John Fortescue in his monumental *History of the British Army*, 'A duel so stern and resolute that it has few parallels in the annals of war. The survivors who took part in it on the British side seem to have passed through it as if in a dream, conscious of nothing but dense smoke, constant closing towards the centre, a slight tendency to advance, and an invincible resolution not to retire. The men stood like rocks, loading and firing into the mass in front of them, though frightfully punished not so much by the French bullets as by the French cannon at very close range. The line dwindled and dwindled continually; and the intervals between battalions grew wide as the men, who were still on their legs, edged closer and closer to their colours: but not one dreamed for a moment of anything but standing and fighting to the last. The fiercest of the stress fell upon Houghton's brigade, wherein it seems that every mounted officer fell ... captains, lieutenants and ensigns, sergeants and rank-and-file all fell equally fast. Nearly four-fifths of Houghton's brigade were down and its front had shrunk to the level of that of the French; but still it remained unbeaten, advanced to within twenty yards of the enemy and fired unceasingly.'

Stewart was hit twice. Houghton, riding along the line and encouraging his men, received several minor wounds and then fell dead with three musket balls in his body. In the 29th, Lieutenant-Colonel Daniel White was mortally wounded. His second-in-command, Major Gregory Way, took over but after a little while reeled from his horse with bridle arm shattered. The battalion colour parties also formed a natural aiming point for the enemy so that the colours themselves quickly became riddled. Two of the 29th's three colour sergeants were already down when seventeen-year-old Ensign Edward Furnace, carrying the King's colour, staggered under the impact of a mortal wound. Seeing his predicament, a subaltern from an adjacent company offered to relieve him of the burden. Furnace refused, remaining upright with the support of the last colour sergeant until the latter, too, was hit. Beside them, the Regimental colour fell as Ensign Richard Vance was struck down; somehow, before he died, Vance managed to pull the tattered silk from its pole and push it inside his coat. Shortly after, Furnace received a second wound and collapsed, his colour falling across his body. None came to raise it, for the attention of all had degenerated into a robotic rhythm of loading and firing that excluded every other consideration.

It was a similar story in the 57th. By virtue of seniority, the battalion's commanding officer, Lieutenant-Colonel William Inglis, had assumed command of the brigade when Houghton was hit. A seasoned campaigner who had fought in the American War of Independence, in Flanders, the West Indies and in the Peninsula since 1809, Inglis recognised that this rate of attrition could not be maintained for much longer. In his ride along the ranks he had reached a point close to his own battalion when his horse was killed under him and he was simultaneously felled by a four-ounce grapeshot in the neck[6]. Believing the wound to be mortal, he propped himself on one elbow and fiercely exhorted his men:

'Die hard, Fifty-Seventh! Die hard!'

They evidently also believed that their commander was dying, for their fire now took on a redoubled ferocity, and from that moment onwards until the regiment's independent history ended a century and a half later it was known as the Diehards. It was in this spirit that one of its company commanders, Captain Ralph Fawcett, at 23 already a veteran of several battles, refused to be carried to the rear when he received a mortal wound; instead, he asked to be placed on a little hillock just behind the line from which he continued to exercise command, instructing his men to aim low and not to waste their ammunition. The King's colour, ripped by seventeen bullets and its staff broken, was carried by Ensign Jackson who, having been hit for the third time, handed it over to Ensign Veitch while he went to have his wounds dressed; on his return Veitch refused to hand it back and was himself severely wounded shortly after. The bearer of the Regimental colour seemed to bear a charmed life, despite the fact that 21 bullets had passed through the silk. Subsequently, Beresford noted in his despatch that the 57th's dead were 'lying as they had fought in ranks, and with every wound in front.'

On the brigade's left Lieutenant-Colonel Duckworth of the 1/48th was shot dead leading his battalion into action, while to its right the ranks of the 2/31st, which had hitherto escaped serious loss, were being as mercilessly culled as any. Amid the drifting smoke and drizzle, men lost all sense of time. The slight tendency to advance noted by Fortescue was caused by moving forward a pace or two every so often so as not to be encumbered by casualties, and was matched by the French giving a little ground.

By now, however, Abercrombie's brigade was coming into line on the left, at an oblique angle to the flank of the French column, with the 2/28th (later the Gloucestershire) Regiment on the right, the 2/39th (later the Dorsetshire) Regiment in the centre and the 2/34th (later the Border) Regiment on the left. While it was doubling forward, the disorganised Spaniards had come streaming back between the company columns. A decade later Sherer recalled:

'I remember well, shot and shell flew over in quick succession; we sustained little injury from either, but a captain of the 29th had been dreadfully lacerated by a ball and lay directly in our path. We passed close to him, and the heart-rending tone in which he called to us for water, or to kill him, I shall never forget. He lay alone, and we were in motion and could give him no succour; for on this trying day, such of the wounded as could not walk lay unattended where they fell: – all was hurry and struggle; every arm was wanted in the field ... A very noble-looking young Spanish officer rode up to me, and begged me, with a sort of proud and brave anxiety, to explain to the English that his countrymen were ordered to retire, but were not flying.'

A number of accounts make the point that at this stage there were 3,000 British muskets opposed to 8,000 French during the sanguinary struggle for the crest, but this requires some clarification. Together, Houghton's brigade and the 2/31st had gone into action with about 2,000 men, but their ranks had already been torn apart by the time that Abercrombie's brigade, with 1,500 men, came into the line. The probability, therefore, is that there were never as many as 3,000 of Stewart's men in the line at any one time. On the other hand, it is known that some of the Spaniards, a little shamefaced like the young officer referred to by Sherer, did return to the firing line, although the numbers involved were comparatively small. Again, the French, being in column, could not deploy anything like 8,000 muskets, but as their frontage was approximately equal to that of the British it is probably fair to say that they had between 2,500 and 3,000 in action, although they lacked the precise fire discipline of their opponents. They were, too, taking very heavy casualties as the British volleys thudded into the packed ranks. Where the French scored heavily was in artillery support, of which the British had none. Soult later recorded that he had 40 guns trained on the British line, of which a large number were providing close support with grape and canister, sometimes sweeping away entire sections with their fire. The odds facing Stewart's division were, therefore, far heavier than the 8:3 ratio of engaged infantry, and they were rising steadily.

Sherer's impressions of this horrific day, though sometimes recorded out of sequence, were still vivid after ten years:

'Just as our line had entirely cleared the Spaniards, the smoky shroud of battle was, by the slackening of the fire, for one minute blown aside, and gave to our view the French grenadier caps, their arms, and the whole aspect of their frowning masses. It was momentary, but a grand sight; a heavy atmosphere of smoke again enveloped us, and few objects could be discerned at all, none distinctly ... The murderous contest of musketry lasted long. To describe my feelings throughout this wild scene with fidelity would be impossible: at intervals a shriek or groan told me that men were falling around me; but it was not always that the tumult of the contest suffered me to catch these sounds. A constant feeling to the centre of the line, and the gradual diminution of our front, more truly bespoke the havoc of death. As we moved, though slowly, yet ever a little distance in advance, our own killed and wounded lay behind us; but we arrived among those of the enemy, and those of the Spaniards who had fallen in the first onset: we trod among the dead and dying, all reckless of them.

'We were the whole time progressively advancing upon and shaking the enemy. At a distance of about twenty yards from them, we received orders to charge; we ceased firing, cheered, and had our bayonets in the charging position, when a body of the enemy's horse was discovered under the shoulder of a rising ground, ready to take advantage of our impetuosity.'[7]

Just who gave the order to charge is unknown, but it was countermanded immediately; Abercrombie's brigade was not to be destroyed as Colborne's had been. Sherer's narrative continues:

'Already, however, had the French infantry, alarmed by our preparatory cheers which always indicate a charge, broken and fled, abandoning some guns and howitzers about sixty yards from us. The presence of the cavalry not permitting us to pursue, we halted and recommenced firing on them. The slaughter was now for a few minutes dreadful; every shot told; their officers in vain attempted to rally them. Some of their artillery, indeed, took up a distant position, which much annoyed our line, but we did not move until we had expended our ammunition, then retired in the most perfect order to a spot sheltered from their guns and lay down in line ready to repulse any fresh attack with the bayonet.'

For both commanders, the crisis of the battle had now been reached. It was unusual for the French to display such iron tenacity in a prolonged firefight, and they were doing so now because they believed they were winning. They had seen off Colborne's brigade and the Spaniards and now Houghton's battalions had shrunk to small scarlet oblongs standing isolated among their dead and wounded. In Soult's eyes their protracted stand, which had cost his men so dear, entirely contradicted every tenet of military logic; even so, however gallantly they had behaved, their end could not be delayed for many more minutes. It was at that moment that Abercrombie's brigade, full of fight, had appeared to ravage the right flank of his assault column and flung it back in disorder. His sole remaining reserve was Werlé's brigade and he could only hope that it retained sufficient élan to restore some momentum to the attack and enable his troops to administer the coup de grâce as quickly as possible.

For his part, Beresford had reached the lowest point in his professional career. The Spaniards had received a mauling and could no longer be relied upon to do any serious fighting; and in Stewart's 2nd Division, which had already fought itself to within an inch of destruction, the ammunition supply had begun to fail. Beresford undoubtedly considered himself to be beaten, and, deeply depressed, his only consideration at that moment was to save as much as he could of his army. Orders were given for Alten's Germans to abandon Albuera village and for Hamilton's Portuguese division to reposition itself so as to cover the line of retreat. These orders were being put into effect when the course of the battle took a sudden and totally unexpected turn.

One of Beresford's staff, 26-year-old Colonel Henry Hardinge, did not agree with the Army Commander's gloomy assessment of the situation. Acting entirely on his own initiative he galloped across to confer with Sir Lowry Cole, whose 4th Division was positioned in reserve behind Lumley's cavalry, urging him to mount an immediate counter-attack on left flank of the French and so stabilise the situation. Cole's division consisted of two brigades only, Lieutenant-Colonel Sir William Myers' Fusilier Brigade (1/ and 2/7th (later Royal) Fusiliers and 1/23rd (later Royal Welch) Fusiliers, and a Portuguese brigade under Brigadier-General Harvey, and while he fully appreciated the point of Hardinge's argument he was reluctant to commit his troops without a direct order from Beresford. Myers joined the discussion, pointing out that the French were on the point of launching their final assault and emphasising the urgency of the situation. Cole gave way but, unlike Stewart, he insisted that adequate precautions should be taken to protect the flank of the counter-attack against cavalry.

The divisional deployment was completed quickly and efficiently. All ten of the light companies, British and Portuguese, were formed in column on the right flank. Then, in line but echeloned back somewhat to the left came the four battalions of Harvey's brigade, consisting of the Portuguese 11th and 23rd Regiments. Myers' brigade came next with, from right to left, the 1/7th, 2/7th and 1/23rd, their left flank being protected by a column formed by a Portuguese light infantry unit of the Loyal Lusitanian Legion. The two brigades were drawn up in battalion columns at quarter distance so that, when the moment came, they could deploy quickly into line.

Those waiting to advance could see that the situation on The Ridge was deteriorating minute by minute. As already mentioned, Abercrombie's brigade had pulled back into dead ground when its ammunition began to fail. Now, the battered remnants of Houghton's brigade were being pushed steadily back by Werlé's triumphant battalions, who already held the summit. To their right, the Polish lancers could be seen hovering in the area of the captured German battery. At length, satisfied that he had done all he could, Cole gave the order to advance. Never was a counter-attack more desperately needed, and never was one more exquisitely timed.

As the battalion columns passed through the intervals between Lumley's squadrons, Latour-Maubourg could hardly believe his eyes. For the second time within hours Allied infantry were advancing unsupported within striking distance of his horsemen. Leaving the major portion of his strength to hold Lumley in check, he launched four regiments at Harvey's brigade. On this occasion, while the attack would be delivered frontally against troops in column rather than, as in the case of Colborne's brigade, against the flank and rear of battalions in extended line, a similar outcome was clearly anticipated. For a moment Cole, knowing that the Portuguese had never been in action before, held his breath. He need not have worried, for Harvey's regiments had been trained to British standards, in which a well-drilled platoon in two ranks could fire up to five volleys a minute. The Portuguese, moreover, were perfectly steady, firing volley after volley that felled horses and riders until the French, having had enough, galloped back whence they had come. Harvey then formed a protective shoulder with which to cover the further advance of Myers' brigade.

The Fusiliers, in their tall, peaked, bearskin caps, were the finest-looking British troops in the field that day, despite their worn uniforms and a recent issue of locally made buff-leather boots that hurt abominably. They tramped steadily upwards, breaking up a firefight that had developed in the smoke and confusion between a Spanish unit and some British troops, the latter possibly survivors of Colborne's brigade. Ahead lay the massed ranks of the French, now in possession of the summit and believing themselves to be on the brink of victory.

Lieutenant John Harrison, commanding one of the 23rd's companies, recalled that only when the brigade was within musket range, i.e. less than 200 yards, and the French had actually opened fire, did Myers' battalions deploy from column into line. There ensued a series of ferocious firefights, which he says took place almost muzzle to muzzle, each being followed by a bayonet charge, in which several enemy battalions were routed in succession. Shortly after this he was shot in the thigh and was being helped to the rear when he noted, with horror, that only a third of the Fusiliers were still on their feet; notwithstanding, their remorseless advance continued.[8]

For all that Napier's version of the battle is burdened by his opinions on Beresford and flawed in some details, it contains the finest account possible of the Fusilier brigade's counter-attack and its consequences.[9] The epic quality of its prose cannot be equalled and, although it has been quoted in numerous regimental and campaign histories, this in itself justifies its being repeated here:

'Such a gallant line, issuing from the midst of the smoke and rapidly separating itself from the confused and broken multitude, startled the enemy's heavy masses, which were now increasing and pressing onwards as to an assured victory: they wavered, hesitated, and then vomiting forth a storm of fire, hastily endeavoured to enlarge their front, while a fearful discharge of grape from all their artillery whistled through the British ranks. Myers was killed; Cole, and the three colonels, Ellis, Blakeney and Hawkshawe, fell wounded; and the Fusilier battalions, struck by an iron tempest, reeled and staggered like sinking ships. Suddenly and sternly recovering, they closed on their terrible enemies, and then was seen with what a strength and majesty the British soldier fights. In vain did Soult, by voice and gesture, animate his Frenchmen; in vain did the hardiest veterans, extricating themselves from the crowded columns, sacrifice their lives to gain time for the mass to open out on such a fair field; in vain did the mass itself bear up, and, fiercely striving, fire indiscriminately upon friends and foes, while the horsemen hovering on the flank threatened to charge the advancing line. Nothing could stop that astonishing infantry. No sudden burst of undisciplined valour, no nervous enthusiasm, weakened the stability of their order; their flashing eyes were bent on the dark columns in their front; their measured tread shook the ground; their dreadful volleys swept away the head of every formation; their deafening shouts overpowered the dissonant cries that broke from all parts of the tumultuous crowd, as foot by foot and with a horrid carnage it was driven by the incessant vigour of the attack to the farthest edge of the hill. In vain did the French reserves, joining with the struggling multitude, endeavour to sustain the fight; their efforts only increased the irremediable confusion, and the mighty mass, giving way like a loosened cliff, went headlong down the ascent. The rain flowed after in streams discoloured with blood, and fifteen hundred unwounded men, the remnant of six thousand unconquerable British soldiers, stood triumphant on that fatal hill.'

Soult managed to form a grenadier unit into a rearguard which, together with the expertly withdrawn French artillery, covered the flight of his broken infantry across the stream and into the woodland beyond. The British, too exhausted and now too few in numbers, did not pursue. Elsewhere, two Portuguese batteries had come forward and begun to punch holes in Latour-Maubourg's ranks while, closely followed by Harvey and Lumley, he sought to conform to the French withdrawal. Five of the KGL's lost guns were recovered, although the battery's howitzer had been towed away by the enemy. The Buffs' Regimental colour was recovered by Sergeant Gough of the 7th Fusiliers and returned to its owners.[10]

Alten's Germans were ordered to retake Albuera village, which they did at some cost, and Hamilton's Portuguese division assumed responsibility for the Allied right flank.

The day's fighting had cost both armies very dear. Soult had sustained the loss of about 8,000 men killed or wounded, including 800 of the latter left on the field. His capture of a howitzer, several colours and about 500 prisoners, a surprisingly high number of whom escaped shortly afterwards, was hardly an adequate return for the loss of one-third of his army. He had failed to relieve Badajoz and he believed that he had been deprived of a well-deserved victory. 'There is no beating these troops,' he wrote of the British after the battle. 'I always thought they were bad soldiers – now I am sure of it. I had turned their right, pierced their centre and everywhere victory was mine – but they did not know how to run!'

Beresford, far from being elated by the sudden recovery in his fortunes, remained deeply despondent, a state of mind reflected in his despatch on the battle. Reading through it the following day, Wellington commented that another such success would ruin the Allied cause; then, conscious of the effect the despatch would have on those at home, he turned to one of his staff with the remark: 'This won't do – write me down a victory.'

What depressed Beresford most were the crippling casualties sustained by the British portion of his army. The Germans and Portuguese had between them lost approximately 600 men, killed, wounded and missing; the Spaniards 1,368; but the British loss was in excess of 4,000. Brigades were coming out of action commanded by captains, battalions by subalterns and companies by sergeants and corporals; the following morning, it is said, one drummer collected the rations for his company in his hat.[11] The grievous extent of the loss is set out below.

	Present	Casualties
Colborne's Brigade		
The Buffs	728	643
2/48th Regiment	452	343
2/66th Regiment	520	339
2/31st Regiment	418	155
Houghton's Brigade		
29th Regiment	507	363
1/57th Regiment	647	428[12]
1/48th Regiment	497	280
Abercrombie's Brigade		
2/28th Regiment	640	164
2/39th Regiment	482	98
2/34th Regiment	500 est	128
Myers' Fusilier Brigade		
1/7th Regiment	⎡ total between ⎤	354
2/7th Regiment	⎢ 1,500 and ⎥	351
1/23rd Regiment	⎣ 2,015[13] ⎦	340

With the British completely exhausted and the Portuguese now holding the line, Beresford requested Blake for Spanish assistance in clearing the field of its thousands of wounded. It beggars belief that the Spaniard should have declined, commenting off-handedly that each of the Allies should be responsible for their own casualties. The result was that the wounded spent the night where they lay, drenched by continuous rain. As if they had not suffered enough, the scum among the camp followers and the local peasantry appeared after dark to strip and rob them, murdering any who dared to resist. Next morning, the field resembled a charnel house, the sights of which remained fixed forever in Captain Sherer's mind:

'Look around – behold the thousands of slain, thousands of wounded, writhing in anguish and groaning with agony and despair. Here lie four officers of the French 100th, all corpses. Here fought the 3rd Brigade; here the Fusiliers: how thick those heroes lie! Most of the bodies are already stripped; rank is no longer distinguished. Here again lie headless trunks, and bodies torn and struck down by cannon shot. Who are these that catch every moment at our coats? The wounded soldiers of the enemy, who are imploring British protection from the Spaniards. It would be well for kings, politicians and generals if, while they talk of victories with exultation and of defeats with indifference, they would allow their fancies to wander to the field of carnage.'

Among those lucky enough to have been brought off the field on the evening of the battle was Lieutenant Latham of the Buffs, unrecognisable but still incredibly alive and still with his King's colour safe within his coat.

Beresford had expected Soult to renew his attack on the 17th but, to his intense relief, he did not and the following day the French withdrew. The siege of Badajoz was renewed although, for various reasons, neither it nor Ciudad Rodrigo fell until the following year.

There were many heroes at Albuera, but only a few survived to receive any reward. Major Guy L'Estrange, who had kept the 2/31st in action after the rest of Colborne's brigade had been swept away, was awarded brevet promotion to lieutenant-colonel and presented with a commemorative gold medal by his brother officers. In due course he became a lieutenant-general and was knighted.

Lieutenant Matthew Latham also received a gold medal from his brother officers and, on learning of the manner in which he had come by his terrible wounds, the Prince Regent personally paid the cost of a surgical operation to repair the worst of the damage. In 1813 Latham was rewarded with a captain's commission in a Canadian Fencible regiment but remained with the Buffs and exchanged back at the same rank the following year. He retired from the Army in 1820 with an annual pension of £100, plus £70 per annum on account of his wounds. Subsequently, his defence of the colour was permanently commemorated by the Buffs with a magnificent silver centrepiece depicting the event.

Lieutenant-Colonel Inglis, who had urged the 57th to 'die hard,' waited for two days before having the French grapeshot surgically extracted from his neck. After a spell of convalescent leave at home he returned to the Peninsula and took part in numerous hard-fought actions, ending the war as a major-general. 'General Inglis,' wrote Napier, 'Was one of those veterans who purchased every step of their promotion with their own blood.' In 1822 Inglis married at the age of 58 and had two sons, both of whom followed him into the service.

The carnage at Albuera also brought promotion to many other officers, since vacancy and merit also played a part in the system, and of course advancement in the careers of a much greater number of NCOs and private soldiers. As a reward for the outstanding leadership displayed by the NCOs during the battle Beresford allowed each battalion in Houghton's and Myers' brigades to submit the name of one sergeant for promotion to the commissioned rank of ensign; selection cannot have been a difficult matter, since so few were left to choose from.

The hardest-hit units, no longer able to function on their own, were formed into provisional battalions until their strength could be restored with reinforcement drafts. It would be two years before the Buffs and the 57th fought another battle. The 29th was sent home to recover and did not fight again during the war, arriving in Flanders just too late to participate in the Battle of Waterloo. The survivors of the 2/7th and 2/48th were absorbed by their respective 1st battalions.

Writing of the astonishing motivation that imbued the British infantry at Albuera, Sir John Fortescue commented: 'Such constancy as was displayed by these battalions is rare and has seldom been matched in the history of war. Whence came the spirit which made that handful of English battalions content to die where they stood rather than give way one inch? Beyond all question it sprang from intense regimental pride and regimental feeling.' True, but to that must be added additional interlinked factors such as the contemporary attitude to the French and the close bonds of comradeship. To give best to the French was unthinkable, and, if it valued its reputation, no battalion would leave the line while others were still in place; likewise, no man would leave the ranks while his comrades were still fighting, for he would have to face them afterwards. It mattered not that on this occasion the French, scenting an easy victory, were at their most formidable; rather the reverse, in fact.

Notes
1. Quoted in Napier's *History of the War in the Peninsula*, Vol III, pp. 409–10.
2. The rising was the result of a victory won by a small British army under Sir Thomas Graham at Barrosa, near Cadiz, the seat of the 'free' Spanish government, on 5 March 1811.
 3. Two former Vistula Legion lancer regiments served with the French Army, retaining the Polish uniform; in June 1811 they were designated the 7th and 8th *Chevau-Léger Lanciers*. Although the French 10th Hussars were credited with the capture of the King's colour of the 66th, there are grounds for believing that it was actually captured by the 2nd Hussars, as part at least of the 10th are known to have been present with Godinot's diversion force.
4. Although the various depictions of Latham defending his colour, including the Buffs' silver centrepiece, show his left arm missing and its staff intact, a photograph taken in old age reveals that it was his right arm which was amputated. It would have been entirely logical for him to have held the remains of the colour with his left hand, i.e. that furthest from the enemy, while he defended it with his right.
5. L'Estrange's method, subsequently known as the Albuera Square, was regularly practised by his regiment until the 1850s.
6. Inglis, the third son of an Edinburgh surgeon, was born in 1764 and received his ensign's commission in the 57th at the age of fifteen. He had joined the regiment in New York two years later and remained with it ever since, save for a period of several months the previous year when he had acted as brigade commander, notably at Busaco.
7. Save for two regiments with Godinot, all the French cavalry was concentrated under Latour-Maubourg opposite the right of the British line. There was none opposite the 34th, on the extreme left of the line, although the numerous French gun teams, glimpsed imperfectly at a distance through the heavy smoke, may have given a contrary impression.
8. For the 23rd, one of six British and two Hanoverian battalions which, at Minden in 1759, had carried out a similar advance, routing French cavalry and infantry in succession, it must have seemed as though history was repeating itself. See the author's *At All Costs!*
9. Napier suggests the counter-attacks by Abercrombie's and Myers' brigades coincided. Given the scale of ammunition expenditure described by Sherer, Abercrombie's brigade must have been in action a minimum of 30 minutes before Myers commenced his advance.
10. Sergeant William Gough was granted an ensign's commission in the 2nd West India Regiment. Some accounts say that he 'recovered' the Buffs' colour, others that he 'recaptured' it, which suggests fighting. Either way, it is reasonably safe to assume that the lancer who took it from Ensign Thomas was by now dead.
11. Houghton's brigade was brought out of action by Captain G. Cimitière, whose history was as unusual as his name. A French emigré serving as a corporal with the 14th Regiment in Flanders, he had used his local knowledge to lead his regiment out of a tight spot and been rewarded with an ensign's commission in the 4th West India Regiment. The following year, 1796, he was, without purchase, promoted lieutenant in the 48th. He received a gold medal for his service at Albuera, became a lieutenant-colonel in 1824 and commanded the 48th until he retired four years later.
12. After the battle the 57th's survivors, recovering from their ordeal in a Spanish inn, agreed to devise a means by which their dead comrades' example should never be forgotten. Ever since, on the anniversary of Albuera, that promise has been fulfilled by the 57th and its successor regiments in a moving ceremony known as the Silent Toast. The officers join the warrant officers and sergeants in the latter's mess, forming a circle. The

commanding officer, flanked by the regimental sergeant major and the junior sergeant, receives a silver cup filled with champagne from the officers' mess sergeant and proposes the toast: 'To the Immortal Memory.' There is no reply and no other words are spoken. The cup is then passed in complete silence from right to left around the circle, with each drinking from it in turn.

13. Cole's despatch says that the 'Fusilier brigade lost 1,000 out of 1,500 men and 45 officers.' The casualties are not in dispute and the impression that two-thirds of the brigade were down is supported by Lieutenant John Harrison's recollections, included in the text. On the other hand, Michael Glover's detailed research on the battle, incorporated in his history of the Royal Welch Fusiliers *That Astonishing Infantry*, gives the brigade's strength as being 2,015 but concurs with the casualty figure of 1,045. Yet, even if the larger figure is accepted, it still produces a loss ratio in excess of 50 per cent, well beyond the level at which units are normally considered to a spent force.

CHAPTER TWO

Scarlet and Grey – The Battles of Chippewa and Lundy's Lane, July 1814

O ne of the causes of the American War of Independence had been the burden of taxation placed upon the colonists to provide for their defence by the regular armed forces of the Crown. The threat formerly posed by the French had been eliminated during the Seven Years' War and, that being the case, ran the argument, there was no further need for British regular troops to be stationed in North America at such prohibitive cost. There was, perhaps, a case to be made for a few garrisons in the west, where the Indians were beginning to oppose the increasing flow of white settlers, and for a small number of troops to man coastal defences along the eastern seaboard, but the general feeling was that any local emergency that might arise could be dealt with by local militias and minutemen.

Much the same feeling existed within the infant United States during the 30 years which followed the end of the Revolutionary War, and in consequence the Regular Army maintained by Congress was tiny. It was moreover, a body upon which the general public was not inclined to look with any favour, for two reasons. The first was that, beyond providing aid for the civil power in extreme circumstances, it was an expensive institution which brought no apparent benefit to the majority of citizens; and the second was that, since the great majority of those serving in the ranks had enlisted out of sheer economic necessity, it was a refuge for the otherwise unemployable in a country where energy and enterprise were respected as nowhere else in the world.

This, then, was the unfortunate relationship which existed between the nation and its army when the United States declared war upon Great Britain on 19 June 1812. One cause of the war was the high-handed attitude of the Royal Navy, which not only stopped American vessels in pursuance of its blockade of Napoleonic Europe, but also impressed their crews. Another was the desire of a vocal political lobby in Washington that Canada should be absorbed into the United States. In the aftermath of the Revolutionary War Canada had provided a new home for the numerous loyalists in the former colonies who had not wished to sever all links with the mother country and whose lives had been made a misery because of their views. Many had lost everything and, understandably, even 30 years after the event, considerable bitterness towards the United States still existed on the Canadian side of the border. Indeed, in the west there was active Canadian support for an Indian confederation under Chief Tecumseh which was resisting white encroachment on their land, thereby providing fuel for the war faction in Washington. None of these problems were insoluble, and all could have been sorted out at the diplomatic level without undue difficulty, given a degree of goodwill; unfortunately that commodity was totally lacking on both sides.

At sea, the small US Navy won a number of single-ship actions with its few superbly constructed frigates, but it was unable to prevent the imposition of a British blockade on the American coast, provoking an anti-war reaction from the New England states, which relied heavily upon maritime commerce for their living.

On land, nothing occurred that might have changed the American public's indifferent opinion of its army. On 17 July the British captured Fort Mackinac, strategically located on the island of the same name in the straits connecting Lakes Huron and Michigan. On 15 August Fort Dearborn, on the site of modern Chicago, was abandoned and its small garrison captured after a brief struggle with Indians allied to the British. The following day Brigadier-General William Hull, with 2,500 men at his disposal, tamely surrendered Detroit to General Sir Isaac Brock, who had only 350 regulars, 400 Canadian militiamen and 600 Indians with him, scarcely a shot being fired.

These events in the west, however, were of less importance than what was about to take place on the Niagara front. Here the 30-mile-wide Niagara peninsula, bounded on the north by Lake Ontario and on the south by Lake Erie, was separated from up-state New York by the Niagara river, connecting the two lakes and with the famous falls approximately half-way along its length. Near the river's mouth Fort George was balanced on the American bank by Fort Niagara, and at the southern end of the river the British had also built Fort Erie, within sight of the American town of Buffalo to the south-east.

In October an American force consisting of 900 regulars and 2,270 militia, commanded by Colonel Solomon Van Rensselaer, was detailed to cross the Niagara. Unfortunately for Van Rensselaer, only his regulars would make the crossing, the militia standing firm upon their constitutional right not to be employed abroad. Brock, having returned from Detroit, was at Fort George and, rounding up 600 British regulars and 600 Canadian militia, he attacked the American position on Queenston Heights on 13 October. The result was a decisive British victory in which 250 Americans were killed and wounded and 700 captured. British losses amounted to just fourteen men killed (one of whom was Brock himself) and 96 wounded. Throughout the engagement the American militia had, to their eternal shame, stood idly by on their own bank of the river while their comrades were overwhelmed. The following month a further invasion of Canada, this time involving 5,000 men under Major-General Henry Dearborn moving north along the Lake Champlain route, had to be abandoned when, once again, the militia element refused to cross the border.

In the spring of 1813 the Americans returned to the offensive, with mixed success. A 1,600-strong force under Brigadier-General Zebulon Pike crossed Lake Ontario and seized York, as Toronto was then called, on 24 April. After a powder magazine exploded, killing Pike and causing 320 casualties among his men, the enraged survivors burned the town's public buildings before returning home a fortnight later. In military terms the expedition achieved nothing and was actually counter-productive since it hardened Canadian attitudes.

Towards the end of May, Dearborn sailed from Sackett's Harbor with 4,000 men and effected a landing near Fort George. The landing was opposed by the 700-strong garrison of the fort under Brigadier-General John Vincent who, rather than risk being bottled up to no purpose, began withdrawing west along the shore of Lake Ontario towards Burlington Bay. Fort Erie was also abandoned and occupied by another American force which had crossed the Niagara, thereby bringing the entire Canadian bank of the river under American control. At last it began to seem as though the Americans were beginning to make some headway, especially when an amphibious raid against Sackett's Harbor, mounted by Lieutenant-General Sir George Prevost, the British commander-in-chief North America, was decisively repulsed by Brigadier-General Jacob J. Brown's small garrison on 29 May.

It was not to be. Dearborn, in poor health, followed up the retreating Vincent slowly. During the evening of 5 June his advance guard, consisting of 2,000 men under Brigadier-Generals John Chandler and William H. Winder, encamped for the night at Stony Creek, near present day Hamilton. Chandler and Winder were that curse of the American military system that would endure until the second half of the nineteenth century, namely political appointees whose abilities fell far short of their ambitions, and in this instance they do not even appear to have protected their camp by posting an adequate picket line. At 02:00 the following morning Vincent's entire command came storming out of the darkness, routing the Americans, taking their artillery and baggage, and capturing Chapman and Winder. Two days later the remnants of the latter's force straggled into Fort George.

At about this time a Canadian renegade named Joseph Willcocks, a newspaper editor and member of the Legislative Assembly, approached Dearborn with an offer to raise a Canadian unit for service with the American army. Driven by self-interest and political venom, Willcocks clearly believed that the United States would prove to be the eventual winner in the war and absorb Upper Canada. That being the case, he reasoned, any assistance he gave now would be amply rewarded with high office when the time came. He was granted a major's commission in the US Volunteers and with his unit of 'mounted scouts,' formed from fellow renegades and malcontents, served as guides to American patrols, simultaneously paying off old scores, looting private property and burning farms. Naturally, the Canadians responded by sniping and it became unsafe for American troops, whose morale had already been broken by the débâcle at Stony Creek, to stray too far from the fort, save in strength. Even this precaution came to naught when a raiding column, 540 strong, was ambushed at Beaver Dams, less than twenty miles distant, with the result that it surrendered to a British lieutenant commanding a much smaller force of Indians. Dearborn was promptly dismissed.

After this, the American garrison at Fort George simply withered away. Together, sickness, the departure of time-expired militiamen and the demand for troops elsewhere had, by the beginning of December reduced its size to some 400 men. When, on 10 December, one of Willcocks' patrols was wiped out, the fort's commander, Brigadier-General George McClure, decided to abandon the post and withdraw across the river, having burned down the nearby village of Newark (now Niagara-on-the-Lake), this task being entrusted to a grateful Willcocks, whose home town it was. Simultaneously, Fort Erie was evacuated.

American officers themselves described the burning of Newark as a 'flagrant act of barbarity', so it is hardly surprising that Lieutenant-General Gordon Drummond, the British commander in Upper Canada, should respond vigorously and at once. During the night of 18/19 December Fort Niagara was captured by a daring coup-de-main. Drummond's deputy, Major-General Phineas Riall, then advanced south along the American bank of the Niagara and, brushing aside New York state militia, burned Lewiston, the Black Rock navy yard and Buffalo in reprisal for the atrocities at York and Newark. On the Niagara front, therefore, the Americans ended the year considerably worse off than they had begun it.

Elsewhere, they had also enjoyed mixed success. On 10 September they emerged the victors from a hard-fought naval action on Lake Erie and as a direct result of this the small British garrison of Detroit, consisting of 800 regulars and 1,000 Indians under Brigadier-General Thomas Proctor, found itself in a position of strategic isolation and, thoroughly demoralised, commenced a disorganised retreat into Canada along the Thames river. Following up with a force of 3,500 regulars and militia, Major-General William Harrison found Proctor's men drawn up near Moravian Town. After firing a couple of volleys, the British regulars fell apart under the impact of a cavalry attack, although the Indians fought on until Tecumseh, their great war chief, was killed, then melted away. Yet, somehow, the American War Department managed to blight even this small but important success by ordering the disbandment of Harrison's militia regiments and posting his regulars to the Niagara front. Harrison, a capable and experienced soldier, resigned his commission in disgust.

The recovery of Detroit in the west was more than balanced by disasters far to the north-east. Here, during the autumn, the Americans had evolved a complex plan for the capture of Montreal. Dearborn's replacement, Brigadier-General James Wilkinson, was to move down the St Lawrence from Sackett's Harbor with 8,000 men and effect a junction with Brigadier-General Wade Hampton who, with a further 4,000 men, was pushing north from Lake Champlain. It was optimistically envisaged that the combined force would then proceed with the capture of Montreal, despite the fact that it was outnumbered by the British garrison and protected by formidable fortifications.

Hampton came to grief first. On 25 October he found himself confronted by a British and Canadian force of unknown size in close country near the Chateaugay river. His opponent, Colonel George Macdonnell, had only 1,500 men at his disposal but by having bugle calls blown at different points around the Americans he created the impression of much greater strength. Hampton tried to break through with a combined frontal and flank attack, but when these failed he meekly withdrew to winter quarters in Plattsburg, although neither side had sustained more than a handful of casualties.

Wilkinson's slow passage down the St Lawrence had been harassed by a British force of 800 regulars and Indians under the command of Colonel J. W. Morrison. On 11 November, near Cornwall, he landed 2,000 of his own regulars under Brigadier-General John Boyd to deal with the threat. When the two forces clashed at Chrysler's Farm, the Americans, coming into action piecemeal, were routed and driven back to their boats with the loss of 249 killed and wounded and 100 captured. The following day, having learned of Hampton's retreat, Wilkinson abandoned the expedition and went into winter quarters at French Mills on the Salmon river. Thus, apart from the recovery of Detroit, the US Army ended 1813 with very little to congratulate itself upon.

Nor did the campaigning season of 1814 begin very differently. Wilkinson resumed his ill-considered offensive against Montreal in March, this time with only 4,000 men, using the Richelieu river as his axis of advance. A few miles beyond the border he mounted an attack on a fortified stone mill at La Colle, only to be sharply repulsed by its 600-strong garrison. His spiritless reaction was to fall back on his base at Plattsburg. For the War Department, this proved to be the last straw and he was summarily removed from his command.

His replacement was Major-General Jacob Brown who, it will be recalled, had successfully resisted the British raid on Sackett's Harbor. Brown was an unusually efficient New York militia officer who was able to get the best out of his troops. He did not believe that a war with Great Britain served the best interests of the United States, although this did not prevent him from doing his duty when the time came. He was particularly fortunate in the appointment of Brigadier-General Winfield Scott as his second-in-command and commander of his 1st Brigade. Scott, a towering presence six feet five inches tall and proportionately broad, was a regular officer who had received a captain's commission in the light artillery shortly before the outbreak of war. A dedicated professional, he placed a high value on the study of military history, constantly adding to his collection of books on the subject. His normally sound judgement could be prejudiced by flashes of impetuosity, and by temperament he could be stubborn and argumentative – indeed, throughout his long career he somehow managed to quarrel with everyone with whom he was professionally associated. As a lieutenant-colonel Scott had assumed command when Van Rensselaer had been wounded on Queenston Heights, negotiating the American surrender. Subsequently exchanged and promoted, he had been present at the capture of Fort George and taken part in Wilkinson's abortive expedition the previous year, being mortified by the performance of the American regulars at Chrysler's Farm.

Brown and Scott established their base at Flint Hill near Buffalo. Neither of them agreed with the saloon bar historians' view of the Revolutionary War, namely that citizen soldiers had thoroughly whipped King George's redcoats from start to finish. If that had indeed been the case, asked the more thoughtful, why had it taken so long to bring the matter to a conclusion, and how was it that the British had won most of the battles? The truth was that the army of the new-born republic had only begun to make tangible progress when it adopted the same high standards of discipline and training as its opponents. That lesson seemed to have been forgotten in the intervening years, especially by Revolutionary War veterans like

Wilkinson, whose skills now lay in politicking rather than fighting a very professional enemy. Now, after numerous humiliating reverses, the War Department was prepared to let younger, harder and more determined officers have their way, and in this respect Brown and Scott were of one mind – in a stand-up fight, the British could only be beaten by thoroughly trained and disciplined troops.

Most of the training of what became known as the Left Division US Army was left in Scott's hands. Throughout April, May and June he drilled the troops endlessly, imposing a firm but fair discipline. Some men lacked uniform altogether while that of the majority was ragged and worn out. Recognising the importance of this item to unit morale, he requisitioned fresh supplies. Instead of blue uniform coatees, however, he received a consignment of grey woollen fatigue jackets, with which he had to make do.[1] He also insisted that the troops pay strict attention to their personal hygiene and sanitation, with the result that the sick list shrank and only two men died from disease during this period.

In the meantime President Madison's administration had agreed to enter into peace negotiations with Great Britain. Far from furthering American interests, the war was actually damaging them. Furthermore, with the downfall of Napoleon clearly imminent, it could only be a matter of time before Wellington's Peninsula veterans were shipped to North America and matters would go from bad to worse. What was needed, Secretary of War John Armstrong informed Brown, was an unqualified success that would strengthen the hand of the American negotiators. After considering various alternatives it was decided that the best prospects were offered by a limited offensive on the Canadian bank of the Niagara, involving the capture of Fort Erie and an advance to the Chippewa river; in the event of Brown winning a victory he was to exploit this by advancing north to capture Forts George and Niagara in cooperation with the American squadron on Lake Ontario, which would also deliver the necessary heavy artillery. The problem was that the American squadron, under Commodore Isaac Chauncey, was balanced by a British squadron under Captain Sir James Yeo, and although each watched the other's movements closely, neither was prepared to risk losing control of the lake by bringing on a general engagement. When approached about the idea of cooperating with the projected Niagara offensive, Chauncey commented that his movements would be governed by Yeo's, adding: 'I shall sail on or about the 10th (July) but I shall not leave this vicinity (i.e. Sackett's Harbor) unless the enemy's fleet leads me up the lake.' Although Brown unwisely took this to mean that Chauncey's ships would be lying off Fort George on 10 July, he had sufficient reservations to discuss the matter with his two senior brigade commanders, Winfield Scott and Eleazar Ripley. Scott, aggressive and confident that the troops were fully trained, urged immediate action. After due consideration Brown, mindful of the risks involved if he had misconstrued Chauncey's intentions, but equally concerned to restore the Army's reputation, decided to proceed.

During night of 2/3 July the Left Division began its crossing. Its overall strength amounted to some 5,000 men, about 900 of whom were left behind to garrison Buffalo, Schlosser and Lewiston, the remainder being organised as follows:

DIVISIONAL TROOPS
Cavalry (Captain Samuel Harris)
One troop each of US Light Dragoons and New York Volunteer Dragoons,
Estimated total 70.

Artillery
Major Jacob Hindman's Battalion of four companies, each with three guns
Artillery Reserve

Engineers
Lieutenant David Douglass's Company

First Infantry Brigade (Brigadier-General Winfield Scott)
9th Infantry (now 5th Infantry)
11th Infantry (now 6th Infantry)
22nd Infantry (now 2nd Infantry)
25th Infantry (now 6th Infantry)
Estimated strength 1,319

2nd Infantry Brigade (Brigadier-General Eleazar Ripley)
21st Infantry (now 5th Infantry)
23rd Infantry (now 2nd Infantry)
Estimated strength 992

3rd Infantry Brigade (Brigadier-General Peter Porter)
Composite regiment of New York Militia
5th Pennsylvania Militia
Willcocks' renegade Canadian volunteers
Indian warriors
Estimated total 926

As the first wave of boats neared the Canadian shore they were fired upon by a British picket. This soon withdrew into Fort Erie, the commander of which, Major Thomas Buck, despatched his small detachment of 19th Light Dragoons to the north to give warning of the American landing. During the morning Brown's troops isolated the fort, incurring a handful of casualties from its cannon. Most believed that they would have to storm the work, yet within a discreditable scene was being played out. Buck's orders from Major-General Phineas Riall had assured him that the defences were quite capable of withstanding any attack 'short of an invasion in force.' The Americans were clearly not the only people capable of producing ambivalent correspondence, for Buck took this to mean that he should surrender the fort when confronted by an invasion in force. Most of his officers believed that further resistance would only result in useless loss of life, but there were others, backed by many of their men, who took the more professional view that their only purpose in being there was to do the Americans as much damage as they possibly could until necessity compelled their surrender. Buck nevertheless accepted the majority view and in mid-afternoon, just as the first of the newly landed American field pieces was being emplaced, he sent out a flag of truce to conclude the details.

Brown had thus secured the first of his objectives at virtually no cost, even before the Left Division had completed its crossing. At about noon on 4 July Scott's 1st Brigade began marching north towards Chippewa. Having covered only four miles, Scott encountered a British force holding the far bank of Frenchman's Creek. This consisted of the light company of the 1st Regiment, both flank companies of the 100th Regiment, two 24-pounder guns under Lieutenant Richard Armstrong RA, and a troop of 19th Light Dragoons under Lieutenant William Horton. In command was an experienced light infantry officer, Lieutenant-Colonel Thomas Pearson, who had been seriously wounded at Albuera and sent to Canada to fill a less physically demanding post as an inspector of militia. Now, once more, he was in the thick of the fighting. He opened fire on the American column, forcing Scott to deploy, then withdrew. He repeated this at every creek along the route, so that it took almost seven hours for the Americans to cover the next thirteen miles. At length he broke contact just short of the unfordable Chippewa river and, having set fire to those houses near the south bank in order to deny them to the enemy, retired across the bridge into Chippewa village, removing the bridge decking as he did so. Scott, following up, crossed a area of cleared farmland, subsequently known as the Plain, measuring approximately 1,200 yards from north to south and 600 yards from east to west, bounded on the left by dense forest and on the north by a thick belt of trees. Passing through the latter, he came under fire from the

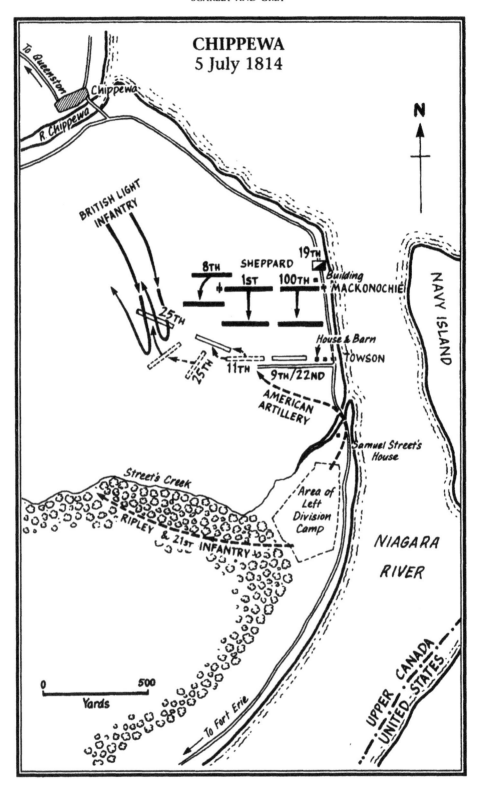

CHIPPEWA
5 July 1814

north bank of the Chippewa, on which gun emplacements had been dug the previous year. The light was now fading, it was beginning to rain and, recognising that he could proceed no further, he withdrew across the Plain and established a camp on the southern bank of Street's Creek. At about midnight Brown arrived with Ripley's 2nd Brigade and the artillery.

Before proceeding further it is necessary to examine what was taking place on the other side of the lines. The regular regiments of the British Army in Canada were of identical quality to those serving in the Peninsula and, having won their battles for the past two years, they saw no reason why they should not continue to do so. However, it was to the Peninsula that the best British commanders were being sent and Canada, being a secondary theatre of war, had to put up with what was left. The senior British officers serving in Canada were competent enough in a run of the mill sort of way, but they lacked imagination and their successful defence of the long frontier for the past two years with very few troops had engendered a sense of complacency; Brock had been a notable exception, but now he was dead.

Major-General Phineas Riall, responsible for the Niagara sector, had been at Fort George when the news of the American landing reached him at about 08:30 on the morning of 3 July. He had acted with commendable speed in mobilising his troops and directing them to concentrate at Chippewa, where the river offered the best line of defence against a continued American advance to the north. By the morning of 5 July he had assembled one squadron of the 19th Light Dragoons,[2] the 1st (Royal Scots) Regiment, the senior line infantry regiment of the British Army with a lineage so ancient that it was known as Pontius Pilate's Bodyguard, the 8th (The King's) Regiment, also of considerable seniority, the 100th (later the Prince of Wales's Leinster Regiment (Royal Canadians)),[3] the 1st and 2nd Lincoln Militia (later the Lincoln and Welland Regiment), mainly of Loyalist stock and fighting on their own home ground, part of Captain James Mackonochie's Brigade, Royal Artillery, with three 6-pounder guns, two 24-pounder guns and one 5½-inch howitzer; and about 300 Indians, giving an overall total of approximately 2,400 men.

Riall was worried that the Americans might make a second landing at Queenston to his rear and to guard against the threat he sent back the 1st Lincolns, for whom he had a high regard. He had no reason to believe that Fort Erie was not still holding out and, having personally scouted the American camp, which his snipers were bringing under fire, he decided to advance south from the Chippewa and drive the enemy back to their boats. His engineers therefore set about replacing the decking of the Chippewa bridge.

47

In the meantime the 5th Pennsylvania and some 380 Indians of Porter's brigade had crossed the Niagara during the previous night and were marching north from Fort Erie. When, at noon, they reached the American camp at Street's Creek they were allowed to rest until Brown, tired of the constant sniping, asked Porter to clear the woodland to the west. Porter asked for volunteers but the Pennsylvanians were tired and hungry and only 200 of them came forward, together with 300 Indians. They entered the woods at about 15:00 and at first they succeeded in pushing the sharp-shooters back. The British committed their own Indians and the 2nd Lincolns, followed by the light companies of the three regular regiments. A wild, savage and frequently hand-to-hand struggle surged back and forth among the trees until the Americans gave way and fled.

At about the same time Porter had entered the forest, Riall's engineers finished their work on the Chippewa bridge and the British main body began to cross. At first its progress was concealed by the belt of trees bounding the northern edge of the Plain, but at length Brown, who was visiting the picket north of Street's Creek, observed the head of the column marching along the river road, then begin to deploy smartly into a battle line across the open grassland. He immediately sent his adjutant, Colonel Charles Gardner, galloping back to the camp with orders to bring up Scott's brigade. Although Scott had just provided his men with the Fourth of July Dinner they had missed the previous day he saw no reason why the celebration should interfere with their training programme and had just assembled the regiments for drill when Gardner arrived. Believing that he was being called forward to support Porter, he passed some disparaging remarks on militiamen in general but said that he had intended to hold his parade on the Plain anyway and formed the brigade into column of march. As he approached the Street's Creek bridge he encountered Brown coming the other way. 'You will have a battle!' shouted the divisional commander. Grumpily, Scott repeated his comments on the militia, adding his doubts as to whether there were more than 300 British south of the Chippewa. Almost immediately, the first roundshot smashed into the head of his column and shell splinters ripped through the ranks.

Riall had deployed his line with the 100th, commanded by Lieutenant-Colonel John Hay, the Marquis of Tweeddale, on the left and Lieutenant-Colonel John Gordon's Royal Scots on the right; there was insufficient space available for Major Thomas Evans' Kingsmen in the line, so they took position in reserve and were then moved behind the Royal Scots' right rear, in echelon. Two 24-pounder guns and the 5½-inch howitzer under Lieutenant Richard Armstrong were placed on the river road to the left of the 100th, with Major Lisle's 19th Light Dragoon squadron some distance behind, and three 6-pounder guns under Lieutenant Edmund Sheppard were positioned immediately to the right of the Royal Scots.

Observing the fine target presented by Scott's brigade as it neared the Street's Creek bridge, Armstrong opened fire at between 500 and 600 yards and was pleased to note that it began to take effect immediately. Riall, watching the approach of the drab grey column, commented that he seemed to be faced by nothing more serious than 'some Buffalo militia.'

The Americans, however, gave no hint that their casualties worried them and continued to come on. About 200 yards north of the bridge Scott wheeled his brigade off the river road and began to form his line parallel to the British. On the right and closest to the road was the combined 9th/22nd Infantry under Major Henry Leavenworth, which was joined by the company-strong picket belonging to the 21st Infantry; then Colonel Thomas Campbell's 11th Infantry; and finally, on the left, Major Thomas Jesup's 25th Infantry. The entire line was now under fire from the British artillery but Scott continued to adjust the position of its units until he was entirely satisfied. Noting that the British light companies were active on the edge of the forest, he ordered the 25th to change front in their direction, despite the fact that this exposed the regiment's right flank to the fire of Sheppard's guns, giving Jesup authority to act as circumstances dictated. Next, realising that the opposing line was now longer than his own and anticipating, correctly, that the British would attack, he ordered the 11th Infantry, now commanded by Major John McNeil, Campbell having been wounded during the deployment, to take ground to its left and wheel through some 45 degrees to the right, so enabling it to rake the enemy's ranks when the time came. The effect of this was to open a gap between the 11th and the 9th/22nd on their right, but Scott was little worried by this and in due course it would be put to good use. On the river road Captain Nathan Towson's artillery company, armed with two 6-pounder guns and one 5½-inch howitzer, had come into action on the immediate right of the 9th/22nd and had opened a duel with Armstrong's gunners. Quite early in this Towson's howitzer landed a shell on a British limber, which blew up with a shattering roar, but was then knocked out itself by a 24-pounder ball. The principal effect of the duel, however, was to reduce the volume of fire directed at the American infantry.

The Americans had carried out these manoeuvres as neatly and as calmly as if they had been on the parade ground instead of under fire on a battlefield. Riall, having been forced to change his earlier opinion, is said to have remarked in some surprise, 'Why, these are regulars!'[4] In his view, however, it mattered very little, since experience had taught him that American regulars would stand only a little longer than American militia.

He had every confidence that his own infantry would follow its normal practice of closing to within short range of the enemy, firing one or two sharp volleys and then driving them off the field with a bayonet charge before they could recover.

He therefore had no hesitation in ordering the Royal Scots and the 100th to advance, forgetting that in so doing they would soon reach a point at which they would mask the supporting fire of their own guns. Scott made no such mistake. Seeing the long scarlet line bearing slowly down in disciplined silence on his brigade, he galloped over to Towson, ordering him to abandon the artillery duel and concentrate his fire on the British infantry. He then rode along the front of the brigade, reminding them that they had just celebrated the national holiday and should now give their fellow Americans another date to remember.

When the range had closed to within 100 yards Scott gave the order to fire. The two British regiments seemed to stagger as their first casualties went down but closed up and continued their advance until they were within 50 yards before returning fire. Both sides now became involved in a murderous firefight at suicidal range, absorbing heavy casualties. In addition, the British suffered severely at the hands of Towson's gunners, who were firing canister obliquely into their ranks. In vain did Gordon and Tweeddale, before they were themselves hit, urge their men to close with the bayonet and finish the matter; losses were mounting, especially among the officers, and there was something about the steady manner in which the Americans continued to load and fire while their own casualties were pulled out of the line that told those in the ranks that these men would not break when attacked with cold steel.

On the western flank of the battle Jesup had used his initiative, as Scott intended. Within the space of ten minutes he lost some 40 men from the fire of Sheppard's 6-pounders and the British light companies; then, deciding that he was doing no good where he was, he charged the latter, driving them deep into the trees. Detaching one company to pursue them, he began moving north with the rest of the regiment until he was level with the Kingsmen, forcing them to change front to meet the threat.

Simultaneously, Brown was urging Ripley's brigade into action. Major Joseph Grafton's 21st Infantry was ordered to make a wide flank march through the forest towards the British rear, but found the going more difficult than expected and in due course emerged from the trees too late to be of use. Likewise, Major Daniel McFarland's 23rd Infantry was slow moving off and only reached the Plain after the serious fighting was over.

The issue was decided by Major Jacob Hindman, Brown's divisional artillery commander, who sent forward Captain John Ritchie's company with two 6-pounder guns and one 5½-inch howitzer, and one 12-pounder gun under Lieutenant James Hall. The new arrivals slotted neatly into the gap between the 9th/22nd and the 11th, and quickly began lacing the ranks of the Royal Scots with canister. Scott was convinced that 'the enemy could not long withstand this accumulation of fire,' and he was right. Slowly, and without breaking ranks, the Royal Scots and the 100th began to give ground by stages and Riall, recognising that the action was lost, ordered a withdrawal across the Chippewa. This was covered by the Kingsmen, Pearson's light infantry, and the light dragoons, who saw the artillery safely off the field. The Americans followed up but were halted by heavy artillery fire from across the river and at length withdrew to their camp.

From start to finish, the battle had lasted about an hour and a half, but its most intense phase, the firefight between the two British battalions and Scott's brigade, probably lasted no longer than 20 to 30 minutes. Riall's casualty return, excluding Indians, recorded 148 killed, 321 wounded and 46 missing; Brown reported 41 killed, 219 wounded and 50 missing. Donald Graves' meticulous research into all aspects of the battle, however, indicates that many of those reported killed, especially among the British, were in fact prisoners and that the total number killed on both sides, including Indians, was in the region of 200. The Battle of Chippewa had been fought between equal numbers of regular troops with neither side possessing a terrain advantage and the outcome had proved beyond any reasonable doubt that the United States' Army had become a force to be reckoned with. Riall's defeat stemmed from his own understandable underestimation of his enemy and, given that the musketry of both sides was equally efficient, from the close-quarter intervention of the American artillery in the infantry battle, resulting in far higher British casualties. If those British officers now captive in the American camp were chagrined by their defeat, they at least had the cold comfort of knowing that it had been inflicted by troops who maintained professional standards similar to their own, and they were honest enough to say so.

A period of three weeks' indecisive manoeuvring following the battle. Riall, his confidence shaken, abandoned the Chippewa line and, having left a strong garrison in Fort George, withdrew to Twenty Mile Creek on the road to Burlington Bay, where he received the first reinforcements sent forward by Drummond. Brown followed up with the Left Division, halting at Queenston Heights. There, day by day, he waited in vain for the sight of Chauncey's sails on the lake to the north. During this period Porter's militiamen, guided by Willcocks' renegades, carried out a series of patrols that, contrary to Brown's repeated orders on the subject, degenerated into looting and burning expeditions. The Americans' every move was reported by the angry population with the result that they were regularly ambushed by the 1st and 2nd Lincoln and 2nd York Militia, which Riall had sent to screen their camp. At length, tired of waiting for Chauncey, Brown moved forward to Fort George on 22 July. After two days spent exchanging gunfire with the garrison he reached the conclusion that he was wasting his time and withdrew first to Queenston and then to Chippewa, where his troops could be more easily supplied.

Meanwhile, Drummond had decided to assume operational command himself and, as well as following up Brown's withdrawal, he despatched a force to scour the American side of the Niagara. Simultaneously, his advance guard, commanded by Pearson and consisting of the 2nd or Light Brigade (the light dragoons, the Glengarry Light Infantry Fencibles, a composite militia battalion, two 6-pounder guns and one 5½-inch howitzer) and the weak 1st Militia Brigade (detachments from the 1st, 2nd, 4th and 5th Lincolns and 2nd York, plus an estimated 50 Mohawk warriors), a total of between 1,100 and 1,200 men, pushed rapidly southwards and by 09:00 on 25 July were in contact with the American outposts. Sending back word to Riall and Drummond, Pearson took up position along Lundy's Lane, a country road running from west to east to meet the river road and continue on to the Niagara. To the west of the crossroads Lundy's Lane crossed a small hill on the summit of which was a church and graveyard. This feature dominated the wide expanse of open farmland to the south and on it he placed his guns. Most of the area has now been covered by the city of Niagara, the Falls themselves being located about a mile to the south-east of what became the battlefield.

Having visited the position, Riall rode back to Queenston to confer with Drummond and the two decided to concentrate their strength along the line of Lundy's Lane. The troops with Drummond, the 89th Regiment (later the 2nd Royal Irish Fusiliers), three companies of Royal Scots, the light companies of the King's and the 41st (later The Welch) Regiment, two 24-pounder guns, a Royal Marine detachment with Congreve rockets, and some 400 Indians, a total of approximately 1,100 men under the overall command of Lieutenant-Colonel Joseph Morrison of the 89th) were ordered forward during the afternoon. A messenger had already been despatched to Colonel Hercules Scott, encamped near Ten Mile Creek, with instructions for him to hurry forward with all the troops at his disposal. These started at about the same time and included five companies of the King's, seven companies of the 103rd, two of the 104th,[5] and three 6-pounder guns with, in reserve, seven companies of Royal Scots and the 2nd Militia Brigade, consisting of detachments from five militia units, giving a total of 1,720 men.

The Americans, encamped on both sides of the Chippewa, had been aware of the British presence to the north throughout the day. Brown, however, was more concerned by reports from one of his own militia officers regarding the British activity on the American side of the Niagara and he was convinced that Drummond's objective was the Left Division's major supply base at Schlosser. Lacking the means to cross the river in strength, he decided to divert British attention with a renewed thrust at Fort George. At about 15:00 he sent for Scott and told him to take his brigade, Harris's dragoons and Towson's guns north to Queenston. As Brown's instructions seemed lacking in urgency, Scott took his time so that it was not until over two hours later that his regiments began tramping over Chippewa bridge. A mile and a half beyond some British light dragoons were spotted at a roadside inn known as Willson's Tavern, but after observing the Americans for a moment or two they rode off. Having reached the tavern and obtained accurate information regarding Pearson's strength and position from Mrs Willson, an American by birth, Scott sent back a courier to inform Brown that he was in contact with a strong detachment of the enemy which he intended engaging. He then resumed his advance towards some chestnut woods a mile to the north of the tavern. The Americans' approach was greeted by war whoops and shots, but evidently the Indians withdrew almost immediately, for Harris's dragoons, having incurred the loss of a man wounded, were able to gallop up the road and into the area of open farmland, beyond which they could see the British line drawn up some 750 yards distant. It was, in Harris's view, a great deal longer than that which had been encountered at Chippewa, and he sent back a man to inform Scott accordingly.

The irony was that if he had arrived just a few minutes earlier he would have found the entire position deserted. When the light dragoon vedette had galloped in from Willson's Tavern its commander had informed Riall that Brown's entire division was advancing. Riall, still nervous after his rebuff at Chippewa, estimated Brown's strength to be in the region of 5,000 men (it was actually closer to 3,000) and, doubting the ability of Pearson's small command to withstand an assault in such force, he gave orders for a withdrawal to Queenston. Hardly had the position been vacated than the retreating troops encountered Morrison's column, with which Drummond had been riding. Drummond, less than pleased, countermanded the order. After some frank speaking with Riall, he gave instructions for the combined force to reoccupy the position and sent back a galloper with instructions for Colonel Hercules Scott's column to hurry forward. As now formed, the British line followed Lundy's Lane with the weak 1st Militia Brigade on the extreme right, followed in succession by the Glengarry Light Infantry, wearing a green uniform similar to that of British rifle regiments, the Royal Scots, the 89th, the light company of the 41st and the light company of the King's holding the crossroads with the composite militia battalion on their left and the light dragoons to their rear. As before, the artillery, now consisting of two 24-pounder guns, two 6-pounder guns, one 5½-inch howitzer and the rocket detachment, under the overall command of Captain James Maclachlane RA, was positioned on the low hill beside the church. The time was now approximately 19:00.

If Brigadier-General Winfield Scott's handling of his brigade at Chippewa had been a model of sound tactical judgement, the reverse was true at Lundy's Lane. Thanks to his unsparing efforts he had undoubtedly

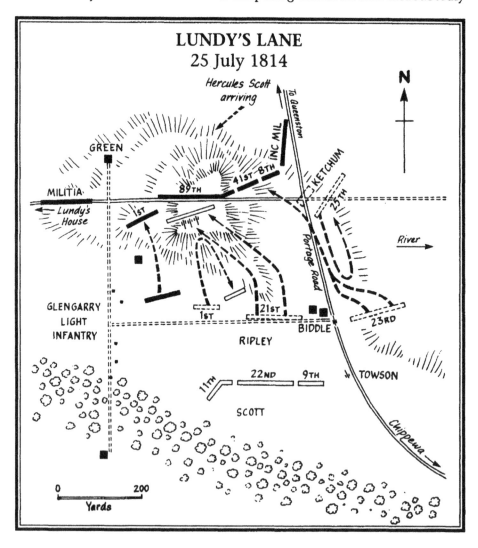

made it the finest formation in the US Army; now, thanks to a series of mistaken decisions, it was to be uselessly squandered.[6] Despite the ominous implications inherent in Harris's contact report, Scott persisted in his intention of giving battle when prudence suggested awaiting the arrival of Brown with the rest of the Left Division. After Jesup's 25th Infantry had been ordered to cover the right flank by advancing north between the river road and the Niagara itself, he deployed the rest of the brigade on the left of the road with the 9th Infantry on the right, the 22nd Infantry in the centre and the 11th Infantry on the left, Towson's guns coming up to conform on the right of the 9th while Harris moved his dragoons into position just behind them.

The Americans had emerged from the chestnut woods at about 19:15. Maclachlane's guns and the rocket detachment opened fire from the hill immediately. The gunfire was accurate and effective, blowing gaps in the ranks of the halted regiments. The 12-pounder Congreve rockets, fitted with solid ball, shell or airburst shrapnel warheads, were less so since they were unstable in flight and rarely hit the target they were intended for. A large proportion simply climbed skywards, but those that managed to maintain level flight had a very damaging effect on the recipients' morale. Unlike cannon shot or howitzer shells, the course of which could to some extent be predicted, the rockets changed direction frequently and without warning; furthermore, their noise, fiery tails and the thunderclap detonations of explosive warheads at head height was extremely alarming.

This was the moment when Scott, realising that he was outnumbered and outgunned, could have withdrawn. He subsequently gave two reasons for not doing so: firstly, he hoped that by standing fast he would overawe his opponents; and secondly, so highly did the rest of the Left Division think of his brigade, its morale could be fatally damaged if it was seen to be withdrawing. Neither reason bears close examination. The truth was that at Lundy's Lane Scott was as over-confident as Riall had been at Chippewa; and, pig-headed as he was, he was determined to repeat his success as soon as Brown appeared with the rest of the division. That, unfortunately for his men, would take far longer than he anticipated.

In the meantime, the 9th, 11th and 22nd were being systematically blown apart. Scott ordered them to open fire, but as this was delivered at extreme range little damage was done and the principal result was to empty the men's cartridge boxes. Towson had tried in vain to respond with counter-battery fire but his guns, being on the flat, lacked the necessary elevation to reach those on the hill and at length fell silent. Harris's dragoons, having lost several men and horses to no purpose, withdrew behind the chestnut wood.

At about 20:00 Scott ordered the three regiments to advance in order to shorten the range, then changed his mind and halted them after they had covered 100 yards. This actually worsened the brigade's situation, for the Glengarry Light Infantry, moving out of the British line in skirmish order, began to engage its left. Drummond, noting the move with approval, despatched the three companies of Royal Scots to support them. Scott could only respond by instructing the 11th to refuse its own left and offer a front. Shortly after this the Americans ran out of ammunition.

It was this and the concurrent transition from fading light to total darkness that saved Scott's brigade from destruction, for the British gunners, deprived of the line of muzzle flashes at which to aim, could only fire at random and by 20:45 their guns had fallen silent save for the occasional shot. The three American regiments had incurred casualties amounting to 60 per cent of their strength and the fact that they were still standing was a tribute to the excellence of their discipline. Even so, Major Henry Leavenworth, commanding the 9th, told Scott that the moment had come to withdraw. Scott had just replied to the effect that they must hang on until Brown arrived when his horse was killed under him. If, at that moment, Drummond had ordered a general advance with the bayonet there is no doubt that Scott's remnants would have been swept off the field. Nevertheless, there were excellent reasons why he did not do so. Because of the darkness, he was unaware of the whereabouts or intentions of the rest of the Left Division, which he still believed outnumbered his own force, and in these circumstances he was understandably reluctant to move out of a good defensive position – especially as a sudden and quite unexpected crisis had developed on his own left flank.

Those responsible for this were Jesup's 25th Infantry who, it will be recalled, had been ordered to cover the right of Scott's brigade by advancing north between the river road and the river itself. No opposition had been encountered and as the light faded Jesup came across an unguarded track which he believed would emerge close to the British left wing. Deploying one of his companies in skirmish order to cover his own left, he led the regiment along the track and found this to be the case. While the attention of the Canadian militia holding the British flank was distracted by his skirmishers, with whom they were exchanging shots, Jesup formed the 25th in line unnoticed, fired a volley and charged home with the bayonet. The two nearest Canadian companies were quickly overrun, the survivors surrendering or scattering into the darkness while the rest of their regiment fell back in some disorder west of the river road, while the light companies of King's and the 41st, together with the left wing of the 89th, conformed to the movement in order to offer a refused flank. Jesup promptly pushed forward a company under Captain Daniel Ketchum to take possession of the now-abandoned Lundy's Lane/river road crossroads. Here it reaped a rich harvest in prisoners as British officers and men, unaware of the American presence in the darkness, simply walked into the trap. Among them was Major-General Phineas Riall who, hit in the arm by a stray round, was looking for a surgeon to dress his wound. Riall is said to have asked Ketchum his name and when told responded with wry humour, 'Well, you've certainly caught us!' At length, having collected more prisoners than he could safely handle, Ketchum fell back on the main body of his regiment where Jesup told him told him to escort the captives to the rear. Shortly after, the party was fired on, almost certainly by a party of rallied Canadian militiamen, and in the ensuing confusion most of the prisoners, save Riall and the officers, who were closely guarded, managed to escape back to their own lines. Soon after this incident Jesup was told what had happened to the rest of Scott's brigade and that no reinforcements had arrived. Believing that the battle was now irretrievably lost, he therefore began marching his regiment to the rear but had only covered a few hundred yards when he encountered Brown, bringing up the rest of the Left Division, led by Ripley's brigade. He therefore halted and awaited further orders.

The arrival of reinforcements was greeted with a thin cheer by Scott's regiments. Soon after, prolonged cheering from the British line indicated the arrival of the first units of Colonel Hercules Scott's column and American morale sank anew. Both commanders now made preparations to renew the battle. Drummond withdrew the Royal Scots from their exposed position, extended his line to the right with the 103rd and 104th as they came up and added the column's three 6-pounders to the guns on the hill. Darkness was now complete save for a moon that struggled to penetrate the slowly dispersing clouds of powder smoke. In these circumstances most commanders would have taken additional precautions for the security of their guns, either by posting pickets ahead of them or absorbing them into the line. Drummond unfortunately did neither, with near fatal consequences.

For his part, Brown was faced with only two alternatives. Confronted with an enemy present in superior strength and the virtual destruction of Scott's brigade, he could withdraw; or, he could renew the assault, using the darkness to conceal his approach, and capture the hill which dominated the British position. Taking a finely calculated risk he decided upon the latter, using Ripley's regulars.

Since Chippewa, Ripley's brigade had been reinforced with Lieutenant-Colonel Robert Nicholas' 1st (now 3rd) Infantry, just 150 men strong. It was decided that this regiment should mount a diversionary attack while Lieutenant-Colonel Joseph Miller's 21st Infantry, which was regarded as the best in the division, advanced obliquely on the hill and carried it with the bayonet, supported on their right by the 23rd Infantry under Major Daniel McFarland and Jesup's 25th.

Save in detail, the plan worked. The sound of the 1st Infantry's approach was detected by Maclachlane's gunners who engaged the regiment with canister, inflicting casualties and forcing it to pull back to the base of the hill. The noise, however, had masked all other sound and the gunners' night vision had been impaired by their own muzzle flashes, so that the approach of the 21st Infantry from the south-east went undetected. Before the gun crews knew what was happening, the Americans had rested their muskets on the cemetery's rail fence, fired a volley, and were coming at them with the bayonet. Some were killed and others were captured, but the rest made off, taking with them the rammers, sponges, buckets and handspikes in accordance with standard procedure, thereby rendering the guns useless to their captors. Alarmed by the sudden uproar, the artillery horse teams bolted through the ranks of the 89th, scattering them. Colonel Morrison, however, was a Peninsula veteran. He quickly restored order and, in conjunction with the light companies of the 41st and the King's, the 89th mounted a series of local counter-attacks with the object of recovering the guns. These failed, largely because the clutter of limbers and ammunition wagons parked on Lundy's Lane broke up the British line before it could come to grips. On Miller's right, however, McFarland's 23rd Infantry, a regiment more used to defeat than victory and seriously lacking in self-confidence, bolted as soon as it came under fire. Nevertheless, on this occasion the officers took hold, rallied their men and led them back into the line. On the American right flank Jesup's 25th took up position to the north-west of the crossroads. By 21:45 the Americans were in firm possession of the objective with their line running approximately along Lundy's Lane. The position was consolidated by the arrival of Biddle's artillery company with the 25th, Towson's with the 23rd and Ritchie's with the 1st, which had come up on the left of the 21st. Porter's militia brigade came up on the American left and, halting short of the lane, presented a partially refused flank to the west.

Drummond's line now ran obliquely from north-east to south-west, two-thirds being north of Lundy's Lane and one-third to the south. Those south of the lane, including most of the 103rd, two companies of the 104th, three companies of Royal Scots, five companies of Kingsmen and the Glengarry Light Infantry, who had been fired upon by their own side as they withdrew during the confusion, actually overlapped the American line by several hundred yards and were in a position to deliver a decisive riposte, despite the presence of Scott's survivors, had Drummond been aware of the fact. Unfortunately, because of the darkness and the extremely fluid situation, he was not. The one thought uppermost in his mind was the recovery of his guns and to achieve this he mounted three frontal attacks in succession, using all his troops north of the lane. Each of these brought the opposing battle lines to within point-blank range of the other for periods of approximately 30 minutes before the British fell back. During the last attack some of 89th, commanded by Major Miller Clifford, actually got among the captured guns and bayonets were crossed in vicious hand-to-hand fighting until the regimental buglers blew Retire.

So close were the contending lines that muzzle flashes clearly revealed the buttons and the whites of eyes in powder-blackened faces opposite. Darkness thickened by dense smoke often prevented the combatants from identifying each other until the last possible moment, the colour of their uniforms being invisible and the shape of their shakos being almost identical; often, the only means of identification was a brief illumination of the differing metal shako plates. The common language also added to the confusion; some men became captives because of it, while others escaped capture. British prisoners were led into the church through a door at one end of the building and escaped by climbing through a window at the other.

Most of the senior officers present were wounded. Drummond was hit in the neck shortly after the loss of his guns but remained in action despite losing a great deal of blood. Towards the end of the battle a ball passed through Brown's right thigh. Jesup received no less than four wounds. Ripley and Porter both had narrow escapes that left their uniforms holed and torn.

By now Scott's brigade had been reorganised into a single composite unit under Colonel Hugh Brady. Brown's intention was that it should remain in reserve behind Ripley's brigade and be used to administer 'the finishing blow to the enemy at some favourable moment, when we could more distinctly see our way;' which, of course, would not be before first light. At about 23:00, however, Scott decided to act on his own initiative by attempting to break the British line with an attack in column. His intention was to take the brigade through the American line between the 21st and 23rd then turn west along Lundy's Lane until he had reached a point on Porter's left, from whence he would launch his attack. He later claimed that he had warned Ripley's regiments of this but clearly his message, if it got through, was misunderstood, for no sooner had his brigade entered the lane than it was heavily fired upon by both sides. Scott had his second horse killed beneath him and the column, badly cut up, broke and fled

westward until it was rallied on Porter's left. Even then he refused to abandon his plan and started to lead the survivors against what he believed to
be the British flank. To his left the 103rd, 104th and Royal Scots quickly
detected the movement and sent volley after volley thudding into the column's ranks until it withdrew. By now there were many, even in this
superbly disciplined brigade, who had begun to doubt their commander's
judgement and only one hundred or so men remained in its ranks. Sensing
the mood, Scott made his way across the American rear to the 25th and
was talking to Jesup when he was incapacitated by a musket ball through
the shoulder.

By midnight both armies had fought themselves to the point of exhaustion. As the firing died away Brown was assured by some of his officers that
not only had the British gone but also that he had won a great victory. He
took no steps to verify the former and if he believed the latter he must
have known it was pyrrhic in character. Knowing that Scott's brigade had
all but ceased to exist, that his guns were out of ammunition, that casualties had reduced the 25th Infantry to a single rank, that Porter's brigade
had already broken once, that the infantry had been reduced to collecting
cartridges from the dead and that there were probably no more than 800
men holding the line, he was well aware that his army could not withstand
another attack. Exhaustion and the pain of his wound combined to dull
his judgement and, agreeing to a suggestion that the troops should withdraw to the camp at Chippewa for food and rest, he designated Ripley as
commander and left the field. On his instructions the American artillery
had already pulled back, save for a damaged 5½-inch howitzer and one 6-
pounder gun in Towson's company which had to be left behind because
no horse teams were available. For the same reason, all but one of the captured British guns were left where they were. Most of the wounded were
loaded into wagons and finally the weary infantry formed column and
marched back along the river road to Chippewa. When Ripley arrived at
the camp he was disgusted to find that, by his estimation, it already contained about 1,000 men, many of whom had left the line with the excuse
of escorting wounded comrades to the rear. Visiting Brown in his tent, he
was ordered by the latter to return to the battlefield at dawn and bring
away the rest of the captured guns.

Drummond had merely retired his troops a few hundred yards into the
darkness. He was aware of his own heavy losses but he knew that Brown's
were probably heavier. He was also absolutely determined to recover his
guns, without which he would be at a fatal disadvantage in future engagements, and his weary troops, some units of which had not been involved
in the previous night's counter-attacks, fully expected the battle to be

rejoined next morning. At first light they formed up and began to move forward, To their surprise and pleasure they encountered no opposition whatever and by 07:00 they were in possession of the hill, now strewn with the casualties of both sides and the carcasses of dead horses. All save one of their guns were recovered, plus the two abandoned by Towson. While part of his division set about collecting the wounded for despatch to Fort George and collecting the dead for burial or cremation, Drummond pushed a strong detachment south to Willson's Tavern. Here, at about 10:00, the Americans appeared from the direction of Chippewa, but after a period during which each side regarded the other without opening fire, they turned about and disappeared.

Despite Brown's orders, Ripley was well aware that the Left Division was in no condition to fight another major action. It was not, in fact, until 09:00 that the three brigades, with only 1,500 men between them, left the camp at Chippewa. The attitude of officers and men left Ripley in no doubt that a renewal of the contest was far from welcome and, when his light troops sent back an inaccurate report to the effect that the British detachment at Willson's Tavern outnumbered him he had no hesitation in convening a council of war. When Porter, Towson and others concurred with his view that the division should withdraw to Fort Erie he returned to Chippewa. Brown was furious but, being on the point of being evacuated to Buffalo with Scott and other wounded officers, reluctantly accepted the majority decision. By 15:00 the Left Division had broken camp and, having thrown its non-transportable supplies into the river, was marching south to Fort Erie, vindictively burning Bridgewater Mills before it left.

Lundy's Lane was the most bitterly contested battle of the war. Drummond's casualty return included 84 killed, 559 wounded, 42 men known to be prisoners and 193 missing, a total of 878. Again, Donald Graves' research, taking into account the American listing of 169 British prisoners, suggests a lower overall figure, probably in the region of 800. Brown reported 173 killed, 571 wounded and 117 missing, a total of 860. The much higher proportion of American dead stemmed largely from the needless immolation of Scott's brigade, which incurred the loss of 109 killed, 350 wounded and 57 missing.

Opinions as to who won the Battle of Lundy's Lane have been divided ever since. Certainly Brown was the tactical victor at midnight, but his decision to abandon the field and with it the captured artillery forfeited his success. He may have assumed, without any real justification, that the battle was over. Against this, and despite his orders for Ripley to return the following morning, he appeared to accept, subconsciously at least, that the Left Division had been fought to its limits. For his part, Drummond could not afford to accept that the battle was over. Both he and his troops were prepared to resume the action at dawn, which the Americans were not. Had the latter chosen to remain on the position overnight, the coming of light would have revealed the full extent of their weakness. The probability is that, after resisting for a while, they would have been driven off the field by Drummond's superior numbers and his ability to manoeuvre against their flanks. Such thoughts must have been running through Brown's mind and in the circumstances his decision to abandon the field was the correct one.

A week later, Drummond followed up the Left Division's withdrawal to Fort Erie, which he found had been strengthened by newly constructed earthworks. On 14 August an attempt to storm the defences proved abortive when a powder magazine blew up with heavy loss of life. The following month Drummond decided to abandon the siege, for which he was ill-equipped.[7] On 17 September, as his guns were being pulled out of their emplacements, the Americans mounted a major sortie. This was repulsed after each side had sustained in excess of 500 casualties, and he withdrew to the Chippewa line. Having been reinforced with their Right Division, the Americans closed up but were unable to make further progress. By the beginning of November the new American commander on the Niagara front, Major-General George Izard, had become anxious to obtain winter quarters for his troops and, having already retired to Fort Erie, and blown up its entrenchments, his troops crossed to the United States. So ended the last American invasion of Canada.

Elsewhere, the scales had begun to tilt against the United States as Wellington's Peninsula veterans began reaching North America in large numbers. During the absence of Izard and his Right Division on the Niagara front Prevost launched an invasion of New York state with 10,000 men and was only prevented from advancing beyond Plattsburg when the British lost control of Lake Champlain. However, with the war now entering its third year, the American militia proved as unreliable as ever. Fighting from within entrenchments, they were able to repulse British attacks on Baltimore in September and New Orleans the following January, but in the open field they remained incapable of standing up to regular troops. At Bladensburg on 24 August 1814 some 6,000 of them, commanded by same incompetent Major-General William Winder who has featured earlier in these pages, were routed and put to flight in a matter of minutes by only 1,500 British regulars, the advance guard of a 5,400-strong landing force commanded by Major-General Robert Ross. Continuing their advance, Ross's troops entered Washington, which they occupied for two days, burning the public buildings in reprisal for American depredations on the Niagara front.[8] They then marched back to their ships, virtually unmolested. As a result of this Secretary of War Armstrong was replaced by James Monroe, a future President of the United States.

The time had come to make peace. The war was producing no benefits for either side and with Napoleon now in temporary exile on Elba the Continental System, one of its primary causes, no longer existed. Despite the continued failings of the militia, the news of Chippewa and Lundy's Lane strengthened the somewhat weak hand of the American peace commissioners, since it proved that the United States could produce regular troops capable of meeting the best in the world on even terms. A peace treaty, based on the status quo ante-bellum, was concluded at Ghent on 24 December.

Many of the officers who served with the Left Division achieved high rank and profoundly influenced the Army's development during the next half century. Brown became General-in-Chief in 1821, but poor health and bad investments marred his later years; he died in 1828, aged 52. Scott ended the war as a brevet major-general. For the next 30 years he concentrated on the introduction of sound training methods, taking the French Army as his model. In 1846 he commanded the American army during its successful campaign in Mexico. He, too, became General-in-Chief and was still serving when the Civil War broke out. He devised the Anaconda Plan for the crushing of the Confederacy but, sickened by political interference in the army's affairs, he retired in November 1861. Ripley also ended the war as a brevet major-general but became involved in an acrimonious feud with Brown and left the army in 1820. Porter returned to politics and held the post of Secretary for War for a year during the presidency of John Quincy Adams. Towson became Paymaster General in 1819 and held the post for 34 years, retiring with the rank of major-general; in 1848 he presided over a court of inquiry into Scott's disbursement of public funds in Mexico. Jesup ended the war as a brevet colonel. In 1818 he was promoted brigadier-general and appointed Quartermaster General, a post he was still holding when he died in 1860.

There is, therefore, because of the legacy of these men, an excellent argument to be made that, the lessons of the Revolutionary War having been forgotten by 1812, the modern United States' Army more properly has its origins in the Niagara Campaign of 1814, and especially in the Battles of Chippewa and Lundy's Lane.

Notes
1. There were just sufficient blue uniforms to equip one regiment; they were given to the 21st Infantry. Shortage of blue cloth also meant that the West Point cadets began wearing grey uniforms in 1814, and they have continued to do so ever since, thereby perpetuating the memory of Left Division.

2. Serving with the squadron was Lieutenant William Arnold, son of the notorious Benedict Arnold who had changed sides during the Revolutionary War.

3. One of the 'lost' Irish regiments disbanded in 1922.

4. Recorded by Scott in his *Memoirs*. The more popular version, 'These are regulars, by God!' first appeared in Charles Elliott's biography of Scott, published in 1937.

5. The 103rd and 104th were disbanded in 1817, although the Canadian Army's Royal New Brunswick Regiment retains an area connection to the latter. No connection exists with the 103rd and 104th Regiments added to the British Army following the Indian Mutiny, these being directly descended from European regiments in the service of the Honourable East India Company.

6. It was typical of Scott that he should decline any responsibility for this. Instead, he blamed the militia officer who had, quite correctly, informed Brown of the British activity on the opposite bank of the Niagara, on the grounds that this had precipitated the action at Lundy's Lane.

7. The unpleasant Mr Willcocks was shot dead by a British or Canadian sniper during the siege. Those of his renegades who survived the war, knowing they faced the noose if they returned to Canada, were forced to make a new life for themselves in the United States.

8. Among the buildings burned was the 'President's Palace' on Pennsylvania Avenue. The sandstone walls of this were so badly marked by the fire that when it was rebuilt they were painted white and the building subsequently became known as The White House.

CHAPTER THREE

Mission Impossible –
The Reliefs of Lucknow

Although in the years prior to and shortly after Independence some Indian politicians chose to regard the Great Mutiny of 1857 as a war of national liberation the idea is not tenable, for without widespread Indian assistance it would have taken the British authorities far longer than they did to contain and finally put down the outbreak; again, the fact that the Mutiny was largely confined to the Honourable East India Company's Bengal Army, leaving the Bombay and Madras Armies almost untouched, in itself confirms that, while the rebellion covered a wide area, large parts of the sub-continent were either untouched by these events or actually hostile to those involved. Yet, it has to admitted that what took place amounted to more than a mutiny, since many of those who took up arms in support of the mutineers included some princely rulers and other elements of Indian society seeking the restoration of vested interests and influence that had been sharply curtailed by the Company's rule.

Most Indians had benefited from the Company's presence, which brought peace, law and stability. On the other hand, in a society that was feudal and innately conservative, deeply religious and dominated by the concept of caste, the Company's application of mid-Victorian zeal for the welfare of its subject people was sometimes dangerously insensitive. Thus, measures permitting widows to remarry and the establishment of a land title system where none had existed previously, resulting in the wholesale confiscation of land regarded as hereditary property, were met with quite unexpected anger. It was, however, Christian missionary activity which caused most anger among Hindus, especially the Brahmins, who saw in it a deliberate attempt to undermine the caste system which formed so fundamental an article of their own faith.

Many of the Bengal Army's sepoys were high-caste Hindus, recruited in the princely state of Oudh, which had been so seriously misgoverned that it had recently been annexed by the Company. This in itself caused widespread resentment, but what angered the majority of sepoys most was the imposition of new conditions of service requiring them to serve outside India if the need arose, since crossing the sea would deprive them of their caste. In such circumstances they were inclined to listen to tales of British shortcomings in the Crimea, simultaneously noting that there were fewer British troops present in India, and ponder the old augury that the Company's rule would end during the hundredth anniversary of the Battle of Plassey. Concurrently, messengers carrying a single chapatti began reaching the villages by night, always with instructions that four more chapattis should be baked and passed on to four more villages; no one knows to this day the origins of these strange arrivals, nor their intended significance, but to simple minds they foretold great and probably violent events.

Normally, potential disaffection among the troops would have been quickly spotted and dealt with by their British officers. However, the formerly good relationship between officers and men, forged in such hard-fought struggles as the Sikh Wars, had become more distant during the years of peace that had followed. Some of the newer generation of junior officers, recently arrived from England, disliked the sepoys and spent as little time as possible with them. Others, more conscientious, saw trouble ahead but their warnings were brushed aside by superiors who, thinking of days past, simply refused to believe that the sepoys would not remain true to their salt.

Matters were brought to a head by the attempted issue of the now notorious greased cartridges for the new Enfield rifle. A clever rumour was started to the effect that the grease was a compound of cow and pig fat and, since the cow was sacred to the Hindus and the pig abominated by Muslims, sepoys of both faiths believed that they would be defiled by contact with it. To many it seemed that the imposition of the cartridges was another step along the road towards enforced Christianity. Some regiments simply refused to accept them and were disbanded, their sepoys thus forfeiting both their pensions and the status in which they were held in their home villages.

Matters came to a head at Meerut on 24 April 1857 when an ill-considered attempt was made to impose the cartridges on the 3rd Light Cavalry. Eighty-five troopers who refused to accept them were court martialled, sentenced to a term of hard labour and publicly stripped of their uniforms before the entire garrison during a parade at which the British regiments pointedly carried loaded weapons and the native regiments did not.

The authorities, somewhat belatedly, had already promised to look into the question of the offending grease but the sepoys were either unaware of this or, more probably, had simply lost confidence in them. By now, most of them felt they had been pushed so far that only three alternatives remained to them. They could accept the cartridges and in so doing damn their own souls; they could refuse them and suffer disgrace and harsh pun-ishment; or they could mutiny and destroy the system that threatened them. On Sunday 10 May, while the British troops were at church parade, the native regiments at Meerut chose mutiny, embarking on a frenzied orgy of destruction and slaughter in which neither their British officers, nor the latters' wives and families, were spared. Then, they set off for Delhi, only 36 miles distant, where similar horrific scenes were enacted.

The mutiny spread like wildfire throughout the entire Bengal Army. Some of the more alert garrison commanders disarmed their native regi-ments before any real harm could be done. Others, slow to react, paid the penalty with their lives. Suddenly, all over northern India, small British garrisons, burdened with their families and refugees seeking their protec-tion, found themselves fighting for their lives. Taken completely by sur-prise, the authorities struggled to put together a field force from the few British troops at their disposal and such Indian troops as remained loyal.

One man who was not taken by surprise was Brigadier-General Sir Henry Lawrence, the Chief Commissioner for Oudh, who was based at Lucknow the state capital, in the centre of the most disaffected area. Lawrence had originally been commissioned into the Bengal Artillery and had spent most of his life in India. Understanding the country and its people as he did, he had long been aware that a mutiny was probable and had taken suitable precautions.[1]

Lucknow was a sprawling, labyrinthine Indian city bordered to its east by the river Gumtee and to the south by a canal. The principal buildings of the city, including palaces, temples and mosques, often enclosed by walls and separated by gardens, lay beside the river. Just to the north of these lay the British Residency, an odd combination of Indian and Italianate architecture, situated within its own enclosure on a small plateau. On all save the northern side the buildings of the city pressed close against the walls and in some areas overlooked them.

In May Lawrence had begun to fortify the Residency, establishing a defended perimeter with gun positions, putting a garrison into a tumble-down fort named the Muchhee Bhowan a half-mile to the north, and lay-ing in supplies of food, forage and ammunition. Plans were also made for the evacuation of the city's European population into the Residency should the need arise.

Lawrence had already disbanded one Oudh irregular unit when, on 14 May, news arrived of the Meerut mutiny. He received warning that the native element of his own garrison, including one cavalry regiment, three infantry regiments and an artillery battery, would mutiny during the evening of 30 May. This intelligence proved to be accurate, although the

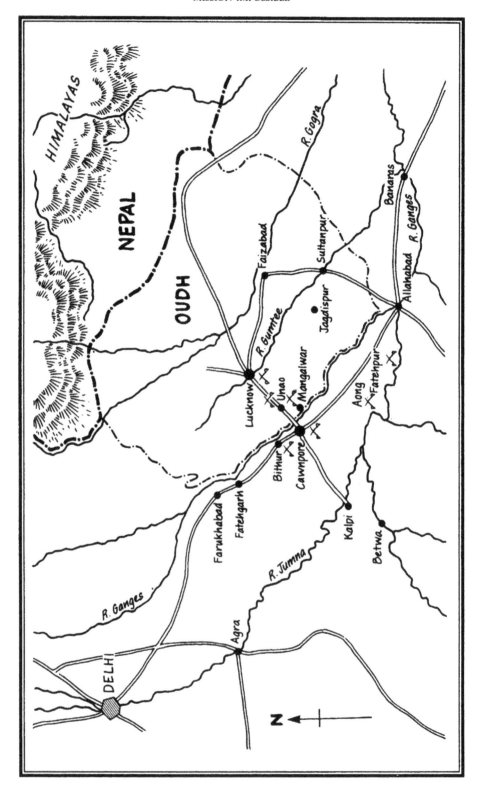

mutineers were chased out of the city and cantonment areas by the under-strength 32nd Regiment (later the Duke of Cornwall's Light Infantry) under the command of Colonel J. E. W. Inglis, and 4/1 Battery Bengal Artillery,[2] a European unit, before they could approach the Residency.

For their own security, Lucknow's European civilians had been brought into the Residency that day. An interesting list of their numbers has survived, paying due heed to the hierarchical social structure of the day. Thus, the entries showing the presence of 69 ladies and 68 ladies' children is followed by those of 171 'other women' and 196 of their children, 125 'uncovenanted servants', and eight employees of the Martinière School, a large building to the south of the city that would feature prominently in later fighting. It was said that at first some of the ladies found themselves 'utterly unable to cope without their husbands and servants,' but when the Residency came under siege they buckled to in the hospital and kitchens, took the strain off the fighting men in as many ways as they could, loaded muskets and even fired them. One of the two surgeons present was Dr William Brydon who, wounded in several places and riding a dying horse, had staggered into the besieged fortress of Jellalabad during the First Afghan War, believing that he was the sole survivor of the massacred Kabul garrison; he was not, but was immortalised just the same by Lady Butler in her *The Remnant of an Army*.[3]

By 12 June it was clear that every British outpost in Oudh had fallen. Lawrence and those with him were entirely alone in the enemy's heartland without any immediate prospect of relief. Towards the end of the month this sense of isolation was heightened by the news that the Cawnpore garrison had surrendered, although the horrible details of its fate did not become known in their entirety for some time. Curiously, despite Lawrence's fears to the contrary, the rebels left Lucknow alone until 29 June, when a force estimated to number 500 infantry, 50 cavalry and one gun was said to have reached Chinhut, some ten miles distant. In fact, the enemy's strength was well over ten times that quoted but Lawrence took no steps to verify the truth and allowed himself to be talked into attacking the rebels. Next day he set off with 300 men of the 32nd, 170 loyal sepoys, about 100 cavalry and eleven guns. Despite the fact that his opponents were trained, professional soldiers, many still wearing infantry scarlet or light cavalry silver-grey, he neglected to take the elementary precaution of reconnaissance and found himself engaged on the most unfavourable terms from the outset. His small force stood not the slightest chance of even winning the firefight and was driven back into the Residency having incurred 200 casualties and lost five guns, one of them a powerful eight-inch howitzer that was later used against the defences, to no purpose. The

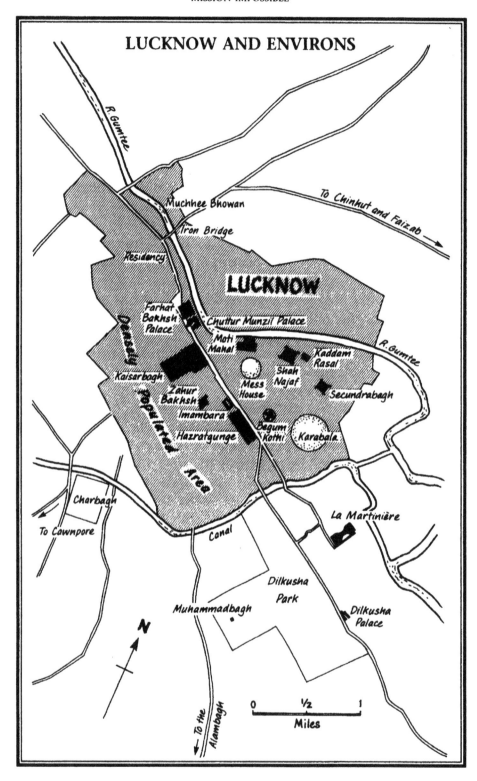

only benefit from the action was that the garrison of the Muchhee Bhowan was ordered to retire within the main perimeter that night, the move being completed without incident. It seems unlikely that the fort, which was blown up to prevent its occupation by the enemy, could have resisted independently for long and, given the subsequent casualties incurred within the Residency itself, it is probable that this too would have fallen without the additional manpower thus made available.

The affair at Chinhut had been a disaster for the Residency garrison. Not only did the rebels close in very quickly around the defences, but many of their fellows also converged on Lucknow, bringing with them every malcontent in Oudh, all of them elated by the British defeat. Many of the large buildings immediately outside the perimeter had not been demolished, an omission for which the garrison began to pay at once.

'Our heaviest losses,' wrote Inglis in his despatch, 'have been caused by fire from the enemy's sharpshooters, stationed in the adjoining mosques and houses of the native nobility, the necessity of destroying which had been repeatedly drawn to the attention of Sir Henry (Lawrence) by the staff of engineers. But his invariable reply was, "Spare the holy places, and private property too, as far as possible." And we have consequently suffered severely from our very tenderness to the religious prejudices, and respect to the right of our rebellious citizens and soldiery. As soon as the enemy had thoroughly completed the investment of the Residency they occupied these houses, some of which were within easy pistol shot of our barricades, in immense force, and rapidly made loopholes on those sides which bore on our post, from which they kept up a terrific and incessant fire, day and night, which caused us many daily casualties, as there could not have been less than 8,000 men firing at one time into our position. Moreover, there was no place in the whole of our works that could be considered safe, for several of the sick and wounded, lying in the banqueting hall, which had been turned into a hospital, were killed in the very centre of the building.

'Neither were the enemy idle in erecting batteries. They soon had from twenty to twenty-five guns in position, some of them of a very large calibre. These were planted all round our post at small distances, some being actually within fifty yards of our defences, but in places where our own heavy guns could not reply to them, while the perseverance and ingenuity of the enemy in erecting barricades in front of and around their guns in a very short time, rendered all attempts to silence them by musketry unavailing. Neither could they be effectually silenced by shells, by reason of their extreme proximity to our position, and because, moreover, the enemy had recourse to digging very narrow trenches, about eight feet in

71

depth, in rear of each gun, in which the men lay while our shells were fly- ing, and which so effectually concealed them, even while working the gun, that our baffled sharpshooters could only see their heads while in the act of loading.'

On 1 July Lawrence was sitting in his room, talking to a Mr Coupar, when a shell passed between them and exploded without causing injury to either. Lawrence brushed aside his staff's suggestion that he should change his quarters with the remark that it was unlikely that the enemy could repeat the performance. Unfortunately, they did, the very next day, and Lawrence was mortally wounded. It might well be said that his long years of civil administration had dulled the edge of his military instincts, but it cannot be denied that his foresight and planning saved hundreds of lives, nor that by his decision to defend the Residency he tied down thousands of mutineers whose presence elsewhere might have been critical.

Inglis, later promoted brigadier-general, assumed command, instituting a series of successful sorties that wrecked the enemy's forward posts and spiked his guns, thereby teaching him that, for all the firepower at his dis- posal, he had taken rather too much for granted. These restored the garri- son's understandably shaky morale, enabling it to endure the constant sniping and beat off periodic attacks. Finding their prolonged fire ineffec- tive and unable to penetrate the defences, the rebels resorted to mining. As soon as this was detected the garrison's engineers, assisted by a number of Cornish tin miners from the 32nd, put counter-measures into effect. Although these stealthy subterranean contests generally ended in favour of the defenders, on 10 August the enemy succeeded in blowing up a 20-foot section of the defences and bringing down the outside wall of a house in the process. With pardonable exaggeration, Inglis recorded that a regiment could have marched through the resulting breach in perfect order. In the event, the few mutineers who tried to rush it were either brought down or fled in the face of a withering fire from the roof of the nearby brigade mess; the poor response in itself suggests that the mine could well have been det- onated by accident.

The garrison also had its enemies within the walls. Because of the cramped living conditions diseases such as cholera, dysentery and small- pox, encouraged by poor sanitation and the difficulties involved in dis- posing of human and animal remains, killed or incapacitated nearly as many as the mutineers' guns. The inadequate diet induced scurvy and other skin diseases; heatstroke and trauma also took their toll. In the hos- pital the wounded and sick, for whom there were insufficient beds, some- times lay crowded together on the floor in rows while flies feasted on their bloodied bandages. To add to these difficulties, Dr Brydon was himself wounded. Nevertheless, whenever the mutineers attacked, those who could walk left the hospital to take their place on the defences or, if they were too weak to fight, busied themselves loading muskets. No doubt what remained in every single mind was that if the Residency fell those within it – men, women and children alike – would be savagely butchered.

The siege dragged on through August and on into September without any prospect of relief on the horizon. The primary purpose of this chapter, however, is not solely to describe its course, but also to examine the relief attempts, which involved some of the most difficult and dangerous operations the British Army has ever been asked to perform.

To understand this it is necessary to place the siege in the overall context of the Great Mutiny. Physical possession of the Residency itself was of no military importance whatever to either side, although as long as it remained in British hands it continued to absorb the enemy's attention. It was, however, of immense emotional and political significance to the rebels and the British alike.

It was estimated that at any one time there were between 50,000 and 100,000 mutineers and their supporters in and around Lucknow. This was natural enough, as they wished to re-establish the independent principality of Oudh. In emulation of their comrades in Delhi, who had proclaimed the aged King Bahadur Shah II as Emperor of Hindustan, they appointed a son of the deposed King of Oudh who was now under guard in Calcutta, as Wali (Governor) and set up an administration to govern the country. Ostensibly, their cause had triumphed, the only reminder that their sojourn in power might only be temporary being the repeatedly patched and mended Union Flag, flown defiantly from the tallest tower of the Residency. Every effort must therefore be made to eliminate the hated symbol.

The official British attitude to Lucknow was ambivalent. The military authorities in India recognised that Delhi had become the epicentre of the rebellion and were concentrating their resources on its capture. Substantial reinforcements, including Crimean veterans, were on their way from the United Kingdom and elsewhere around the world, but they would take time to arrive. There were strong arguments against sending what would, of necessity, be a small relief column to Lucknow, not least the consideration that within Oudh the enemy was concentrated in overwhelming strength. Nevertheless, the electric telegraph and the popular press at home ensured that the general public, already outraged by the frightful atrocities that had accompanied the outbreak of the mutiny, were fully aware that in the shot-battered Residency fewer than 1,000 Britons, including women and children, were fighting for their lives alongside their own soldiers and a handful of loyal sepoys. For the British as well as the rebels, therefore, the Residency had become a symbol and, whatever the military considerations, it was politically quite unacceptable that those within should be abandoned without any attempt to reinforce or relieve them.

On 30 June Brigadier-General Sir Henry Havelock arrived at Allahabad, a town containing a major arsenal, situated on the Ganges just south of the Oudh frontier, from which the local rebels had been dispersed. His orders stated that 'He should lose not a moment in supporting Sir Henry (Lawrence) at Lucknow and Sir Hugh Wheeler at Cawnpore, and should take prompt measures for dispersing and utterly destroying all mutineers and insurgents.' Such a brief was absurdly ambitious in the prevailing circumstances. Again, while the use of the vague and in this context meaningless term 'support,' rather than the more specific 'reinforce' or 'relieve,' might perhaps be generously construed as permitting Havelock considerable discretion, its more probable intention was to absolve those who drafted the order from any responsibility if disaster struck.

Havelock, the son of a failed Sunderland shipbuilder, was a Regular Army officer who had chosen to perform his service in India for the very good reason that, having no money of his own, it was cheaper to do so. Now he was aged 62, and some considered him to be too old for the job, but he had a wide-ranging experience of active service, including the epic siege of Jellalabad, a reputation for being cool in action, and was entirely reliable.

It took some days for him to concentrate his supplies, transport and troops, which included three British regiments, the 64th, the 78th and 84th (later, respectively, the North Staffordshire Regiment, 2nd Seaforth Highlanders and 2nd York and Lancaster Regiment) and one Company European regiment, the Madras Fusiliers (later the 1st Royal Dublin Fusiliers[4]), the 3/8th Battery Royal Artillery with four guns and two howitzers, a detachment of Sikhs and about twenty volunteer cavalry. Also present was an irregular cavalry unit of dubious value. As all the regular units were under strength Havelock had less than 2,000 men with which to commence this apparently impossible undertaking.

By the time he left Allahabad on 7 July the fate of the Cawnpore garrison was known. Following their surrender on 27 June Wheeler and his men had been treacherously massacred; their womenfolk and children, it was said, were now being held in captivity as hostages in Cawnpore by the Nana Sahib, otherwise known as Dondhu Pant, Maharaja of Bithur, a town to the north of Cawnpore, who had assumed leadership of the insurgents in that area.[5]

Havelock's first task, therefore, was to secure the release of the women and children. This made no difference to his planned axis of advance which would, in any event, have taken him north to Cawnpore, then across the Ganges into Oudh and eastwards to Lucknow. An advance guard, commanded by a Major Renaud, had left a week earlier and was already well on the way to Cawnpore. On learning of the massacre Renaud took his own indiscriminate revenge, burning the villages he passed through and hanging from the trees every man of military age who could not prove his innocence. Recognising that in the long term such measures were counter-productive, Havelock ordered him to desist unless the villages were clearly in insurgent hands.

The march of the main body from Allahabad commenced by easy stages, mainly because many of the infantry were recruits whose feet had not yet hardened sufficiently. It was also the hot season, when temperatures regularly soared well above 100°F, and because heat-stroke cases were common most marches took place at night. Sensibly, woollen serge tunics and formal headgear were consigned to the regimental baggage, being replaced by shirt-sleeve order and forage cap, the latter with a white cover and neck cloth which, by association, became known as a Havelock.

On 11 July the main column caught up with Renaud four miles from Fatehpur. Havelock's intention was to rest the following day, but while the troops were waiting for their breakfast a rebel force, consisting of approximately 3,500 men and twelve guns, closed in on the encampment. Believing that they had only Renaud's small force to deal with, the mutineers came on full of fight but pulled up sharply when all of Havelock's regiments deployed into line. To their horror they discovered that the new Enfield rifle, with which the British were armed, was extremely effective at ranges beyond the reach of the old Brown Bess musket they had chosen to retain; nor can it have helped when Captain Francis Maude, commanding 3/8 Battery, personally laid a gun that brought down the rebel commander's elephant with the first shot. Seeing the wavering opposite, Havelock gave the order to attack. Panic stricken, the enemy fled before bayonets could be crossed, abandoning all their guns from which Maude was able to re-equip his battery with five 9-pounders and one 24-pound howitzer, the standard armament of a British field battery at the time. From start to finish, the incident had lasted a mere ten minutes. The full extent of the mutineers' loss is not known, but it cannot have been excessive. It would undoubtedly have been much heavier if an irregular cavalry unit serving with the British had not refused to carry out a pursuit; Havelock promptly disarmed it and sent its members on their way. No British casualties had been sustained as a result of enemy action, but twelve men had dropped dead from heat-stroke.

Three days later and ten miles further on, Havelock defeated another enemy force at Aong. This time the rebels put up a much stiffer fight and were only dislodged by a flank attack, the unexpected delivery of which put them to flight, leaving their baggage and stores strewn across a wide area. Among the British casualties was Renaud, mortally wounded. As a direct result of this action Havelock, who lacked any sort of bridging train was able follow up his success and secure the only bridge across the Pandu Nadi river which, though normally fordable, was now swollen by seasonal rains.

It was now necessary for the Nana Sahib to take the field in person or lose all credibility with his followers. Believing, correctly, that the British would advance on Cawnpore along the Grand Trunk Road, he set up a strong blocking position with 8,000 men and eight guns some seven miles outside the city. Havelock, however, had been informed of his dispositions by two very courageous loyal sepoys who had been sent to infiltrate the rebel army the day before, and on 16 July his main body, under cover of a feint directed at the enemy centre, swung off to the right and, concealed by mango groves, carried out a rapid advance which brought it opposite the rebel left. Unable to redeploy quickly enough to meet this unexpected threat, and with most of its guns now masked by their own troops, the Nana Sahib's army was simply rolled up as the 78th Highlanders, pipes skirling, overran a battery with a ferocious bayonet charge, then, with the 64th, cleared a village in the centre of his line. With most of his troops now in flight, the Nana Sahib summoned reinforcements from the city, including several guns which for a while halted the British infantry, advancing in line some way ahead of their own ox-drawn artillery. Unwilling to lose the momentum of the advance, Havelock rode along the ranks, pointing at the enemy battery and urging them on:

'The longer you look at it, men, the less you will like it. Rise up! The brigade will advance!'

Together, the Madras Fusiliers, the 64th, 78th and 84th clambered to their feet and began moving forward again. 'It was irresistible,' wrote Havelock in his despatch. 'The enemy sent round shot into our ranks until we were within three hundred yards, and then poured in grape with such precision and determination as I have seldom witnessed. But the 64th, led by Major Sterling and my aide-de-camp, who had placed himself in their front, were not to be denied. Their rear showed the ground strewed with wounded; but on they steadily and silently came, then with a cheer charged and captured the unwieldy trophy of their valour (a 24-pounder gun). The enemy lost all heart, and after a hurried fire of musketry gave way in total rout. Four of my guns came up and completed their discomfiture by a heavy cannonade; and as it grew dark the roofless barracks of our artillery were dimly descried in advance, and it was evident that Cawnpore was in our possession.'

The victorious column bivouacked for the night outside the city, from within which a series of explosions indicated that the mutineers were blowing up the arsenal and therefore leaving. No resistance was encountered the following morning but on reaching the house known as the Bibighur it was discovered that the hostages, women and children alike, had been slaughtered and mutilated in the most barbaric circumstances the previous day.[6] Blood covered the entire floor of the building, the interior walls of which were also splashed and smeared scarlet while human hair still adhered to the marks made by sword and cleaver cuts. The dead and dying had then been flung down a well in the courtyard until it could hold no more.

The massacre marked a turning point in the Mutiny. The British, fighting for their own survival and to rescue the hostages, were already highly motivated, but after the discoveries at Cawnpore they would fight for vengeance with a savage zeal that was utterly alien to their nature. For the soldiers of the 84th the spectacle was particularly horrible as the victims included some of the regiment's own womenfolk. Some men kept scraps of bloodstained clothing or trinkets which they subsequently took into action with them. The head of one of Wheeler's daughters was discovered and, when a lock of her hair was cut off to send to her relatives, several of the 78th Highlanders also asked for and were given locks. When asked why they were counting the strands they replied with cold, hard fury that they had sworn to kill a rebel for every one of them. Thus far, neither side had sought or given quarter, but from this point on, for the British, the war had become one of extermination.

The troops had marched 126 miles in eight days, during which they had fought several pitched battles against heavy odds and captured 24 guns. It was hardly surprising, therefore, that after discovering the horrors of the Bibighur, they should have located a stock of liquor and rendered themselves insensible for a while.

Nevertheless, Havelock was determined that, if it was humanly possible, the tragedy of Cawnpore would not be repeated at Lucknow. With some difficulty, he collected sufficient boats to bridge the Ganges and, having left a small garrison at Cawnpore, he commenced his march into Oudh on 25 July. He beat the rebels on several occasions in the area of Unao, approximately one third of the way to Lucknow but by the second week of August casualties and cholera had reduced his strength to about 1,500 effectives and he was short of artillery ammunition for his ten guns. With the rebels massing in his path, his lines of communication threatened and the Nana Sahib massing a fresh army at Bithur on his flank, he reluctantly reached the conclusion that, for the moment, it would be necessary to retire to Cawnpore and await the reinforcements he had already requested. During what must have been one of the lowest moments of his career, he wrote to Inglis at Lucknow, urging him that 'When further defence becomes impossible, do not negotiate or capitulate. Cut your way out to Cawnpore.'

This was quite unrealistic, as Inglis indicated in his reply:

'It is quite impossible, with my weak and shattered force, that I can leave my defences. You must bear in mind how I am hampered; that I have upwards of 120 sick and wounded, and at least 220 women and about 230 children, and no carriage of any description, besides sacrificing twenty-three lakhs of treasure and about thirty guns of sorts. In consequence of the news received, I shall soon put this force on half rations. Our provisions will last us then until about the 10th of September.

'If you hope to save this force, no time must be lost in pushing forwards. We are daily being attacked by the enemy, who are within a few yards of our defences ... My strength now in Europeans is 350, and about 300 Natives, and the men are dreadfully harassed; and, owing to part of the Residency having been brought down by round shot, many are without shelter. Our native force having been assured, on Colonel Tytler's authority, of your near approach some twenty-five days ago, are naturally losing confidence, and if they leave us, I do not see how the defences are to be manned.'

In the meantime, Havelock had mounted a punitive expedition against Bithur, where the Nana Sahib, now on his home ground, had collected about 4,000 men and several guns. For some reason he chose to give battle in front of an unfordable stream crossed by a single bridge. The engagement took place in furnace temperatures that cost the British numerous casualties from heat-stroke, but after an hour's hard fighting the mutineers broke and were driven into the stream or across the bridge and through the town. The Nana Sahib's palace and several other buildings were burned to the ground and in December much of his personal treasure, including gold and silver plate and boxes containing the then enormous sum of £200,000 in gold coin, was recovered from the well in which it had been concealed. The entire hoard was claimed by the government, not one penny being allocated as prize money to the troops; in the nature of things, it would have been very surprising indeed if some of the latter had not already found less official ways of benefiting from the find. Now a fugitive who would be hunted implacably by the British, the Nana Sahib played little further part in the Mutiny.[7]

The long-awaited reinforcements, including the 5th (later Royal Northumberland) Fusiliers, the 90th Light Infantry (later 2nd Cameronians), 2/3 and 1/5 Batteries Bengal Artillery, and a contingent of Sikhs from the Punjab had reached Cawnpore by 15 September, raising the strength of the relief column to over 3,000 men. With them came Major-General Sir James Outram, who had been designated commander of the enlarged force and also Civil Commissioner for Oudh. Outram knew Havelock well, the two having served together during the recent campaign in Persia, and, conscious that Havelock had produced the first clear-cut British victories since the Mutiny began, he did not wish his own appointment to be interpreted as an adverse reflection upon him. He therefore issued an order to the effect that while he would personally accompany the column as a volunteer, Havelock would remain in command until Lucknow had been relieved. Technically, such an order was illegal, but it was also extremely generous.

Despite Inglis' gloomy prediction that his rations would not last beyond 10 September, he was still holding out. The relief force began crossing the Ganges again on 18 September and made unexpectedly good progress, defeating an enemy force at Mangalwar three days later. The following day the enemy were found not only to have abandoned their positions covering the vital bridge spanning the river Sai, but also failed to demolish the bridge itself. That night the column bivouacked at Bani, just sixteen miles from Lucknow, within sound of the guns bombarding the Residency.

Such obvious neglect was indicative of rebel disorganisation rather than demoralisation. In an attempt to satisfy their various factions, the rebels had chosen leaders from among them, dispensing with the services of real soldiers such as Barhat Ahmad, who had defeated Lawrence at Chinhut. Consequently, any decisions taken tended to be those of a parliament of fools. Among the mutineers themselves, too, the bonds of discipline had relaxed to the point that regiments had fragmented into bands led by barrack-room lawyers or brigands on the make. Be that as it may, at this period the rebels certainly did not consider themselves to be beaten men, and, moreover, there were 60,000 of them in Lucknow. Very probably, their intention was to allow Havelock to advance until he was in their midst, then destroy his relief column within sight of the Residency garrison.

On 23 September the relief column moved off at 08:30. Twelve miles were covered without incident before the rebels were encountered, drawn up approximately four miles south of Lucknow. Their line, some two miles long, was partially protected by a marsh and its left rested on the Alambagh, the summer place of the former kings of Oudh, located within a large garden enclosed by a high wall with a turret at each angle. Their strength was estimated as being 10,000 infantry with ample artillery in support, and 1,500 cavalry.

As the marsh inhibited a direct assault, Havelock decided to attack the enemy right with a wide turning movement. While this was in progress rebel artillery, previously concealed by trees, opened fire on the marching column, inflicting serious casualties. At this Major Vincent Eyre's 1/5th Battery, which had previously been bombarding the enemy's line, switched its fire to the offending guns. Equipped as it was with 24-pounder guns and two eight-inch howitzers, Eyre's battery could be classed as heavy rather than field and the weight of its shells soon silenced its opponents. It then engaged the mutineer cavalry which, unable to charge because of the marsh and unwilling to endure the concentrated rain of shot, broke and bolted. As the flank attack began to develop the enemy infantry, their cavalry gone and many of their guns silenced, also broke, those who attempted a stand in the Alambagh being hounded out by the 5th Fusiliers. Led by Outram, the Volunteer Cavalry, the strength of which had now risen to 168, pursued the beaten army as far as the canal that marked the southern edge of the city.

That same day Havelock received news, unconfirmed but accurate, that Delhi had fallen amid a great slaughter of mutineers, that the so-called Emperor of Hindustan was now in custody, and that his sons had been shot dead by Major William Hodson, the commander of Hodson's Horse.

Immensely heartened, Havelock and Outram spent the next day deciding how best the Residency could be relieved. The essence of their difficulty was that the Residency was situated on the far side of the city and both knew that street fighting could be prohibitively expensive. Three possible axes of advance were open to them. The first involved bridging the Gumtee, moving north along the river through more open terrain, then recrossing the river by an iron bridge just to the north of the Residency. This had obvious advantages, as the final stage of the advance would be covered by the guns of the Residency itself. Outram, however, insisted that the plan was not feasible, pointing out that three days of continuous rain had so softened the ground that movement of artillery across country would be extremely difficult, and in this he was almost certainly right. The second alternative was to seize the Char bridge over the canal and proceed to the Residency by the direct route through the city. This, too, was rejected, as the rebels were known to have loopholed the buildings on either side of the route and dug trenches across the streets. The third alternative, suggested by Outram, who had previously served as Resident in Lucknow and knew the area well, was to seize the Char bridge, turn east, keeping the canal on the right of the advance until the palaces lining the river were reached, then approach the Residency through their various parks. Street fighting could not be avoided altogether, but this plan offered the best prospects for success and was adopted. Havelock also decided that in the event of failure he would fall back on the Alambagh, in which he left a 300-strong garrison, the sick and wounded and the baggage.

Shortly after 08:00 on 25 September the column moved off, encountering strong opposition long before it reached the Char bridge. This was centred on a two-storeyed building, subsequently known as the Yellow House, to the right-front of the advance. Several enemy guns opened fire from positions near the building, as did infantry from the building itself, from the loopholed walls surrounding its garden, and from a belt of high grass nearby. As Outram had feared, the monsoon rains had rendered the adjacent fields impassable to artillery, although the road approached the bridge along a low causeway and still provided a firm surface. While the British infantry took temporary cover in the lee of the causeway Captain Maude's 3/8 Battery RA pushed two of its 9-pounder guns forward and, firing wheel to wheel, these replied to the enemy artillery. Their detachments began to fall at once but were replaced immediately by men from the battery's other sections; Outram and Maude, standing among the gunners to encourage them, both received minor wounds. At length the enemy's fire had slackened sufficiently for the infantry to clear the vicinity of the Yellow House, forcing the rebel gunners to limber up and retire. By then, Maude's battery had sustained 21 casualties.

The advance on the bridge was resumed but was again halted when the leading infantry came under fire from a battery of five (some sources say six) guns, one of them a 24-pounder, dug in on the far bank of the canal, and from mutineers in gardens and walled enclosures on either flank. Once more, while Outram set about clearing the enclosures, Maude pushed his two leading guns forward, this time to engage in a murderous duel at only 150 yards' range. One gun detachment was wiped out immediately by a bursting shell, but another ran forward to take its place. As more men continued to drop beside the guns, some infantrymen of the 84th responded to Maude's request for help by acting as ammunition carriers and assisting in running up the carriages. By every known law of probability, the two 9-pounders should have been blown to kingdom come yet, somehow, the impossible happened. Within ten minutes they were so clearly winning the firefight that Brigadier-General James Neill, commanding the advance guard in Outram's temporary absence, ordered an assault on the bridge. A forlorn hope consisting of ten men of the Madras Fusiliers, led by Havelock's son and ADC, ran forward onto the structure only to be met by a blast of grapeshot that left only the latter standing.

Before the enemy could reload, the bridge was rushed by elements of the Madras Fusiliers, 5th Fusiliers and the 84th, who bayoneted the gunners then tumbled their guns and ammunition into the canal.[8]

It might be thought that Maude's battery had suffered enough for one day, but at this moment it came under fire from two guns and some infantry that had returned to the vicinity of the Yellow House. On this occasion, however, the menace was quickly disposed of. The 90th Light Infantry, located near the rear of the column, immediately charged and captured the guns, which were then towed off by Captain William Olpherts, commander 2/3 Battery BA, using his own teams and limbers.

Once the bridgehead had been secured the column swung right into a narrow lane while the 78th Highlanders acted as flank guard until its tail had passed. The mutineers, who had probably expected the relief force to take the direct route to the Residency, seem to have been caught wrong-footed, for it was not until the column entered the area of palaces, temples, mosques and gardens that it began to encounter really determined opposition. Here the rebels were concentrated in enormous numbers so that the column was forced to fight its way forward foot by foot along the narrow lanes. Eyre's 24-pounders were ideal tools for this sort of work, blasting the way ahead for the infantry, who, with vengeful shouts of 'Remember Cawnpore!' drove the enemy from one position after another at the point of the bayonet. Nevertheless, the rebels, firing from within loopholed buildings, were able to exact a toll in return. One of Eyre's 24-pounders, pushed too far forward, had to be abandoned for this reason. At considerable risk, it was recovered after dusk when a Private Duffy of the Madras Fusiliers crawled out to tie a drag rope to the trail while Olpherts attached the other end to a team of bullocks he had brought up.[9] By now, under heavy fire from the Kaisarbagh (King's Palace), the head of the column had worked its way into the Chuttur Munzil (Old Palace) and halted so that the remainder, still winding its way along the tortuous route, could close up. To everyone's surprise the 78th Highlanders, recalled from their task as flank guard, rejoined the column near its head instead of its tail, having lost their way among the twisting alleys and captured the enemy's guns in the Kaisarbagh on the way.

Outram felt that, having reached the Chuttur Munzil, it would be sensible to permit a few hours' rest during which the entire column could enter the building. It would then, he thought, be possible to reach the Residency by breaking through the walls of the intervening buildings, a course of action that would go far to reduce casualties. However, in his self-imposed capacity as a volunteer, he was unable to insist and Havelock, knowing that only 500 yards now separated the column from the Residency, was impatient to finish the business.

The route lay along a street intersected with trenches and flanked on both sides by loopholed houses. While storming its way forward the column incurred the heaviest casualties of the entire operation, including Brigadier-General Neill shot dead at close quarters. At length, however, it reached the Residency gates amid scenes of jubilation and joyful relief. Havelock and his senior officers, aware that the garrison was half-starved, were startled to be served a dinner which included mock-turtle soup, beef cutlets and champagne. Nevertheless, the impossibility of pleasing everyone was demonstrated by one *Grande Dame* who haughtily asked an exhausted, battle-stained officer whether Queen Victoria was still alive!

Outram took over at once, relieving Havelock and Inglis of the terrible strain they had endured for months. The tail of the column did not come in until the following evening and only then was it possible to assess the cost of the previous day's fighting. It amounted to an horrific 31 officers and 504 men killed or wounded, and in itself this meant that Outram would be unable to comply with the government's orders to evacuate the Residency and escort its occupants to Cawnpore. In real terms, the relief amounted to nothing more than a reinforcement, enabling him to hold an extended perimeter around the Residency as well as the Alambagh to the south of the town. Had the food supply situation been as bad as Inglis genuinely believed it to be the addition of so many mouths to the garrison would have been little short of disastrous. Fortunately, Outram's personal knowledge of the Residency led him to a swimming pool beneath the building. This was found to contain a huge quantity of foodstuffs stockpiled by Lawrence prior to the siege – sufficient, in fact, to support the enlarged garrison for over two months. For some reason Lawrence had never mentioned the matter to the commissariat officers and they, in turn, did not suspect the existence of the room.

In some ways, the reinforcement of the garrison was counter-productive. It was true that, despite their numbers, the rebels had been unable to prevent it, but it was also true that Havelock and his column, who had for so long been a thorn in their side, were now also besieged and virtual prisoners. This was most unfortunate at a time when mutinies, though fewer in number, were still breaking out. Again, the fact that Outram was now too weak to evacuate the Residency meant that the army would have to mount a second and much stronger relief column to extract the garrison and its dependents before turning its attention to restoring order elsewhere. In the meantime, the siege continued as before with even greater emphasis on mine warfare. Couriers regularly made the hazardous journey to and fro between the Residency and the Alambagh carrying messages written in classical Greek script to prevent their being understood by the mutineers; in due course, and with the assistance of a school encyclopedia, the two garrisons set up semaphore stations in order to communicate with each other. On 27 October a message was received to the effect that the advance guard of the second relief column, commanded by Brigadier-General Hope Grant and consisting of units that had captured Delhi, had reached Cawnpore. On 6 November Hope Grant was in touch again, reporting that he had crossed the Sai and was now waiting for the arrival of General Sir Colin Campbell, the new Commander-in-Chief India, with the main body.

Campbell had probably seen as much fighting as any man alive. The son of an impoverished Glasgow carpenter, his uncle, then a serving officer, had obtained a commission for him while he was still a boy. Since then he had served in the Peninsular War, the War of 1812, the First Opium War, the Second Sikh War and on what later became the North-West Frontier of India. Recalled from retirement on half-pay to command the Highland Brigade during the Crimean War, he had, as a result of his actions at the Alma and Balaklava, become a national hero. As a strategist he was inclined to be cautious, but he was a sound tactician and a hard fighter who, when he attacked, believed in the infantry coming to close quarters as quickly as possible, supported in appropriate circumstances by the artillery firing at point-blank range. Some people found his preference for Scottish regiments, and in particular the 93rd (later the Argyll and Sutherland) Highlanders, the original 'thin red line' with which he had defeated a Russian cavalry probe at Balaklava, a little tiresome, forgetting, perhaps, that he always saw to it that those same regiments were in the forefront of the battle.

It was unusual for the Commander-in-Chief India to take the field personally, but with Outram and Havelock besieged in Lucknow and Brigadier-General John Nicholson, the real driving force behind the siege of Delhi, now dead, the shortage of suitable senior officers was so acute that Campbell felt he had no alternative. He experienced no difficulty in joining Hope Grant, who was nominated column commander, although he retained tactical control himself.

On the morning of 10 November two bedraggled figures made their way into his camp. One was a native spy in Outram's service; the other, who towered over him, was wearing native clothes, had his skin stained with a mixture of oil and lampblack, and concealed a head of fair hair beneath his turban. His name was Thomas Kavanagh and he was a 36-year-old clerk, the father of fourteen children. At Lucknow he had been employed in counter-mining, a task no one enjoyed but at which he became adept. On hearing that Outram was anxious to inform Campbell of the enemy's dispositions and advise him of a better route to the Residency than that which had cost his own relief column so dear, Kavanagh had volunteered for the mission despite the obvious dangers involved. The two had slipped out of Lucknow the previous night, talked their way out of the hands of an enemy patrol that had picked them up, lost their way and been forced to flounder across a swamp, but finally made contact with a British outpost. Campbell described their achievement as 'one of the most daring feats ever attempted.' Kavanagh was rewarded with £2,000, which he used to pay off his numerous debts, and a post in the Civil Service. The recommendation that he should be awarded the Victoria Cross was not initially accepted on the grounds that he was a civilian, this decision being overturned on appeal.

Faced with little opposition, Campbell relieved the Alambagh on 12 November. When the garrison was added to his own troops he had almost 5,000 men and 49 guns available for the relief operation. These included units that had fought at Delhi, including the 8th (later The King's) Regiment and the 75th (later The Gordon) Highlanders, now few in numbers, lean and tired-looking, their skins burned to the colour of mahogany, their original uniforms long since worn out and replaced by slate-grey clothing; the 93rd, only recently arrived in India, splendid in feathered bonnets, scarlet and tartan, over 700 of them wearing their Crimean medal ribbons; men from several regular line infantry regiments, some of them besieged in the Residency, their various uniforms adapted to meet the needs of campaigning under the hot Indian sun; tall, bearded Sikhs from the Punjab, dressed in khaki set off with coloured turbans and sashes; the 9th Lancers, still in blue, with white 'pagris' wound around their forage caps; the wild irregulars of Hodson's Horse, willing to follow their leader anywhere; and a naval brigade under the command of Captain William Peel, RN, consisting of 250 sailors and marines from HMS *Shannon*, armed with ships' heavy 24-pounder guns that would be used in street fighting or to smash breaches in walls.

The column's chief engineer recommended that Campbell should approach the Residency along the opposite bank of the river as far as the iron bridge. Havelock, it will be recalled, had rejected this alternative because the ground had then been too waterlogged to support the movement of his guns. This objection was no longer valid as the ground was now firm and dry, but instead Campbell chose to rely on the information supplied by Outram and decided to remain on the near bank, keeping as close to the river as possible. Such an axis of advance would avoid many of the tortuous alleys in which Havelock's force had sustained such heavy casualties, and on this occasion, as the canal was now dry, it would not be necessary to fight for a bridgehead on its far bank. Against this, there were several large, walled, fortified palaces and mosques along the way, all of which the rebels could be depended upon to defend tenaciously.

Campbell was able to deploy one cavalry brigade, consisting of two 9th Lancer squadrons, one squadron each from the 1st, 2nd and 5th Punjab Cavalry and Hodson's Horse, and three infantry brigades of varying strength. Brigadier-General Greathead's brigade contained the remnants of the 8th, the 2nd Punjab Infantry and what today would be called a composite or provisional battalion formed from detachments of units besieged in Lucknow; Brigadier-General Russell's brigade, with the 23rd (later Royal Welsh) Fusiliers and part of the 82nd (later the South Lancashire) Regiment, was even weaker; by far the strongest of the three, and intended to form the cutting edge of the relief, was Brigadier-General Adrian Hope's brigade, containing the 93rd Highlanders, half of the 53rd (later the King's Shropshire Light Infantry), the 4th Punjab Infantry and a weak composite battalion.

The force began moving forward at 09:00 on 14 November. The enemy was found to be lining the walls of the Dilkusha Park, from which they were driven by artillery fire. They attempted a further stand at the Martinière school but gave way when threatened with an infantry assault. The column then closed up to the canal, beating off several weak counter-attacks.

The next day was spent bringing up the heavy baggage and provision train to the Dilkusha Park. This was very necessary because Campbell intended evacuating the Residency garrison almost as soon as he had broken through, but it proved to be a very difficult operation as the long convoy of wagons was subjected to constant attacks which the rearguard, consisting of 200 men of the 93rd Highlanders, was sometimes hardpressed to contain. Nevertheless, using a semaphore from the roof of the Dilkusha palace, Campbell was able to inform Outram that he would attempt to break through next day and the latter replied that he would make the necessary preparations. Campbell's graphic despatch to Lord Canning, the Governor-General, describes the course of events once the canal had been crossed:

'I advanced direct on the Secundrabagh early on the 16th. This place is a high-walled enclosure of strong masonry of 120 yards square, and was carefully loopholed all round. It was held very strongly by the enemy. Opposite it was a village at a distance of a hundred yards, which was also loopholed and filled with men.

'On the head of the column advancing up the lane to the left of the Secundrabagh, fire was opened on us. The infantry of the advance guard was quickly thrown into skirmishing order, to line a bank to the right. The guns were pushed rapidly onwards, viz., Captain Blunt's troop, Bengal Horse Artillery, and Captain Travers,' Royal Artillery, heavy field battery. The troop passed at a gallop through a cross-fire from the village and the Secundrabagh, and opened fire within easy musketry range in a most daring manner. As soon as they could be pushed up a stiff bank, two 18-pounder guns, under Captain Travers, were also brought to bear on the building. While this was being effected, the leading brigade of infantry, under Brigadier the Hon Adrian Hope, coming rapidly into action, caused the loopholed village to be abandoned; the whole fire of the brigade then being directed on the Secundrabagh.'

The 93rd Highlanders were then deployed with five companies, commanded by Lieutenant-Colonel Leith Hay, opposite the southern wall of the palace and the rest, under Lieutenant-Colonel Ewart, opposite the eastern wall. For ninety minutes, while Travers' two 18-pounders focused their fire on a small section of the wall close to the gate, they engaged in a fire-fight with those lining the walls, evidently to some effect as the gunners, serving their weapons at suicidally close range, sustained relatively few casualties. By the end of this period the guns had battered a small hole, between three and four feet square, through the tough masonry.

Campbell's intention was that part of the 93rd should fight their way through this tiny breach and then open the gates for the rest. When his drummer beat the Advance the whole line surged forward, the 93rd with a terrifying yell of long-suppressed rage that boded ill for those within the walls. The Highlanders had not reached India in time to witness first hand the worst of the mutineers' atrocities, but they were fully conversant with all that had happened and now there was no thought in their minds other than to close with and kill the perpetrators, man to man and steel to steel. Pipe Major John McLeod and his pipers struck up *The Haughs of Cromdell*, otherwise known as *The Old Highland Charge*, the sound of which raised the men's fury to berserk level. First through the breach was Captain Burroughs, slashing at those beyond with his broadsword. Close behind came Lance-Corporal John Dunley, then more and more kilted figures, including Lieutenant-Colonel Ewart and his fourteen-year-old drummer, James Grant. Leading the rush to open the gate, Burroughs went down under a sword-cut to the head. Fortunately, the resilience of his feathered bonnet saved him from the worst effects, although he was temporarily stunned and would certainly have been killed had not Dunley intervened to defend him until the fight surged past. The struggle for the gates was bitter in the extreme, but the sheer ferocity of the Highlanders' attack ensured success. With the opening of the gates the rest of the regiment, the

53rd, the 4th Punjab Infantry and the brigade's composite battalion poured through, hounding the rebels into the courtyard, along passages, up stairways and through room after room. Here and there shots would crack out, but there was neither time nor space to reload amid the screaming, hacking, frenzied struggle and the business was usually settled with the bayonet or sword. Ewart had personally killed eight of the enemy, including two native officers from whom he took a Colour, when he was wounded and set upon by five more. Seeing the Colonel now fighting for his own life, Private Peter Grant intervened and killed them all. In similar incidents Colour Sergeant James Monro saved the life of Captain Welch and Private David MacKay captured another set of the enemy's Colours. When the slaughter was over, not a rebel was knowingly left alive within the Secundrabagh; over 2,000 were later carried out.

The storming of the palace had cost the 93rd Highlanders 22 killed and 75 wounded. It might be thought that the regiment had done work enough for one day, but the afternoon was wearing on and Campbell was anxious to break the back of the enemy's resistance by capturing the next objective, the Shah Najaf mosque, about 500 yards to the northwest, before dusk. The 93rd and the brigade's composite battalion re-formed outside the Secundrabagh and advanced on the Shah Najaf together with the heavy guns of Captain Peel's Naval Brigade. Campbell's despatch continues:

'The Shah Najaf is a domed mosque with a garden, of which the most had been made by the enemy. The wall of the enclosure of the mosque was loopholed with great care. The entrance to it had been covered by a regular work of masonry, and the top of the building was crowned with a parapet. From this, and from the defences in the garden, an unceasing fire of musketry was kept up from the commencement of the attack. This position was defended with great resolution against a heavy cannonade of three hours. It was then stormed in the boldest manner by the 93rd Highlanders, under Brigadier Hope, supported by the battalion of detachments under Major Barnston, who was, I regret to say, severely wounded; Captain Peel leading up his heavy guns with extraordinary gallantry within a few yards of the building, to batter the massive stone walls. The withering fire of the Highlanders effectually covered the Naval Brigade from great loss, but it was an action almost unexampled in war. Captain Peel behaved very much as if he had been laying the *Shannon* alongside an enemy's frigate. This brought the day's operations to a close.'

By the time the despatch was written, Campbell had received official confirmation that he had been appointed Colonel of the 93rd. Unfortunately, his entirely justifiable pride led him to gild the lily somewhat with regard to his regiment's part in the capture of the Shah Najaf, which was undoubtedly a tougher nut to crack than the Secundrabagh. The guns continued to batter the masonry wall without apparent result until sunset and during this period the 93rd sustained the loss of three killed and fifteen wounded in their exchange with the enemy lining the walls. As dusk began to fall the mutineers' buglers could be heard sounding the Advance followed by the Double. This suggested that the garrison was about to make a sortie in strength and Hope took appropriate precautions. By last light, however, the enemy's fire had died away completely. A patrol under Staff Sergeant John Paton, sent out to examine possible ways into the enclosure, discovered that the rebels had abandoned the position, escaping through a gate at the rear. Reasons for their doing so may have included the complete lack of survivors from the Secundrabagh, the concurrent break-out operations of the Residency garrison, which had succeeded in securing several important buildings behind them, and the fact that Peel's guns were doing greater damage than was apparent from the outside.

The Shah Najaf was promptly occupied and next morning the 93rd's adjutant, Lieutenant McBean, accompanied by Sergeant Hutchinson and Drummer Ross, climbed a minaret to wave the regiment's Colours for the benefit of the Residency garrison, now just 400 yards distant. They quickly became a target but Ross, disregarding not only McBean's orders to come down but also the musket balls zipping past his ears, proceeded to blow *Cock o' the North*. In response came the faint sound of the 78th's own pipers and the dipping three times of the Residency flag.

Just two major objectives, the Mess House and the Moti Mahal, now separated Campbell's and Outram's troops. The Mess House had been used by the 32nd prior to the Mutiny and its capture is described by Campbell:

'Captain Peel kept up a steady cannonade on the building ... (which) was defended by a ditch about twelve feet broad and scarped with masonry, and beyond that a loopholed mud wall. I determined to use the guns as much as possible in taking it. About three p.m., when it was considered that men might be sent to storm it without risk, it was taken by a company of the 90th Foot, under Captain Wolseley, and a picket of Her Majesty's 53rd, under Captain Hopkins, supported by Major Barnston's battalion of detachments under Captain Guise, and some of the Punjab Infantry under Lieutenant Powlett. The Mess House was carried immediately with a rush. The troops then pressed forward with great vigour and lined the wall separating the Mess House from the Moti Mahal, which consists of a wide enclosure and many buildings. The enemy here made a last stand, which was overcome after an hour, openings having been broken in the wall, through which the troops poured, with a body of Sappers, and accomplished our communications with the Residency. I had the inexpressible satisfaction, shortly afterwards, of greeting Sir James Outram and Sir Henry Havelock, who came out to greet me before the action was at an end.'

A point of interest regarding the storming of the Mess House was that two future field marshals and commanders-in-chief of the British Army, Captain Garnet Wolseley of the 90th and Lieutenant Frederick Roberts, Bengal Artillery now serving on Campbell's staff, were participants. The former incurred Campbell's wrath by exploiting the breakthrough into the Moti Mahal with his own and some Sikh troops, who were the first to reach the Residency garrison, an honour which the General intended should fall to the 93rd. Wolseley believed that the incident cost him a recommendation for the Victoria Cross, but his career was not damaged.[10]

The most difficult part of Campbell's task had now begun. He not only had to cover the evacuation of the garrison, its sick and wounded, the women and children and anything that might be of value to the enemy, but also to make provision for a very serious threat that was developing to his rear. Just for once, the rebels had managed to reach a strategic decision and had persuaded Tantia Topi, one of their most prominent commanders and a supporter of the Nana Sahib, to march on Cawnpore with an army of mutineers and other dissidents from the state of Gwalior. The probability was that the small force left by Campbell to defend the city would be overwhelmed and that the vital bridge across the Ganges would be lost. If that happened, it would leave Campbell's entire column, including those evacuated from the Residency, trapped between two large rebel armies.

The first priority, however, was to complete the evacuation, the course of this being described by Campbell in his despatch dated 25 November:

'Having led the enemy to believe that immediate assault was contemplated, orders were issued for the retreat of the garrison through the lines of our pickets at midnight on the 22nd. The ladies and families, the wounded, the treasure (twenty-three lakhs of rupees and the King of Oudh's jewels), the guns it was thought worthwhile to keep, the ordnance stores, the grain still possessed by the commissariat of the garrison, and the state prisoners, had all been previously removed. Sir James Outram had received orders to burst the guns which it was thought undesirable to take away; and he was finally directed silently to evacuate the Residency of Lucknow at the hour indicated. The dispositions to cover their retreat and to resist the enemy, should he pursue, were ably carried out by Brigadier the Hon Adrian Hope; but I am happy to say that the enemy was completely deceived and he did not attempt to follow. On the contrary, he began firing on our old positions many hours after we had left them. The movement of the retreat was admirably executed, and was a perfect lesson in such combinations. Each exterior line came gradually retiring through its supports, until at length nothing remained but the last line of infantry and guns, with which I was myself to crush the enemy if he had dared to follow up the pickets. The only line of retreat (was) through a long and tortuous lane, and all these precautions were absolutely necessary for the protection of the force.'

It was decided that Outram would maintain a British presence at Lucknow by holding the Alambagh, which was a great deal easier both to defend and relieve than the Residency. Havelock, worn down by fatigue, strain and the effects of dysentery, died there on 25 November; he was to be remembered by his generation as the embodiment of the Christian soldier.

On 27 November, having left 4,000 men and 35 guns with Outram, Campbell began the 40-mile march from the Alambagh to Cawnpore, from which no news had been received for several days. Anxieties began to rise along the slow-moving convoy as the rumble of distant gunfire became audible. At about noon a native runner from Major-General Windham, commanding at Cawnpore, reached the head of the column with a letter for Campbell, written two days previously. Windham, it seemed, had already been in action against Tantia Topi's army, which was present in great strength and possessed ample artillery. It was probable that his troops would have to retire into the entrenchment covering the bridge and urgent assistance was therefore requested. Campbell was not altogether confident in Windham, who lacked experience, and, aware that he had only about 1,000 men at his disposal, could leave nothing to chance. Leaving his infantry to protect the convoy he rode ahead with the cavalry and horse artillery to discover the present state of affairs for himself. By the time he arrived it was clear that the rebels were in possession of the city and had overrun the British camp. On the other hand, Windham's troops were still resisting in their entrenchment and the bridge was, for the moment, intact.[11] It took until the following day for his own bullock-drawn heavy guns and the infantry to come up, enabling him to take effective counter-measures.

'All the heavy guns attached to General Grant's division, under Captain Peel RN and Captain Travers RA, were placed in position on the left bank of the Ganges and directed to open fire and keep down the fire of the enemy on (i.e., against) the bridge. This was done very effectively, while Brigadier Hope's brigade, with some field artillery and cavalry, was ordered to cross the bridge and take position near the old dragoon lines. A cross-fire was at the same time kept up from the entrenchment to cover the march of the troops. When darkness began to draw on the artillery parks, the wounded and the families were ordered to file over the bridge and it was not till 6 p.m. the day of the 30th that the last cart cleared the bridge.'

During the next week Tantia Topi, whose army numbered 14,000 with 40 guns, mounted several attacks, all of which were repulsed. Having reorganised his transport and sent on the civilians and the wounded to the safety of Allahabad on 3 December, Campbell was left with both hands free to plan his counter-stroke. This was delivered three days later against both wings of the rebel army, which quickly dissolved in rout. Once again, Captain Peel and his seamen distinguished themselves, manhandling their heavy 24-pounders forward with the skirmish line and simply blasting away anyone in their path. The pursuit was pressed for fourteen miles and resulted in the capture of sixteen guns and an immense quantity of ammunition, stores, vehicles and bullocks.

The defeat of Tantia Topi and the Gwalior rebels marked the turning point in the history of the Mutiny. For the first time the country people, sensing who the ultimate victors would be, came in to trade. Campbell, his mission completed, wished to turn his attention to putting down the rebellion elsewhere, but Canning insisted that since Oudh had become the principal rallying point for the mutineers its early conquest would produce valuable political dividends throughout the sub-continent and beyond.

Thus it was that many of those who had been besieged in Lucknow or taken part in its reliefs, all of whom had performed prodigies, found themselves marching once more on the city, where Outram's force at the Alambagh was still maintaining itself. On this occasion however, Campbell had a 20,000-strong army at his disposal, including 9,000 Gurkha volunteers under Jung Bahadur.

The capture of Lucknow, completed on 21 March 1858, does not form a part of this story. It cost Campbell 1,200 casualties but thousands of rebels died and the rest fled. They dispersed throughout the state to be dealt with piecemeal. Simultaneously, vigorous action by General Sir Hugh Rose, whose troops included elements of the Bombay and Madras armies as well as contingents from some of the princely states, stamped out the rebellion in Central India. In November the last formed bodies of mutineers in both theatres were defeated; they had brought nothing but destruction and death wherever they went and by now both the people and most of the local rulers had turned against them. All that remained were a few armed gangs that were remorselessly hunted down. By the end of the year it had become possible to begin returning responsibility for the troubled areas to the civil police.

There were several important consequences of the Mutiny. In 1858 the East India Company was deprived of its powers of government, these being directly assumed by the Crown. Secondly, the Indian Army was thoroughly reorganised and restructured to ensure that the circumstances giving rise to the Mutiny could not arise again. Most remarkable of all was the fact that, while the terrible events of the Mutiny could never be forgotten, both sides recognised that they had been guilty of untypical acts of savagery that were best put behind them. For the remaining 90 years of the Raj they would live, work and fight together, and when their paths diverged at Independence they parted as friends. During the Second World War a few Indian politicians attempted to evoke echoes of the Mutiny but the response was trivial when compared with the two million Indians who volunteered for active service in the armed forces of the Crown, and the millions more who undertook some form of war work.

Notes

1. His brother, Sir John Lawrence, was chief commissioner of the recently annexed Punjab where, by his ruthless energy he not only disarmed every suspect regiment before the idea of mutiny could take root, but also recruited over 30,000 Sikhs to the British service, enabling him to despatch his deputy, Brigadier-General John Nicholson, to Delhi with substantial reinforcements for the besieging force. See *At All Costs!* Chapter 3.

2. The contemporary designation used by both the Royal Artillery and the Bengal Artillery for batteries was to refer to them as companies within a battalion, then the arm of service, viz.: 4th Company, 1st Battalion, Bengal Artillery. However, as this contrasts awkwardly with modern usage I have adopted the more simplified format of 4/1 Battery Bengal Artillery, 3/8 Battery RA, etc.

3. Brydon had entered the East India Company's service in 1835. Having narrowly escaped one massacre, been besieged twice, seen battle and sudden death at close quarters and been wounded on several occasions, by 1859 he probably felt that enough was enough and left India for the peace and quiet of his native Scotland, where he died fourteen years later.

4. One of the 'lost' Irish regiments disbanded in 1922.

5. Wheeler was one of the Company's elderly generals who refused to believe that the sepoys would mutiny. This view was reinforced by his Indian wife, who was on good terms with the Nana Sahib and who had been assured by him that there was nothing to fear. Having managed to hold out in an untenable entrenchment for three weeks, Wheeler agreed to surrender in return for the Nana Sahib's promise of safe passage down the Ganges to Allahabad. The men and many of the women were massacred as they were embarking on boats for the journey. Four survivors managed to get clear and reach safety after many hardships.

6. Ironically, Bibighur means 'the lady's house', the building having been the home of the native mistress of a British officer. Depictions of the interior appearing in the British press showed the walls scrawled with inscriptions such as 'Countrymen Avenge Us' which, if they existed, can only have referred to the earlier massacre beside the river.

7. Many of the rebels themselves probably considered the Nana Sahib to be something of a liability. He sought refuge in Nepal whence unconfirmed reports suggested he had died in October 1859.

8. Maude's Battery received an honour title for its performance at Lucknow, as did 6/13 Battery RA and 4/1, 2/3 and 1/5 Batteries BA.

9. Duffy received the Victoria Cross, as did Maude and Olpherts for their respective parts in the battle. Maude's was a representative award chosen by ballot within his battery.

10. Six members of the 93rd were awarded the Victoria Cross for their part in these operations. They were: Captain Stewart for leading an attack on two enemy guns at the Mess House; and Staff Sergeant Paton, Lance Corporal Dunley, Private MacKay, Colour Sergeant Monro and Private Peter Grant for actions already described. Three more, including Lieutenant-Colonel Ewart, were recommended for the award but did not receive it.

11. Windham, in fact, had already sallied forth on 26 November and given Tantia Topi's advance guard a bloody nose. Next day, however, Tantia Topi arrived unexpectedly with his main body and drove him back to the entrenchment. On capturing the British camp the rebels plundered the kits of the units forming Campbell's relief column; in an unbelievably mean-spirited response, the government insisted that the troops should pay for the replacements out of their own pockets.

CHAPTER FOUR

The Taking of the Taku Forts, 1859 and 1860

For many years the Honourable East India Company made huge profits from its lucrative opium trade with China, bribing local officials to permit entry of the drug to which increasing numbers of Chinese had become addicted. The overall effect of the opium scourge on Chinese life can be compared to that of cocaine and other substances on Western nations today and, understandably, even the normally lethargic Imperial government was moved to take action, issuing an edict banning the trade and ordering the confiscation of existing stocks. What followed was the inevitable consequence of each side regarding the other as barbarians whose ways were totally incomprehensible.

Today, a frequently expressed and cynical view of the Foreign Office is that it exists for the convenience of foreigners. In mid-Victorian Britain, however, it stood unequivocally for the protection of British interests around the world, on the basis that the *Civis Britannicus* should have the same respect once universally accorded to the *Civis Romanus*. Thus, when those British traders who refused to comply with the Imperial edict were imprisoned in their own warehouses, notably in Canton, there was not the slightest hesitation in resorting to arms to rectify the situation. The fact that the loathsome commodity of opium was the proximate cause of the dispute, or that the subsequent conflict became known as the First Opium War, was unfortunate, but that was by the by; what was at stake was nothing less than the national honour.

The ensuing conflict was a one-sided affair. At sea the Chinese war junks, however numerous, were no match for the Royal Navy's frigates, and on land the Imperial government's troops, badly led and armed with ancient muskets, spears and tridents, were repeatedly routed, although their courage was respected. In August 1842, after the ports of Shanghai, Ningpo, Foochow, Canton and Amoy had been captured, the Chinese signed the Treaty of Nanking, granting trading rights at these as well as ceding Hong Kong, which became a British colony. Furthermore, British residents in China were accorded privileges which effectively placed them above the law.

Naturally, there was considerable resentment among the Chinese, who largely disregarded the Treaty's provisions. The Imperial government, more concerned with widespread internal unrest, lacked both the means and the will to enforce them. Harassment of British merchants and mercantile interests continued, culminating in the boarding of the British schooner *Arrow*, registered in Hong Kong, and the arrest of several crew members, in October 1856. Demands for the release of the men were rejected on the grounds that they were pirates. The Royal Navy promptly bombarded Canton. When the local mandarin responded by burning every British business, Rear Admiral Sir Michael Seymour, Commander-in-Chief of the East Indies and China Station, requested reinforcements in the form of a flotilla of gunboats and 5,000 troops from India, intending to occupy the city.

Because of the Indian Mutiny, it was not until late the following year that the necessary resources became available. On 28 December 1857 Canton was again bombarded and by the New Year was firmly under British control. In the meantime the British government's plenipotentiary, Lord Elgin, had been instructed to demand compensation for the lives lost and property damaged, strict observance of the Treaty of Nanking, and diplomatic representation at the Imperial Court. In the last he had the support of the French, who were ostensibly angered by the murder of one of their missionaries – though in reality more concerned that their own interests in China should not be overridden by the British – and were prepared to contribute modest forces, should the need arise. The United States and Russian governments, by now well aware of the benefits that would accrue from increased trade with China, also gave their approval.

There were two major problems. The first was that the Imperial authorities denied access to the Forbidden City, deep in the heart of Peking, to all but a tiny handful of senior officials and mandarins, of whom only a very few were ever ushered into the divine presence of the Emperor himself. Therefore, went their reasoning, if the Chinese could not look upon the Son of Heaven themselves, it was unthinkable that barbarians from the world's outer edges should be permitted to do so. Secondly, it was clear from Chinese intransigence that Elgin, with Seymour's help, would only get what he wanted in Peking itself. That would involve an overland march of some 80 miles from Tientsin, lying at the junction of the Grand Canal with the Pei-ho river, 34 miles upstream from Taku, where the latter flowed between muddy banks into the Gulf of Chi-li.

Aware of the expedition's purpose, the Chinese had begun constructing mud-built shore batteries on both sides of the estuary. The work, however, had not progressed far when, in May 1858, Seymour's ships began entering the river, so that when the Chinese guns opened fire they were quick-

'That Astonishing Infantry': The Albuera Counter-Attack

Left: Gilbert Holliday's painting of the Colour Party of the 29th Regiment at Albuera. The surviving Colour Sergeant tries to support the mortally wounded Ensign Edward Furnace, carrying the King's Colour. On the ground, Ensign Richard Vance rips the Regimental Colour from its staff and pushes it inside his coat to prevent capture. *The Worcestershire Regiment Museum Trust.*

Below: Captain Ralph Fawcett, though mortally wounded, continued to command his company of the 57th Regiment, known as 'The Die-Hards' after Albuera.

Above: Lady Butler's famous painting of Albuera, 'Steady the Drums and Fifes'. *PWRR & Queen's Regimental Museum, Dover Castle.*

Scarlet and Grey: The Battles of Chippewa and Lundy's Lane

Below: Scott's Brigade going into action at Chippewa. At first their grey coats gave the British commander, Major General Phineas Riall, the impression that they were militiamen, but, observing their precise drill and steadiness under fire, he quickly changed his opinion. *Anne S. K. Brown Military Collection, Brown University Library.*

Above: Colonel Joseph Miller's 21st Infantry closing in on the British artillery position at Lundy's Lane. *ASKB.*

Below: Colonel Miller's infantrymen overrunning the British guns at Lundy's Lane. Although most of the uniform details are hopelessly incorrect, the topography is accurate and the illustration gives a good impression of the confusion in which this phase of the battle was fought. Later, as a result of their severe losses, the Americans relinquished their gains. *ASKB.*

Mission Impossible: The Reliefs of Lucknow

Above: Battery position at the Residency, Lucknow. As the picture suggests, even hospital patients were expected to take their turn manning the defences. *ASKB.*

Below left: The 93rd Highlanders fight their way into the breach at the Secundrabagh. *Courtesy, Regimental Headquarters, The Argyll and Sutherland Highlanders.*

Below right: The close-quarter fighting inside the Secundrabagh was savage in the extreme. A watercolour by Orlando Norrie. *Courtesy, Regimental Headquarters, The Argyll and Sutherland Highlanders.*

The Taking of the Taku Forts

Above: An overall view of the gunboats' attack on the Taku Forts, 25 June 1859. The landward defences of the forts are not shown, but the ilustration does emphasise the great expanse of mud confronting the landing party attacking the fort on the left. *National Maritime Museum, Negative No 58/1364.*

Below: The landing party wallows across the low-water mud towards the South Fort at Taku, evening 25 June 1859. *National Maritime Museum, Negative No A7542.*

Left: Ensign John Chaplin and Private Thomas Lane succeed in planting the Queen's Colour of the 67th Regiment on the central tower of the Small North Fort. Both men were awarded the Victoria Cross for their part in the action. *Courtesy The Royal Hampshire Regiment Museum.*

Below: The exterior of the Small North Fort with British and French flags flying from the central tower. The extensive belt of sharpened bamboo stakes surrounding the fortifications is clearly visible. The bodies in the foreground are those of the garrison who tried to escape over the walls. *Courtesy The Royal Hampshire Regiment Museum.*

Left: The interior of the Small North Fort after its capture, showing scaling ladders still in position, guns of various type and vintage and, on the extreme right, what appears to be a 'jingal', an enormous musket fired from a wall mounting, much favoured by the Chinese. *Courtesy The Royal Hampshire Regiment Museum.*

Dargai

Right: Colonel H. H. Mathias, Commanding Officer of the 1st Battalion The Gordon Highlanders at Dargai. *The Gordon Highlanders Museum, Negative No GH2615.*

Below: The pipers of 1st Gordon Highlanders, taken shortly before Dargai. Piper Findlater is on the extreme left of the rear rank. *The Gordon Highlanders Museum, Negative No PB415/16.*

Above: Lieutenant Colonel Mathias leads the 1st Gordon Highlanders' attack on Dargai. The piper in the foreground is Piper George Findlater who was shot through both ankles but continued to play. He is in approximately the correct position but is incorrectly shown wearing a lance corporal's stripe. *ASKB.*

Below: The final stages of the Gordons' attack at Dargai. For the sake of effect the artist has also shown Piper Findlater, together with Lance Corporal (Piper) Milne, who was shot through the chest. Others depicted include men of the 1st/2nd Gurkha Rifles, 2nd Derbys and 3rd Sikhs. *ASKB.*

The Storming of San Juan Ridge, Cuba

Above: Lieutenant Colonel (later President) Theodore Roosevelt with officers and men of the Rough Riders (1st US Volunteer Cavalry) photographed on a hill overlooking Santiago, Cuba. *US Army, Courtesy of the Patton Museum, Fort Knox, Ky.*

Below: The start of the assault on San Juan Ridge, supported by the fire of Lieutenant John Parker's Gatling machine gun detachment, seen here on the left. *ASKB.*

Above: The Americans secure the crest of San Juan Ridge. The blockhouse in the background, though still offering resistance, was abandoned shortly after. *ASKB.*

Mounted Action: The Charges at Beersheba and Huj, Palestine

Opposite page, top: Turkish machine gun teams with rangefinder in position near Beersheba. *Trustees of the Imperial War Museum, London.*

Below: 'The Charge of the Australian 4th Light Horse Brigade at Beersheba', by George Lambert. The supporting wave is about to pass over the Turkish trenches, which have been captured in hand-to-hand fighting by the leading wave. (In poor condition.) *Australian War Memorial.*

Right: Capturing the Beersheba wells intact was critical to the success of Allenby's entire plan. Such was the speed with which the 4th Light Horse Brigade stormed into the town that the Turks were able to destroy only two and damage two more, one of which is being examined by British engineers. *Trustees of the Imperial War Museum, London.*

Above: Australians watering their mounts at Beersheba station. *Trustees of the Imperial War Museum, London.*

Below: 'The Charge of the Warwickshire and Worcestershire Yeomanry at Huj', by Lady Butler. *Courtesy The Queen's Own Warwickshire and Worcestershire Yeomanry Charitable Trust.*

Leading the Way: US Rangers at the Pointe du Hoe and Omaha Beach

Above: US 2nd Rangers' Command and Aid Post in a shell crater on the Pointe du Hoe. *US Army Military History Institute.*

Below: The first supplies to reach the isolated 2nd Rangers on the Pointe du Hoe are carried across the rocky beach. Note the size of the craters caused by the naval bombardment. *USAMHI.*

Above: Colonel Rudder (arrowed) and the survivors of 2nd Rangers prepare to leave the Pointe du Hoe on D+2. *USAMHI.*

Crown of Thorns: The Struggle for Hill 112

Below: Churchill infantry tanks and an M10 tank destroyer breaking harbour for the attack on Hill 112. *Trustees of the Imperial War Museum, London.*

Above: 17-pdr anti-tank gun and burned-out tractor unit hit by mortar fire in 'Death Valley', with the slopes of Hill 112 beyond. *Trustees of the Imperial War Museum, London.*

Below: The summit of Hill 112 before it had been ravaged by the worst of the fighting. *Trustees of the Imperial War Museum, London.*

Dak To: Ngok Kom Leat and Hill 875

Left: Men of the 503rd Parachute Infantry patrolling in the jungles of the Central Highlands, South Vietnam. *USAMHI.*

Below: Members of IV/503rd Parachute Infantry pinned down among the piles of shattered timber covering the slopes of Hill 875. *USAMHI.*

Bottom: IV/503rd light machine gun team photographed shortly before the final assault on Hill 875. *USAMHI.*

ly silenced by his gunboats. The expedition reached Tientsin without further incident and there the representatives of the Imperial government, anxious that no further face should be lost, readily concluded a treaty that accepted every one of Elgin's demands, including the establishment of legations at Peking, recognition of the legitimacy of the opium traffic and the opening of further ports to foreign trade. Accordingly, Seymour withdrew and it seemed that the Second Opium War was over.

Unfortunately the Chinese had no more intention of being bound by the Treaty of Tientsin than they had by the Treaty of Nanking. The Cantonese quickly began harassing British merchants again and the Pei-ho and Yang-tse river were closed to British shipping. By the spring of 1859 it had become apparent not only that the Imperial government would not permit foreign diplomats to reside in Peking, but also that the coast defence batteries covering the mouth of the Pei-ho at Taku had been developed into formidable fortresses. Obviously, the Imperial government had to be taught another sharp lesson.

It was equally unfortunate that the officer who would have to administer this was Rear Admiral Sir James Hope, who had relieved Seymour as commander-in-chief in April 1859. Hope was certainly not lacking in courage, but his powers of judgement had been questioned during the Crimean War and could not be relied upon. In fairness to him, however, once the decision had been made to force the entrance to the Pei-ho again, his options were very limited. The approach to the river mouth was restricted by mud flats to a navigable channel approximately 200 yards wide. In itself this would not have been an obstacle to progress had not the depth of water over the bar at high tide been limited to eleven feet, dropping to two feet at low tide. Thus, although larger warships were available, the task of subduing the Chinese defences would have to be left to the gunboats.

In June he sailed north with eleven of them, HMS *Plover, Banterer, Forester, Haughty, Janus, Kestrel, Lee, Opossum, Starling, Nimrod* and *Cormorant*. These wooden-hulled, shallow draught vessels had been built in large numbers during the Crimean War for service in the confined waters of the Baltic and Black Seas. They had a three-masted gaff rig but in action were driven by a single screw drawing power from a 40 or 60hp steam engine. Their varied armament included 68-, 32- and 24-pounder guns and 24-pounder howitzers; most of Hope's flotilla carried four guns apiece, the exceptions being *Nimrod* and *Cormorant* , which carried six. Each had a crew of between 35 and 45 officers and men.

It was immediately apparent to Hope that the Chinese had spared no effort in strengthening their river defences. The large fort on the south side now had mud ramparts almost half a mile long, with three commanding towers within the perimeter. A similar fortification had been built on the north bank and a little way upstream could be seen two smaller forts, one on each bank. Furthermore, the navigable channel had clearly been blocked against the passage of anything larger than a rowing boat by a series of formidable obstacles.

Hope sent in a message to the Chinese commander, demanding the removal of the barriers. He was assured that they were only there to keep out pirates and promised that the channel would be cleared

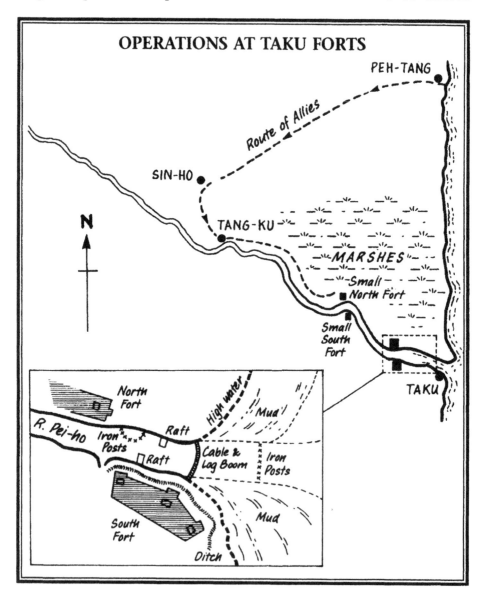

OPERATIONS AT TAKU FORTS

presently. Instead, the Chinese continued to work on their fortifications. On 21 June he issued an ultimatum to the effect that if the obstacles had not been removed in three days' time, he would remove them by force, anticipating little more trouble than Seymour had encountered the previous year.

Nevertheless, as a precaution he sent a reconnaissance party to examine the obstacles in the channel after dark on 24 June. Consisting of three armed boats under the command of Captain George Willes, this first encountered a line of pointed iron stakes at the mouth of the river; supported by tripods sunk into the river bed, the intention being to disembowel any large vessel passing over them. Pressing on upstream until they were opposite the centre of the Large South Fort, the party next encountered a floating boom consisting of one stout hemp and two chain cables, supported by floating logs at thirty feet intervals. Leaving two boats to fix a demolition charge to the centre of the boom, Willes passed over it in the third and some 300 yards beyond came across two huge rafts, moored so as to leave only a narrow zig-zag channel between them, with another line of iron stakes beyond. With Chinese sentries pacing the bank nearby, Willes crawled onto one of the rafts to examine its construction, reaching the conclusion that it would withstand any amount of ramming by the small gunboats. He then dropped down to the boom, where the demolition charge fuze was lit, and the three boats pulled for the gunboats. The explosion attracted several harmless cannon shots from the South Fort, but caused little or no damage as the boom was still firmly in position the following morning.

Although the information gathered at considerable risk by Willes and his party would have made many commanders consider their position very carefully, Admiral Hope, a prey to wishful thinking, decided to attack that very morning. His plan required nine of the gunboats to anchor below the barrier of iron stakes and cover the forts while two more broke through each of the obstacles in turn, clearing the way upstream. If the Chinese resisted, their guns would have been silenced and the forts stormed by a 500-strong landing party of marines and sailors provided by the larger warships anchored off the bar, carried ashore in steam pinnaces, ships' boats and junks. The operation was timed to commence at high water, which occurred at 11:30, and herein lay the plan's fatal flaw, for with every hour that passed the ebbing tide would reveal an ever-widening expanse of glutinous mud, intersected by creeks, that the landing party would have to cross in the teeth of the enemy's fire.

In the event, because of the difficulties of working the ships in the narrow, fast flowing navigable channel, the last of them did not drop anchor until after 13:00, and even then two, *Banterer* and *Starling*, were stuck fast on mud banks in positions which prevented all their guns from bearing. Hope, aboard *Plover*, led the line, with *Opossum*, commanded by Willes, alongside, the task of the latter being to breach the outer barrier. At 14:00 her crew passed a cable around one of the iron stakes and the gunboat went full astern, but so well secured was it that 30 minutes of continuous effort were required before it was uprooted.

Until now the Chinese forts had remained silent, but as soon as *Plover*, followed by *Opossum*, passed through the gap in the barrier and was approaching the floating boom, flags were hoisted, embrasures were unmasked and a large number of guns opened a sustained and accurate fire that indicated the Chinese had been training hard. The gunboats returned this but as the engagement was taking place at point blank range – the Large South Fort now lay only 200 yards to port and the Large North Fort twice that distance ahead – they began to suffer severely; furthermore, though Chinese guns were being dismounted, they were promptly replaced, as were the gunners being killed around them.

By 15:00 both ships were in a poor state, their hulls, bulwarks, boats, masts and rigging being steadily battered to pieces. *Plover* was in the sorrier state, with 31 of her 40-strong crew killed or wounded and only two guns left in action. The dead included her captain, Lieutenant Rason, cut in two by a roundshot, and Captain McKenna of Hope's staff. Hope was himself wounded in the thigh but refused to leave the deck.

Lying at anchor outside the bar was flagship of the US Navy's Asiatic Squadron, commanded by Commodore Josiah Tattnall. As a midshipman Tattnall had fought against the British during the War of 1812, but for him that lay in the past and he was not enjoying the spectacle of two of their gunboats being knocked apart. He had his steam launch called away and, disregarding the Chinese fire, travelled upstream until he was alongside *Plover*. Clambering aboard, he suggested to Hope that the launch be used to evacuate the wounded. Hope had already accepted gratefully when Tattnall observed that his boat's crew had become involved in the fighting.

'What have you been doing, you rascals?' he shouted as they returned, powder-stained, to their own craft. 'Don't you know we're neutrals?'

'Beg pardon, sir,' came the reply, 'They were a bit short-handed on the bow gun and we thought it no harm to give them a hand while we were waiting.'

Tattnall could only grin at Hope before remarking, 'I guess blood must be thicker than water!' It was a remark that would go down in the history of both navies.

By 15:00 *Plover* was little more than a wreck. Hope gave permission for her to drop downstream and transferred to *Opossum*, simultaneously calling forward *Lee* and *Haughty*.

'Your stern is on fire!' hailed one of *Haughty's* officers as she passed *Opossum*.

'Can't be helped!' replied Willes. 'Can't spare the men to put it out – we've only just enough to keep our guns going!'

Aboard *Opossum*, Hope was felled by a tangle of falling rigging, emerging with three broken ribs. Strapped up, he insisted on being lifted into a boat to visit *Lee* and *Haughty*. At length *Opossum*, now barely fightable, dropped down-river. *Lee* became a special target for the Chinese gunners and was hit so repeatedly below the water-line that her pumps were unable to cope. When her commander, Lieutenant Jones, was informed that unless the shot holes could be plugged from the outside she would sink, he declined to order a man over the side because the combined risks posed by the swift tide and the propeller would almost certainly be fatal. Boatswain Woods, however, declaring that just at the moment the chances of being killed were much of a muchness wherever he was, went over the side with a supply of shot plugs and a line tied around his waist and, despite being swept to within inches of the propeller several times, managed to plug several holes. His courage deserved a better reward, for the ship continued to fill and eventually had to be run aground to prevent her foundering.

Her place was taken by *Cormorant* and *Kestrel* and the battle raged on. Aboard *Cormorant*, Hope, now seated in a chair on deck, lost consciousness once and finally allowed himself to be taken to the hospital ship at the bar, handing over command to Captain Shadwell. *Kestrel*, riddled, went down at 17:30.

Six of the gunboats had now been sunk or disabled, but shortly afterwards the fire from the forts began to tail off. It is easy to blame Shadwell for what followed, but he sincerely believed not only that the Chinese had had enough, but also that an assault by the landing party on the Large South Fort stood a reasonable chance of success. What he seems to have ignored is that it was now low water and, in consequence, no less than 500 yards of mud flats separated the landing point from the fort. Nevertheless, after a hurried council of war aboard *Cormorant*, the decision to attack was taken at 18:30.

The seamen and marines, including a 60-strong French contingent, were already waiting in their boats and junks. At 19:00 they were taken in tow by *Opossum* and a small local steamer, the *Toey 'Wan*. As they were cast off within easy rowing distance of the shoreline all seemed to be well. That the North Fort remained silent and guns were only firing at long intervals from the South Fort suggested the enemy was running short of ammunition. The gathering dusk, too, would reduce the accuracy of their fire, it was hoped.

As the boats touched down, however, the entire frontage of the Large South Fort erupted in flame and smoke. Men could be seen crowding the ramparts, ignoring the covering fire of the gunboats. Slopping through boot-tugging mud covered with weed, intersected by channels and tidal pools, the men struggled forward into a blizzard of roundshot, grape and rockets supplemented at closer quarters by musketry and even arrows. Shadwell, who had decided to lead the assault in person, was wounded as soon as he stepped ashore. With casualties mounting rapidly, more men had to be detailed to carry the wounded back to the boats to save them from being smothered in mud so soft as to be waist-deep in places. Of the 500 men who had landed, less than 150 crossed the tidal channel halfway between the water's edge and the fort, and of these only fifty, their paper cartridges soaked and useless, reached the ditch below the ramparts. Their one scaling ladder was reared against the wall and ten men were climbing it when a volley from above killed three and wounded five of them. The ladder was then thrown down and broken. Nothing remained but to retire to the boats.

If anything, the withdrawal was even more harrowing than the advance. The Chinese, past masters in the pyrotechnic arts, sent up rockets and burned blue flares by the light of which they continued to fire on the landing party. As several boats had been sunk and the tide was now rising, many had to wait in waist- or even neck-deep water before they could be picked up. The last of them was not taken off until 01:00. Altogether, the landing party's losses amounted to 68 killed and nearly 300 wounded, over 70 per cent of those employed.

Next day a party was sent in to burn three of the grounded gunboats that could not be got off, and then the flotilla retired to Hong Kong. Public opinion at home was outraged by the news of the reverse. Never, in a century of minor operations of this sort had the Royal Navy been so humiliated, and by the despised Chinese of all people. This failed to take into account that every aspect of the Chinese defence had been thoroughly thought through, and that during the engagement itself the Chinese had fought with determination and an exemplary if unexpected efficiency. The root causes of Hope's failure lay in his over-confidence and in underestimating his enemy. It was simply beyond the capacity of the resources at his disposal to force the entrance of the Pei-ho and he failed to recognise the fact.[1]

Neither the British nor French governments could afford to let the matter rest. In March 1860 an ultimatum was despatched to Peking demanding ratification of the Treaty of Tientsin, together with an apology for firing on Admiral Hope's ships and compensation for the losses incurred. No self-respecting government could be expected to comply with the last two demands and a reply was neither expected nor received. In May a joint expeditionary force, consisting of some 11,000 British and Indian troops under Lieutenant-General Sir James Hope Grant and 6,700 French under Lieutenant-General Cousin-Montauban, began assembling at Hong Kong. A point of technical interest was provided by the British contingent's Armstrong 12-pounder rifled breech-loading field guns, which would be going into action for the first time.

The defences of the Taku Forts were known to have been further strengthened since the previous June and, as direct frontal assault had proved such a dismal failure, it was decided that they would each be captured in turn from the rear, following a landing at Peh-tang, a few miles north of the Pei-ho estuary. To the surprise of many, and the intense anger of some, Admiral Hope, now recovered from his wounds, was placed in command of the naval aspects of the operation, although his brief was restricted to providing gunfire support from the mouth of the river while the forts were under attack.

Some consideration had been given to the hot, humid climate, the British regiments wearing a cool, loosely-woven red tunic of Indian manufacture in place of their tight scarlet serge. Head-dress consisted of either a cloth-covered wicker helmet – the forerunner of the famous Wolseley helmet – or, more commonly, a low peaked cap with a white cover and neck-cloth.

The landing at Peh-tang took place on 30 July. It was not opposed, although the troops had to wade across a mile-wide expanse of mud-flats before they reached the shore proper. Because of this, it took another ten days to land the artillery, cavalry and supplies. During this period a detailed reconnaissance of the way ahead was carried out, revealing that extensive marshland restricted the only practicable route that could be followed by a large force lay along a causeway passing through Sin-ho to Tang-ku on the Pei-ho, some three miles above the Taku Forts, and that the Chinese had constructed entrenchments across this at Sin-ho.

Grant's force, consisting of two divisions, the 1st under Major-General Sir John Michel and the 2nd under Major General Sir Robert Napier,[2] and a cavalry brigade, left Peh-tang on 12 August. The plan was for Michel's division to advance directly along the causeway against the Sin-ho entrenchments while Napier's and the cavalry executed a wide right-flanking movement. The flank march involved two hours of trudging through mud and wading numerous wide canals used for the manufacture of salt, while masses of Tartar horsemen hovered around the column. Some of them, seeking easy pickings among the baggage, were held off by the guard's Enfield rifles and finally chased away by the cavalry. At length Napier's advance guard and artillery reached firmer ground on the left of the enemy entrenchments. Their appearance so unsettled the Chinese that when, following a preliminary bombardment, Michel's troops attacked along the causeway they broke and ran. During the engagement the new Armstrong field guns performed well and 'their range and accuracy excited great admiration.'[3]

After the engineers had bridged the canals the force moved on to Tangku two days later. A week's delay followed while more guns, ammunition and supplies were brought forward. At this point a fundamental disagreement arose between Grant and Cousin-Montauban. The Frenchman wanted to attack the now-notorious Large South Fort first, despite the fact that this would involve a river crossing and separate the force from its supply base. Grant, on the other hand, was for attacking the Small North Fort, arguing that after it had been taken its guns could be trained on the weaker faces of the other forts, compelling each to surrender in turn; and as Grant commanded the greater part of the troops he got his way.

Even so, the defences of the Small North Fort were formidable. In succession there was a deep dry ditch; an open space obstructed by an abatis; then a flooded ditch 45 feet wide and 15 deep; a densely planted 20-foot-wide belt of 'panjis', i.e. sharpened bamboo stakes capable of penetrating a boot or disembowelling a man if he fell on them; another flooded ditch; and another belt of panjis leading up the 15-foot-high crenellated and loopholed mud walls of the fort itself. Swamps restricted any advance on the fort to a narrow frontage on which a bridge over the first wet ditch had been destroyed and the drawbridge over the inner wet ditch had been raised.

Work on the besiegers' batteries was carried out mainly at night. The Chinese illuminated the scene with their blue lights and flares, which made the newer recruits feel nervous and exposed, although the enemy's harassing artillery fire caused little trouble. By the evening of 20 August 44 guns and three 8-inch mortars had been emplaced.

At 05:00 the following morning these opened fire. Simultaneously, the thunder of gunfire from the river mouth indicated that Admiral Hope's ships were engaging the Large North and South Forts. After a while a mortar shell burst in one of the Small North Fort's magazines. There was a deafening explosion and the entire structure vanished in a dense cloud of smoke. In the ensuing silence it seemed at first as though the garrison had been wiped out, but as the smoke cleared the Chinese returned to their guns. A second major eruption in the Large South Fort indicated that the warships were also finding their mark.

Shortly after 06:00 Napier, in overall command of the attack, considered that the time had come for the assault to go in. Because of the narrow frontage available, the storming party, under the tactical command of Brigadier-General Reeves, was only 2,500 strong, drawn mainly from the 44th (later the 1st Essex) and the 67th (later 2nd Hampshire) Regiments, commanded respectively by Lieutenant-Colonels MacMahon and Thomas, and a party of Royal Marines carrying pontoons for use in crossing the wet ditches. General Cousin-Montauban, evidently still sulking after losing his argument with Grant, sent along only 400 men and pointedly turned up without his sword, thereby demonstrating that the matter was nothing to do with him. On the other hand, the French were the better equipped for the assault, bringing with them light bamboo ladders, carried by coolies, that could be used both as bridges to cross the wet ditches and to scale the walls.

Neither the abatis, which had been knocked to pieces during the preparatory bombardment, nor the dry ditch, caused the attackers undue difficulties. The Chinese, however, crowded onto the walls and opened a heavy and sustained fire with their muskets, concentrating on the Royal Marine pontoon carriers, fifteen of whom were shot down by a single volley. Brigadier Reeves was also seriously wounded and command passed to Colonel MacMahon.

At the wet ditches the French swarmed across, the coolies standing up to their necks in water to support the ladders. The pontoons having been abandoned, many of the British also used the ladders. Others were forced to swim or flounder their way to the far side. One of the first over was a Major Anson of Grant's staff, who immediately set about cutting the drawbridge ropes; some accounts suggest that he used his own sword, but it seems more probable that he was provided with an axe by a corporal of the 67th. Napier had already brought forward two howitzers to the edge of the dry ditch and, seeing the drawbridge fall, he ordered them to open fire on the gate beyond. In due course they created a breach sufficiently wide for entry in single file, but by then the issue had been suddenly and dramatically decided.

By now the base of the wall was packed with men, their units inevitably intermixed, seeking a way in. Onto them the Chinese, now unable to use their muskets, rained down grenades, cannon shot, large stones, jars of quicklime and 'stinkpots' that gave off choking clouds of smoke. The

French were struggling to erect their ladders, which were thrown down by the enemy as soon as they were emplaced. Most of the narrow gun embrasures had survived the bombardment, but some had been damaged and into one of them scrambled a courageous Frenchman. For a moment it seemed as though he would be first to penetrate the interior of the fort. He fired his rifle at the nearest defender, took another handed up to him by a comrade, fired it, and then fell back, speared through the face.

Near the gate Lieutenant Nathaniel Burslem and Private Thomas Lane, both of the 67th, also clambered up to an embrasure and, despite the fact that they both sustained serious wounds, used a pick to enlarge it until it was wide enough. In the meantime, Lieutenant Robert Rogers and Private John McDougall of the 44th, who had been among the first to swim the ditches, had been joined by Lieutenant Edmund Lenon and Ensign John Chaplin of the 67th, the latter carrying the Queen's Colour of his regiment. Driving the point of his sword deep into the mud wall and supporting the hilt, Lenon made a step for Rogers to fight his way into an embrasure. Others followed Lenon's example, jamming their bayonets into the wall, enabling Lenon, Chaplin, McDougall and others to join Rogers. Shortly afterwards, Burslem and Lane broke through their embrasure. There was now a steady stream of men from both regiments coming over the wall, from which the defenders were being pitched into the courtyard below. At this point its was noticed that the French, too, had broken in, led by a drummer named Fauchard, and that close behind him came the colour bearer of their 102nd Regiment of the Line. Suddenly, all other considerations forgotten, a deadly race developed between the Allies as to which of them could plant their flag first on the summit of the high central tower, which could be seen crowded with large numbers of the enemy. At the bayonet's point the British stormers fought their way up the long ramp, enabling Chaplin to win, although he was wounded three times in the process. At this point the Chinese resistance, which had been extremely tough, completely collapsed. Some of them hid in huts and corners from which they were winkled out, while others, trying to escape over the walls, were either impaled on their own panjis or drowned in the wet ditches. It was estimated that they sustained 400 casualties out of the 500-strong garrison. British losses amounted to 21 killed and 184 wounded, French losses being proportionally less.

The capture of the Small North Fort had been a desperate business. Yet, for all the obstacles in their path, the attackers had, as one eye witness put it, 'meant to get in.' The Victoria Cross was awarded to Lieutenant Rogers and Private McDougall of the 44th; to Lieutenants Burslem and Lenon, Ensign Chaplin and Private Lane of the 67th; and to Hospital Apprentice

Andrew Fitzgibbon, aged 15, of the Bengal Medical Establishment, attached to the 67th Regiment, for his courage in tending the wounded under fire during the assault. Both regiments received a number of brevet promotions and in the 67th Colour Sergeant Davidson was subsequently promoted to ensign.[4]

The Small South Fort was abandoned by the enemy at once. The commander of the Large North Fort blustered briefly but then allowed the French to take possession of it without firing a shot. To their astonishment and delight the 2,000-strong garrison, who were expecting to be massacred, were simply disarmed and told to go home. Within the fort were some of the guns taken from the ships lost by Admiral Hope the previous year. The mandarin commanding the now-isolated Large South Fort, Hang Foo, surrendered the following day. Over 600 guns of various calibres were counted in the two South Forts alone.

The rest of the story is soon told. The Allies advanced up the Pei-ho to Tientsin and then began marching on Peking, defeating a Chinese field army in two sharp engagements. At this point the Imperial government indicated its willingness to talk but then behaved with incredible stupidity, kidnapping the Allied negotiators and holding them as hostages against a further advance. Disregarding these threats, Grant closed in on the capital and was preparing to storm it when, on 13 October, Prince Kung, deputising for the fleeing emperor, capitulated, agreeing to every one of the Allied demands, including the surrender of Kowloon on the mainland opposite Hong Kong, the payment of a substantial indemnity, and the ratification of the various treaties. When the surviving hostages were handed over, Grant learned to his horror that half the party had died as a direct result of the tortures to which they had all been subjected. In reprisal, he had the Yuen-Ming-Yuen, a group of palaces set in beautiful gardens, burned to the ground.[5] The Allied force then withdrew to the coast, leaving a garrison at Tientsin. Apart from a brief undeclared war with France in the 1880s, the Imperial government avoided conflict with the Western powers for the next 40 years, when it provided unofficial support for the Boxer Rising of 1900.

Notes

1. To transpose the engagement into a more modern perspective, it was as though eleven corvettes and a weak infantry battalion had tried to fight their way into one of the heavily defended river estuaries in Hitler's Atlantic Wall.
2. The name Napier was very familiar indeed in mid-Victorian Britain. General Sir Robert Napier was created Lord Napier of Magdala following his command of a successful punitive expedition against Abyssinia (Ethiopia) in 1867–68. General Sir Charles Napier conquered the Indian principality of Sind during a remarkable campaign in 1843, famously advising the Governor General of his victory, at least in the version of the satirical journal *Punch*, with the Latin cryptogram 'peccavi' (I have sinned). Admiral

Sir Charles Napier restored order in the eastern Mediterranean with naval actions along the Lebanese coast and a decisive victory on land which forced the Egyptian army to evacuate Beirut in 1840, subsequently commanding the Allied Baltic Fleet during the Crimean War.

3. The Armstrong guns were a few years ahead of their time. The vertical vent pieces could crack or even be blown out of the gun on firing. As was usual in such cases the users blamed the manufacturers, the latter responding by accusing the gunners of not tightening the breech screw sufficiently. The root of the problem lay in inadequate sealing of the chamber and during the 1870s the Army reverted briefly to rifled muzzle-loading guns.

4. Rogers and Chaplin both became major-generals in due course. On leaving the Army Lane joined the Kimberley State Police Force in South Africa. Fitzgibbon shares with Drummer T. Flinn the claim to be the youngest winner of the Victoria Cross, both being aged fifteen years and three months at the time of their respective actions, although only Fitzgibbon's age can be authenticated. He graduated to the rank of Apothecary, dying in Delhi in 1883.

5. The Imperial Summer Palace, lying outside the walls, had already been thoroughly looted of its treasures. The British blamed the French, whose conduct they thought disgraceful, although this did not stop them attending the subsequent sale. The Essex Regiment's museum at Chelmsford contains a fine enamel cloisonné vase, and the Royal Hampshire Regiment's museum at Winchester has a beautifully embroidered collar, both taken from the palace. Captain (later General) Charles Gordon of the Royal Engineers was also present and rescued numerous artefacts, including a beautiful carved throne, all now in the Royal Engineers' museum at Chatham.

CHAPTER FIVE

Dargai, 20 October 1897

For a century the tangled mountains of the North-West Frontier of India provided the British and Indian Armies with a school for soldiers, a hard, unforgiving school in which mistakes cost lives and, above all, a school in which the only certainly was the unexpected. Prominent among the frontier tribes were the Afridi, of whom it was said that robbery, murder, treachery and merciless blood feuds were the very breath of life. The same, to varying degrees, might have been said of all the tribes along the frontier, the Wazirs, Mahsuds, Orakzai, Mohmands and Yusufzai. Masters of the ambush and guerrilla war, they fought constantly among themselves and regularly against the British, who could provide much dangerous sport when there was nothing more pressing to occupy their minds. Sometimes a serious incident would require the despatch of a punitive expedition which would fight its way into the tribal territory and destroy the offending villages. In due course, after they had had enough of fighting, the tribesmen would let it be known that they were willing to submit. A 'jirga' or council would be held, attended by the tribal headmen and the senior British military and political officers. A fine would be imposed, the troops would leave and all would remain quiet for a while. Then, in a few years' time, the whole process would be repeated. Such events, however, tended to be local in character and it was unusual for large areas of the Frontier to be affected simultaneously.

Yet, the frontier tribes had another side to their character. Hospitality, for example, was regarded as a sacred trust. Devious with each other, they would react honestly if dealt with the same way. It could take years to win their trust, but once earned it could result in friendship for life. Many enlisted in regiments of the Indian Army and, having served their time loyally, would return home with their pensions and a mellower impression of the British Raj. Against this, the tribes were to a man devout Muslims to whom the killing of infidel Christians and Hindus was entirely impersonal and certainly no matter for conscience searching.

At the beginning of 1897, while those at home were preparing to celebrate Queen Victoria's Diamond Jubilee, the Frontier was quiet, although the term was relative, and seemed likely to remain so. In July, however, it suddenly exploded in revolt along its entire length, presenting the authorities with the most formidable challenge they had ever faced, or were likely to again.

There was only one cause capable of uniting tribes normally at each other's throats, and that was militant Islamic fundamentalism. Fanatical clergy were at work, notably the Mullah of Haddah among the Mohmands, the Mullah Powindah in Waziristan, the Mullah Sayid Akhbar in the Khyber region, and especially the Mullah Sadullah of Swat, known to the British as the Mad Fakir. Eyes blazing with fervour, Sadullah travelled from village to village preaching 'jihad' (holy war) against the infidel, accompanied by a thirteen-year-old boy whom he claimed was the last surviving heir of the Great Moghuls and would soon ascend the throne of his ancestors in Delhi. The situation was aggravated by Abdur Rahman, King of Afghanistan, who had recently produced a tract praising the concept of jihad and, displeased with the results of a recent frontier demarkation, urged the mullahs to drive the infidels from their land, although he had no intention of taking the field himself. Perhaps these factors would not on their own have been sufficient to provoke a general rising, but also present on the Frontier were agents of Sultan Abdul Hamid II of Turkey, determined to make trouble for the British in revenge for a humiliating diplomatic snub he had received at their hands. The line taken by these agents was to hint that Great Britain had been seriously weakened by its quarrel with the Sultan, and since the truth of this would not suffice, lies would do just as well. The Suez Canal and Aden were now in Turkish hands, they claimed, so that whereas reinforcements from the United Kingdom would normally take three weeks to reach India, they would now take six months; and, that being the case, the jihad would be over long before they could arrive. Being simple people with a limited knowledge of geography and no means of verifying the truth, the tribesmen accepted what they were told and were much encouraged.

The fuze which actually detonated the explosion had been in place since the previous year when a government clerk, a Hindu, was murdered in northern Waziristan. As the culprit was never brought to justice a fine of 2,000 rupees was imposed on the area. One village, Maizar, refused to pay its share and on 10 May 1897 the political agent, Mr Gee, arrived there to settle the dispute, accompanied by a military escort of some 300 men. The troops were offered hospitality to lull them into a false sense of security, then were treacherously attacked by over 1,000 tribesmen. After all three British officers had received mortal wounds the Indian officers took charge and embarked on a difficult fighting withdrawal from the village, despatching several cavalrymen to summon reinforcements. These reached the force during the evening, having covered nine miles in 90 minutes, and enabled it to break contact. Losses among the Indian soldiers amounted to 23 officers and men killed, and a large number of wounded; it was estimated that about 100 of their attackers were killed.

During the weeks that followed the rising spread like wildfire along the Frontier, the garrisons of fortified posts having to fight desperately for their lives against an enemy who, inflamed with religious fervour, launched repeated attacks regardless of losses. At the end of August disaster struck. The forts guarding the Khyber Pass were held by an irregular and locally raised unit known as the Khyber Rifles, officered entirely by Afridis. Raised after the Second Afghan War, they had given good service in the past but had become seriously unsettled by the mullahs' propaganda. On 23 August the rebels closed in around the forts. That at Ali Musjid was simply abandoned, while the garrison at Fort Maude offered only a token resistance before falling back on a relief column from Fort Jamrud. Next day it was the turn of Landi Kotal, which resisted successfully for 24 hours before treacherous elements opened the gates; some of the garrison joined the rebels, some were allowed to leave after handing over their weapons, but others, remaining true to their salt, managed to fight their way through to Jamrud. Control of the pass, the vital communications route between India and Afghanistan, was not regained until December. Such was the fury of the tribal assault that those holding the smaller posts stood little or no chance of survival.

On 12 September the heliograph station at Saragarhi, midway between Forts Gulistan and Lockhart, covering the important Samana Ridge to the south of the Khyber and held by the 36th Sikhs, was attacked in overwhelming strength. The garrison, consisting of twenty men under Havildar Ishan Singh, beat off two frenzied attacks during the morning, strewing the surrounding rocks with bodies. However, some of the Afridis, taking advantage of an area of dead ground, began picking away at the brick wall until part of it collapsed, creating a breach. The Sikhs ran from their fire positions to repel the renewed assault but were too few in number and in ferocious hand to hand fighting were forced back into their barrack block, where they fought to the last man. One sepoy, barricading himself in the guard room, shot down or bayoneted twenty of his assailants before perishing in the flames of the burning building; another, one of the post's signallers, remained in heliograph contact with Fort Lockhart until the end. Jubilant, the Afridis swarmed to join their comrades who had invested Fort Gulistan that morning. Held in much greater strength, this proved to be a tougher nut to crack and, despite casualties, was still holding three days later when the tribesmen, flayed by the shellfire of a relief column advancing from Fort Lockhart, abandoned the siege and dispersed into the hills. Thanks to the 36th Sikhs, the Samana Ridge forts remained in British hands and in recognition of the fact the regiment was awarded the unique battle honour 'Samana'.

Such desperate actions as these marked the high water mark of the rising, although months of fierce fighting lay ahead before the Frontier was pacified. The government of India had been taken aback by the sheer scale and ferocity of the revolt but reacted by despatching strong punitive columns to Malakand and against the Wazirs, Mohmands, Afridis and Orakzais. Considerations of space inhibit describing even the more important actions save one, that fought by the 1st Gordon Highlanders at Dargai, which has passed into the legends of Frontier warfare.

A contemporary general inspection report describes the battalion as being 'A particularly fine one. The officers as a body are an exceptionally nice set; the warrant officers and NCOs seem to be very efficient, and the privates have an admirable physique.' Like every good unit, the Gordons reflected the personality of their commanding officer, Lieutenant-Colonel H. H. Mathias, whose bullet head, determined jaw, bristling moustache and level blue eyes indicated a no-nonsense, instinctive fighter. In many ways Mathias was a commander well ahead of his time, paying attention not only to the more obvious aspects of his profession but also to the physical condition of his men and their morale. In 1896 the battalion won the Queen's Cup for shooting and it was regarded as having the best signallers of any British regiment in India. Field exercises took place regularly, one advanced feature being the instruction of NCOs in military sketching, in those days an essential element in reconnaissance, usually taught only to officers. Mathias kept his men fit with a programme of athletics, hill-racing and football, contests being held between companies and against neighbouring units. There were also regimental concert parties and other activities to combat the boredom of cantonment life. The impression given is that the 1st Gordon Highlanders was a highly trained, efficient battalion, entirely at ease with itself and held in high regard; it was, too, an experienced battalion, having taken part in the Chitral Expedition of 1895.

In April 1897 the Gordons, based at Rawalpindi on the Punjab side of the North-West Frontier Province boundary, moved up to their hot weather station in the Murree Hills, expecting to remain there throughout the summer. At the beginning of August, however, in response to the rapidly deteriorating situation on the Frontier, it returned to Rawalpindi whence it was immediately despatched to Jamrud. Here it formed part of a force that prevented the rebels advancing further along the Khyber.

By October the British counter-measures had begun to take effect. Nevertheless, it was appreciated that the tribes would not submit until the war was carried onto their own territory and it was decided to advance deep into the Tirah region. In this area it was estimated that together the Afridis and Orakzais could field between 40–50,000 men and for this reason the Tirah Field Force, commanded by Lieutenant-General Sir William Lockhart, was the largest punitive expedition ever assembled on the Frontier. It consisted of two divisions (the 1st under Major-General W. P. Symons and the 2nd under Major-General A. G. Yeatman-Biggs), two flanking columns, a strong lines of communication element and a reserve brigade. Altogether, 11,892 British and 22,614 Indian troops were involved, accompanied by almost 20,000 followers who performed menial but essential tasks; there were also 8,000 horses, 1,440 ponies for the sick and wounded, over 18,000 mules and an enormous number of camels, carts and baggage ponies. Lockhart's plan was to concentrate at Kohat and enter Tirah from the south by crossing the Samana Ridge at a pass west of Fort Gulistan. He would then force two more passes which would bring him to his ultimate objective, the Tirah Maidan, a wide fertile valley upon which the surrounding tribes relied for subsistence, rarely if ever visited by Europeans before.

Together with the 1st Dorsetshire Regiment, the 15th Sikhs and the 1st/2nd Gurkhas, the Gordons constituted Brigadier-General F. J. Kempster's 3rd Brigade, which formed part of the 2nd Division. The Tirah Field Force left Kohat on 7 October, its route taking it past the now deserted ruins of Saragarhi signal station. By 15 October, marching by easy stages, it had reached Shinawari, but beyond this point progress across the Samana Ridge was blocked by a substantial force of tribesmen holding the village of Dargai, located at the summit of a towering spur that dominated the only road. The crest was lined with sangars, while the rocks themselves contained numerous fissures that provided natural rifle pits. Immediately below the village were precipitous cliffs, broken here and there by goat paths, and below these was a steeply sloping open space several hundred yards wide, forming a glacis that could be swept by fire from above. An attacker who succeeded in crossing this would then find his further upward progress restricted to goat paths or funnelled into the narrowing approach to the village itself, where he could be picked off with ease. Nature, therefore, had endowed Dargai with better defences than many a purpose-built fortress.

Lockhart had only the 2nd Division in hand, the 1st Division still being on the march some sixteen miles short of Shinawari. He nonetheless decided that the former would take Dargai at once, conduct of the operation being entrusted to Lieutenant-General Sir Power Palmer, normally responsible for the force's lines of communication, as Yeatman-Biggs was ill. Palmer's plan was for Brigadier R. Westmacott's 4th Brigade to mount a frontal attack on the village, covered by two mountain batteries, while Kempster's 3rd Brigade made a wide detour to the west, threatening the defenders' right flank and rear.

The troops moved off during the early hours of 18 October. The route of Kempster's brigade, which Palmer accompanied, took it up a dry water-course that had its source near the western summit of the spur. The higher they climbed, the rougher became the going, the narrower the stream bed, the larger the boulders and the steeper the slope. After five miles had been covered the Gurkhas, in the lead, gave the appearance of flies walking up a wall. A point had now been reached at which the mules were unable to cope with the precipitous going and Palmer decided to send back his guns and the field hospital, escorted by the Dorsets and part of the 15th Sikhs. The Gordons, bringing up the rear, had perforce to halt and let them through. From about 09:00 onwards the steady thumping of guns indicated that the mountain batteries were engaged in their preliminary bombardment of Dargai. At about 11:00 heliograph contact was established with Westmacott's brigade, which was making slow but steady progress, often in single file, up the direct route towards the village. By noon the Gordons, after a stiff two-hour scramble, had joined 1st/2nd Gurkhas and 15th Sikhs on the slopes above the source of the water-course, attracting sporadic long range fire. The coordination between the two brigades had been excellent, for Westmacott's battalions were now in position to launch their assault. Under a hail of fire from above, the 2nd King's Own Scottish Borderers and 1st/3rd Gurkhas swarmed across the open slope and up the goat tracks to the village. The tribesmen hastily abandoned their positions and fled, sped on their way by a few long range volleys from Kempster's men. The capture of Dargai had been a model operation, costing the Borderers only six casualties and the Gurkhas thirteen. Undoubtedly, the enemy's resistance would have been far stiffer had not Kempster's brigade threatened their rear, always a sensitive area in tribal warfare.

By mid-afternoon both brigades had been concentrated at Dargai. For the reasons quoted below, Palmer decided to abandon the position, despite the fact that two large groups of tribesmen, one estimated to be over 4,000 strong, could be seen converging on the spur from their camps in the Khanki Valley. Westmacott's brigade, less two companies of Borderers, led off first. Between 16:00 and 17:00, with the sun falling towards the western skyline, Kempster's brigade prepared to follow, covered initially by the

15th Sikhs. They, in turn, were covered by the Gordons and the two Borderer companies as they disengaged and passed through. By now the tribesmen, having reoccupied the sangars along the crest, were directing an increasingly heavy fire at those on the open slope below the cliffs, making the officers their special target. Major Jennings Bramly was killed and Lieutenant Pears was wounded; Second Lieutenant Young had his helmet shot off; and Lieutenant Dalrymple Hay, feeling blood running down his cheek, discovered that it had been grazed by a bullet.

When the moment came, Colonel Mathias released the Borderers then ordered three of his own five companies back into fresh fire positions from which they could support the withdrawal of the remaining two. One of the latter had succeeded in disengaging, as had half of Captain F. W. Kerr's company, when a body of the enemy broke cover some 30 yards distant, fired a ragged volley and charged the small group remaining. Six of them were dropped almost at bayonet point, four of them falling to Private W. Rennie, and the rest made off when they were engaged by Captain Miller Wallnutt's company from its new fire position. While this was taking place Lieutenant Young, Surgeon-Captain Gerrard and Colour Sergeant Craib, went out and rescued a wounded man who was in immediate danger of being hacked to death.

Darkness put an end to the fighting. In addition to the casualties mentioned above, the Gordons had sustained another man killed and seven wounded. Dead and wounded alike were carried down the rough two-mile track to the road, on reaching which the battalion formed up and marched the six miles back to the camp at Shinawari.

The reasons given by Palmer for abandoning Dargai include the following:

1. The 2nd Division was not strong enough to hold the position, guard Shinawari camp and maintain communications between the two.
2. There was no water supply between Dargai and Shinawari, and no supply of firewood at Dargai.
3. The continued occupation of Dargai would have revealed the proposed axis of advance into tribal territory, which was not desirable.
4. The 1st Division was still a day's march short of Shinawari.

The reader might agree that some of these look extremely thin, while others might be regarded as excellent reasons for not having mounted the operation in the first place. As it was, the Orakzais could claim to have repulsed a British attempt to capture the position, and at this stage of the revolt the mere suggestion of a tribal victory was the last thing that was wanted. Nevertheless, for the better part of the next day Lockhart, lulled into a false sense of security by the arrival of the 1st Division, refused to

THE DAGAI HEIGHTS

Dargai Village

Sangars

Enemy's position

Sangars

Sangars

Ⓒ

Ⓑ

Ⓐ

From the Chagru Kotal

Ⓐ The point from which the Gordons charged

Ⓒ The furthest point reached by some of the 2nd Gurkhas before the Gordons came up.

Ⓑ The exposed strip

accept the reality of the situation, expressing the opinion that the continued work of improvement on the road, protected as it was by strong covering parties, would in itself deter the enemy from re-occupying Dargai. However, when he was informed that evening that Dargai Heights were now held by an estimated 12,000 Afridi and Orakzai, he reacted with commendable speed. Because it knew the ground, the 2nd Division, reinforced by elements of the 1st Division, would again clear the spur. This time, there would be no subtlety of manoeuvre against the enemy's flank and rear; what he intended was a straightforward frontal attack in strength, supported by the fire of the divisional artillery, supplemented by an additional battery. At this point personalities began to have a bearing on subsequent events. Lockhart detested Westmacott, and decided that Kempster, whom he merely disliked, would deliver the assault, under the control of Yeatman-Biggs, who had returned to duty.

When the troops, having been briefed on the operation, marched out of camp at 04:30 on 20 October, their muttered opinion of the generals was ripe, to say the least. No doubt Kempster,[1] whom they loathed, received the lion's share of the blame, which in this case was a little unfair as the decisions had not been his.

By 10:00 the guns were pounding the summit, which the Gordons also brought under long range rifle fire. The enemy, secure in their sangars and rocky clefts, were little affected by this; they had, moreover, strengthened their defences and from one point they were also able to direct a crossfire across the all-important open slope below the cliff. Thus, when the 1st/2nd Gurkhas rose to attack, the entire summit erupted in a wild storm of fire. Under the impact of thousands of bullets the dusty surface of the slope was churned into a dust cloud in which it seemed nothing could live. Gurkhas could be seen falling and their casualties strewed the ground. Despite this, three companies reached the cover of a rocky shelf approximately halfway across, but further progress was impossible. Worse still, every attempt by their comrades to reach them resulted in more men shot down. Jubilant, the tribesmen began waving their flags, beating drums and shouting defiance.

Kempster ordered the 1st Dorsets to make the attempt. A few managed to sprint across the fatal 150 yards to the safety of the ledge, but as a whole the battalion was stopped in its tracks. It was then the turn of the 2nd Derbyshire Regiment,[2] but they fared no better. As each attack failed the frenzy of the tribesmen reached higher levels of exultation.

It was now mid-afternoon and, despite the carpet of dead, dying and wounded covering the lower half of the slope, Dargai Heights still remained firmly in enemy hands. The crisis of the battle having been reached, Yeatman-Biggs ordered Kempster to commit the Gordons and the 3rd Sikhs, his last reserves. The latter were providing an escort for the guns on a lower spur and had to await relief by a Jhind state infantry battalion, but the Gordons moved off at once.

As they clambered up the narrow path they were not encouraged by the steady stream of dead and wounded being carried past in the opposite direction. At length they formed up in dead ground screened by some low scrub at the lower edge of the slope. Nearby, grim-faced Derbys, Dorsets and Gurkhas lay firing at the enemy, now capering among the rocks and yelling derisive insults.

It is a matter of record that Highland infantry, heirs to a long and violent history in which the carrying of arms and settlement of disputes by force was usual, have always launched their attacks with a unique speed and a berserk ferocity that was very difficult and often impossible to stop. Colonel Mathias knew how best to awaken these qualities in his men and, having been told that his assault would be preceded by three minutes' concentrated artillery fire on the summit, he used the interval to address them very briefly, his voice cutting like a whiplash through the sounds of gunfire, musketry, savage drumming and yells:

'The General says this hill must be taken at all costs – the Gordon Highlanders will take it!'

There was a moment's silence. The men knew the terrible risks involved, but the Colonel had given his word on their behalf and not one of them would let him down.

'Aye!' It was a spontaneous roar from 600 throats.

'Officers and pipers to the fore!'

It was now, as the sun glinted on the officers' drawn broadswords and the Pipe Major took his place, throwing his plaid and drones across his shoulder with infinite swagger, that the inherited instincts of countless bloody if long-forgotten clan battles began to surface, causing the scalp to crawl and the hackles to rise. Like their forebears of old, they, led by their chief men and pipers, were going out to meet the enemy, steel to steel. Suddenly, the supporting gunfire ceased.

'Bugler – sound Advance!'

Like a tidal wave the Gordons poured out of cover and onto the deadly open slopes. The pipers struck up the regimental march, *The Cock o' the North*,[3] a fine ranting tune that skirled across the hillside, evoking a response from every man present. Yelling, the entire battalion swept upwards. Mathias, still up with the leaders, had unleashed the full fury of his Gordons and knew that they would give the shortest shrift to anyone who got in their way.

Perhaps the sudden appearance of the battalion caught the enemy unawares. If so, the respite was only of seconds' duration. Once again, the crest blazed with fire and, once again, the dust was stirred into a fine mist by the pelting hail of bullets. And now the Gordons began to go down. Lieutenant Lamont was killed outright at the head of his men. Major Macbean, shot through the thigh, crawled to a boulder and continued to cheer on the assault. Lieutenant Dingwall, hit in four places and unable to move, was carried to safety by Private Lawson, who then returned to bring in the wounded Private Macmillan, being hit twice while doing so. The pipers, who could neither run nor take cover and still play, continued to walk upright and thus became a special target for the enemy. Lance-Corporal Milne, among the first to set foot on the slope, continued to march upwards until shot through the chest. Piper George Findlater suddenly felt his feet knocked from under him by a sharp blow. Sitting up, he discovered that he had been shot through both ankles but, disregarding alike the enemy's fire, the pain and the fear that he might never walk normally again, he continued to play his comrades into action. Mathias was hit but kept moving. Major Downman got a bullet through his helmet. Other men felt rounds twitching at their kilts and tunics. Major Macbean, reaching for his water bottle after the assault had passed by, found it empty save for the bullet responsible for draining the contents.

It took less than two minutes for the leading companies to reach the ledge where the Gurkhas were sheltering, although it seemed far longer. There they paused briefly to get their breath back while the others closed up. Then, with a wave of the broadsword and a sharp shout of 'Come!' the officers led a second rush across the ledge to the foot of the escarpment. This time the Gordons were accompanied by kukri-wielding Gurkhas, keen to exact payment for the long hours they had spent pinned down. Another pause, and then the Gordons were scrambling up the goat paths towards the summit. Already the enemy's triumphant drumming had stopped and his firing become ragged. Instinctively the tribesmen understood that the green-kilted soldiers could not be stopped and, recognising the murder in their attackers' eyes, they began shredding away. Those with a mind to stay quickly changed it when, far below, they saw the 3rd Sikhs crossing the open slope, big, bearded, turbaned men coming steadily on behind a line of levelled bayonets. There were, too, large numbers of Dorsets, Derbys and Gurkhas who, inspired by the Gordons' assault, were rushing forward to join in the attack.

Thus, when the Gordons finally reached the summit, they found the sangars contained only a handful of dead and wounded. The reverse slopes of the spur, however, were black with the running figures of thousands of tribesmen, into whom a rapid fire was opened, sending many tumbling among the rocks.

Mathias, out of breath and bleeding, reached the summit alongside Colour Sergeant Mackie.

'Stiff climb, eh, Mackie?' he remarked. 'I'm not quite so young as I was, you know.'

'Och, never you mind, sir,' replied the colour sergeant, slapping his commanding officer on the back with a familiarity justified by events, 'Ye were goin' verra strong for an auld man!' If the compliment was unintentionally back-handed, the admiration was genuine, as Mathias found when his Gordons, now laughing and joking, gathered round to give him three cheers.

Yeatman-Biggs was determined that the tribesmen would not be given a second chance to reoccupy the heights and detailed the Gurkhas and the Dorsets to hold them. The Gordons volunteered to carry down their wounded, an act of kindness that was greatly appreciated. Afterwards, as they marched to their own bivouac, each regiment they passed broke into spontaneous cheering, officers and men pressing forward to shake their hands and offer their water bottles, a small gesture but a very generous one considering that no further supplies could be obtained until the following day.

As the Widow of Windsor's parties went, the second capture of Dargai Heights was small in scale but it was as bitterly contested as any. The cost was three officers and 33 other ranks killed and twelve officers and 147 other ranks wounded, the majority of these casualties being incurred on the lowest 150 yards of the open slope. The Gordons' share amounted to one officer and six other ranks killed and six officers and 31 other ranks wounded. In the circumstances this was little short of astonishing but can be attributed to the speed with which the attack was delivered across the most exposed portion of the open slope, this being cited in later tactical manuals.

Mathias was to receive many congratulatory telegrams on behalf of his battalion; from the Queen and from the British Army's Commander-in-Chief, Field Marshal Lord Wolseley, from the Gordons' 2nd Battalion, from the regiment's friendly rivals the Black Watch, and from Caledonian societies all over the world, including the United States.

Yeatman-Biggs recommended that the Victoria Cross be awarded to Lieutenant-Colonel Mathias, Piper Findlater and Private Lawson. In Mathias' case the supreme award was denied, thanks to an incredibly priggish decision by the War Office that neither general officers nor battalion commanders were eligible for the Cross, presumably because they were doing nothing less than their duty.[4] Queen Victoria made her own feelings known in no uncertain manner by promptly appointing him as one of her aides de camp with the rank of colonel, although he continued to command the battalion until its return to Scotland the following year. Piper Findlater[5] and Private Lawson received the award in the field. In addition, Colour Sergeants J. Mackie and T. Craib, Sergeants F. Ritchie, D. Mathers, J. Donaldson and J. Mackay, and Lance-Corporal (Piper) G. Milne were awarded the Distinguished Conduct Medal, the last mentioned being decorated personally by the Queen when he was invalided home.[6]

The Tirah Field Force fought many more battles as it penetrated deeper into tribal territory, but none was as fiercely contested or as critical as Dargai. Early in November it reached its objective, the Tirah Maidan, a beautiful, fertile valley one hundred square miles in extent, flanked by pine-clad slopes and dotted with copses. There were numerous houses, each of which, significantly, was fortified against its neighbours. In the storerooms were piled high the fruits of the recent harvest – Indian corn, beans, barley, honey, potatoes, walnuts and onions. The entire valley was deserted, the inhabitants having taken their families with them into the hills. Lockhart despatched columns into every corner of the Tirah, where the resistance encountered clearly indicated that the tribes had no intention of submitting. Reluctantly, he decided that if they would not talk he would begin laying waste the valley. The troops, many of whom came from farming stock, did not enjoy the work, but the sight of groves being felled and columns of smoke rising from burning buildings produced the desired result. With the exception of the ungovernable Zakha Khel, who did not submit until the following April, the tribes sent in their leaders to a jirga where they accepted their punishment: they would give up 800 serviceable rifles, pay a fine of 50,000 rupees and return all the property they had stolen during the rising. On 7 December, with the worst of the winter snows approaching, the evacuation of the Tirah Maidan began. The withdrawal of the 1st Division was comparatively uneventful, but that of the 2nd Division was subject to constant ambushes and attacks that inflicted 164 casualties and were obviously not the work of the Zakha Khel alone. Nevertheless, so thoroughly had the rising been put down that during the next twenty years only five major punitive expeditions were required to police troublesome areas, and never again was fighting so widespread along the Frontier.

It would be absurd to suggest that any love was lost between the British and the tribes, but there was a great deal of mutual respect and during both World Wars thousands of the latter volunteered for service with the Crown. There was even a sense of loss when the British left India, for now no one remained for their young men to prove themselves against, even their hereditary Hindu enemies having been removed far to the south of them by the creation of the Islamic state of Pakistan. Yet the world was to hear of them again, for when the Soviet Union launched its disastrous occupation of Afghanistan in 1979 the Frontier again became an arsenal and huge numbers crossed to fight alongside their co-religious kindred in the Mujahideen. For all its size, the Soviet Army was unable to cope. In the end, therefore, the mullahs' promise of a successful jihad had been fulfilled, albeit a century after it was made and against a very different kind of infidel.

Notes
1. Kempster had an unfortunate personality and was so unpopular throughout the Tirah Field Force that its members coined the verb 'to be kempstered,' that is, generally mucked about. For all that, he was a capable enough officer in action.
2. Later the Sherwoood Foresters.
3. The Cock o' the North was the nickname of the Duke of Gordon who had raised the regiment 104 years earlier.
4. At the time the Victoria Cross warrant also incorporated a clause to the effect that in the event of subsequent 'scandalous conduct' the award would be forfeit. This rarely happened but when it did there was an understandable public outcry in protest. King Edward VII put an end to this sort of sanctimonious humbug.
5. To quote from a footnote in Chapter 26 of the Gordon Highlanders' regimental history, *The Life of a Regiment*: 'The incident of the wounded piper continuing to play, being telegraphed home, took the British public by storm, and when Findlater arrived in England he found himself famous. Reporters rushed to interview him; managers offered him fabulous sums to play at their theatres; the streets of London and all the country towns were placarded with his portrait; when, after his discharge, he was brought to play at the Military Tournament, royal personages and distinguished generals shook him by the hand; his photograph was sold by thousands; the Scotsmen in London would have let him swim in champagne, and the daily cheers of the multitude were enough to turn an older head than that of this young soldier. A handsome pension enabled Findlater to rest on his laurels and turn his sword into a ploughshare on a farm near Turriff. He re-enlisted for the Great War, though not fit for foreign service.'
6. Throughout their subsequent history the Gordon Highlanders celebrated the anniversary of Dargai wherever they were stationed. Thanks to government economies that have reduced the Army's strength to the lowest level for 300 years, the regiment no longer has an independent existence, having merged with the Queen's Own Highlanders to form a new regiment, The Highlanders (Seaforth, Gordons and Camerons). This will, however, continue to celebrate the anniversary of the action.

CHAPTER SIX

The Storming of San Juan Ridge – Cuba, 1 July 1898

At 21:40 on the night of 15 February 1898 two explosions took place aboard the second-class battleship USS *Maine*, lying in Havana harbour. The first was comparatively small, but the second, which followed immediately, shattered the superstructure and blew out a large area of the hull's starboard plating, sending debris and bodies soaring up to 200 feet in the air and illuminating the entire harbour with its flash. Very quickly, the *Maine* slid beneath the surface to settle in the soft mud below. Of the ship's complement of 354 officers and men, 252 were either killed instantly or drowned and a further eight died in hospital.

Although the Spanish authorities did everything in their power to assist, a suggestion by Captain Charles D. Sigsbee, the *Maine's* commander, that the proximate cause of his ship's destruction was external in source and could have been a mine electrically detonated from the shore, was eagerly seized upon by a virulently anti-Spanish press at home, to the extent that this explanation became an article of faith. John Harris, however, having scrupulously examined both sides of the argument in his book *Without Trace* , reached a more probable and certainly less emotive conclusion. Spontaneous combustion within coal bunkers, often accompanied by explosion if there was a concentration of coal dust in the air, was a sufficiently common danger for standard safety measures to have been introduced. Likewise, the deterioration of old munitions to a volatile state, especially in hot climates, was not thoroughly understood at the time and was to cause several major explosions aboard warships in the years following the loss of the *Maine*. It seems likely, therefore, that an explosion in a coal bunker triggered a sympathetic and infinitely more powerful detonation in a neighbouring magazine aboard the battleship.[1]

Perhaps it is not altogether coincidence that Sigsbee attracted unfavourable comment for poor internal housekeeping while commanding the veteran *Kearsage* in 1886 and also, in later years, while commanding the battleship *Texas*.[2] Again, the Spanish government, desperately anxious to avoid war with the United States, had nothing whatever to gain from the *Maine's* destruction and no trace of any electric cable was ever found either

by its own or the American courts of inquiry. The only possible beneficia-
ries of such an act would have been Cuban rebels anxious to inflame
Spanish–American relations, and their participation in the tragedy has
never been seriously considered. Be that as it may, the American press,
notably that section of it controlled by William Randolph Hearst, was convinced of foul play and exercised so strong an influence on public and political opinion that on 25 April 1898 President McKinley's administration
declared war on Spain.

The origins of the American involvement in Cuba had their roots in
events which had taken place 30 years earlier. In 1868, following the depo-
sition of Queen Isabella II, the Cubans demanded their independence from
Spain, which still supported slavery and imposed high taxes on them while
denying them a share in their own government. A ten-year guerrilla war
ensued, costing the lives of about 200,000 Cubans and Spaniards. The
United States, while refusing to intervene directly, was sympathetic to the
rebels and provided them with unofficial support. The war ended when
Spain promised reforms but apart from the abolition of slavery in 1886
these did not materialise. Rebellion broke out again in 1895 and made considerable headway until General Valeriano Weyler y Nicolau, a veteran of
the earlier war, arrived to take command of the Spanish troops. Weyler, a
very capable general, brought the situation under control by subdividing
the affected areas with lines of blockhouses and barbed wire to restrict the
rebels' mobility, and deprived them of food and support by removing the
non-combatants from their homes to centralised 'concentration' camps.[3]
By the end of 1896 these measures had confined the insurgents to the eastern end of the island.

Within the United States the Hearst group and other sections of the press
generated a powerful ground swell of anti-Spanish feeling by their biased
reporting of the war, feeding their readers with a diet of atrocities allegedly
committed by Weyler and his men. Subsequent studies revealed that in the
field the behaviour of the Spanish troops had been no worse than that of
other armies in similar situations and that their officers had, in fact, exercised restraint on their men. What could not be denied was that thousands
of non-combatants, including women and children, were dying in the 'concentration' camps, not as a result of deliberate policy, but because of poor
administration, overcrowded accommodation, poor rations and bad sanitation, creating the very conditions in which diseases quickly reached epi-
demic proportions.

The outraged American public, sensing the latent power of their young
nation, brought immense pressure on the McKinley administration to
intervene on behalf of the Cuban rebels; so, too, did the influential press

barons. Strong representations were made to the Madrid government which, painfully aware that throughout the past 100 years Spain had declined to the level of a fourth-rate power, did what it could to avoid direct confrontation. During 1897 it ended the 'concentration' camp system, recalled Weyler and offered the Cubans home rule, none of which was reported in the American press.

The effect of these concessions was most marked in Cuba itself, where the rebels, sensing Madrid's weakness, believed that by continuing the war they could obtain full independence. For their part, Spaniards resident in Cuba and those Cubans who wished to retain the link with Spain bitterly resented the American intrusion into their affairs, to the extent that the US Consul General in Havana, General Fitzhugh Lee, a former Confederate cavalry commander and nephew of General Robert E. Lee, reported that American nationals in the island were in potentially serious danger. Furthermore, Lee doubted whether the rebels would be capable of forming a government and asked for the despatch of naval vessels for the protection of American interests. The idea found support in Washington, notably with Theodore Roosevelt, the Assistant Secretary of the Navy, and to avoid further injuring Spanish pride, it was decided that the exchange of friendly naval visits between the United States and Spain, suspended since 1895, would be resumed. A Spanish cruiser, the *Vizcaya*, was to visit New York, and the *Maine* would go to Havana, where she arrived on 25 January 1898 to a correctly courteous if not warm welcome.

The subsequent destruction of the battleship destroyed any prospect of peace and the outbreak of war was greeted with scenes of wild enthusiasm in the United States. An increase in the regular army's strength from 28,000 to 60,000 men was authorised and some 200,000 volunteers swamped the hastily set up recruiting offices. Volunteer units were formed, of which the most famous was the 1st US Volunteer Cavalry, otherwise known as the Rough Riders, in which Theodore Roosevelt, a man of immense energy with a firm belief in direct action and the quality of grit, served as a lieutenant-colonel.

The problem was that the small regular army, which, since the end of the Civil War had been responsible for the security of the western frontier, was simply not equipped to cope with such a huge expansion. Everything was in short supply and even long-established regular units had to put up with what they could get. Thus, Captain W. C. Brown, commanding E Troop 1st Cavalry, was to note in his diary, 'War was declared on April 25th, yet on the last day of May my troop was still in all respects on the reduced basis called for by a state of profound peace and, of the essentials needed to bring it to war strength, many of its recruits had not yet enlisted; its horses were still on the horse ranches of the West awaiting the arrival of the remount purchase; and its arms and equipment were still in the store houses at various arsenals, or in process of manufacture.' It was, perhaps, typical of the times that the very next day, having been told that his troop was to fight dismounted, Brown received a substantial quantity of saddlery and tack, plus eight carbines, twelve revolvers, and fifteen sabres.

The navy, on the other hand, was fully prepared and went into action immediately in accordance with the overall strategic aims of the war, which were to attack Spain's major overseas possessions, namely the Philippine Islands in the Pacific, and Cuba. On 1 May Commodore George Dewey's Asiatic Squadron destroyed the Spanish naval presence in the Philippines at the Battle of Manila Bay, clearing the way for an expeditionary force that reached the islands at the end of June. However, Rear Admiral William T. Sampson's Atlantic Fleet, consisting of five battleships and two armoured cruisers, failed to prevent the arrival of Admiral Pascual Cervera with four modern cruisers and three destroyers at Santiago de Cuba on 19 May. Here, protected by forts covering the entrance to the deep natural harbour, the Spanish warships remained blockaded, their presence providing the Americans with an objective against which to strike. It was decided that the V Corps, commanded by Major General William R. Shafter, would effect a landing at Daiquirí, some miles to the east, and capture the city.

Aged 63, Shafter had joined the army as a volunteer during the first year of the Civil War and had earned the Congressional Medal of Honor for gallantry. After the war he had been granted a Regular commission and served on the Frontier during the Indian Wars. He had attained the rank of brigadier-general only as recently as 1897, but his untarnished record, seniority and friends in the War Department ensured that on the outbreak of war he received a commission as a major-general of volunteers and with it his present command. He was, unfortunately, not a man to inspire confidence in his subordinates. As years of sedentary garrison duty had resulted in his weight rising to 300 pounds, he therefore possessed a somewhat gross appearance, and his understandable inability to move quickly was further aggravated by gout. Coarse mannered and inclined to bully, he alienated many of those with whom he came in contact. Despite this, his major deficiency as a commander was one which he shared with the majority of his contemporaries and for which he was not to blame – he had no experience whatever of handling large formations.

V Corps consisted of three divisions and one independent brigade. The Cavalry Division, commanded by Major-General Joseph P. Wheeler, a former Confederate officer, contained two brigades each of three regiments;[4] the 1st and 2nd Infantry Divisions, commanded respectively by Brigadier-

Generals J. F. Kent and H. W. Lawton, each contained three brigades of three infantry regiments; the Independent Brigade, under Brigadier-General J. C. Bates, contained two infantry regiments. With the exception of 1st US Volunteer Cavalry in the Cavalry Division and one volunteer regiment in each infantry division, all of Shafter's troops were regulars. The army's standard weapon for infantry and cavalry alike was the .30-calibre Krag-Jörgensen rifle, which had been introduced in 1893. This had a five-round magazine into which rounds were loaded in succession, but the American musketry doctrine of the day stressed the importance of single aimed shots and discouraged the filling of magazines save when rapid fire was required to repel an attack. Although all of Shafter's Regular units were equipped with the Krag-Jörgensen, the sheer scale of the Army's expansion meant that there were not enough to go round, and because of this the volunteer units were armed with the old single-shot .45-calibre Springfield rifle. There was also a shortage of smokeless ammunition for the Krag-Jörgensens and none at all for the Springfields. V Corps' artillery included two field artillery batteries with six 3.2-inch guns apiece, two batteries of assorted heavier weapons, and one four-gun Gatling machine gun battery. No smokeless propellant was available for the field batteries and this was to have serious consequences once battle was joined.

Shafter's command began assembling for its mission at Tampa, Florida, where chaos reigned supreme for several weeks. The local railway system, never having been designed to transport 17,000 men and everything they needed for a campaign abroad, all but collapsed under the strain placed upon it. Stores of every description, guns, ammunition and transport wagons jammed the quays and were loaded without thought of disembarkation requirements simply to make working space. Sufficient thought had been given to the problems of fighting in Cuba to recognise that the cavalry would have little opportunity for mounted action, but the troops were still being sent to do battle in tropical, humid heat wearing their blue woollen uniforms, the one exception being the Rough Riders, which had sensibly outfitted themselves in khaki cotton drill. This unit consisted mainly of cowboys and prospectors from Arizona, Montana, New Mexico and Oklahoma, with a leavening of Eastern college men who were regarded as dudes but secretly admired.

At length, despite serious shortages of equipment, it was clear that V Corps was as ready as it would ever be. The troops, together with 272 teamsters and 107 stevedores to assist in unloading, were finally aboard the transports, in the holds of which were 2,295 horses and mules, 193 wagons, seven ambulances, sixteen 3.2-inch guns, four 7-inch howitzers, four 5-inch siege guns, eight 3.6-inch mortars, one Hotchkiss and four Gatling machine guns, and one dynamite gun.[5] This, the largest military expedition ever to have left the shores of the United States, set sail under naval escort on 14 June and arrived off Santiago four days later. Together, Shafter and Admiral Sampson went ashore to confer with the local rebel commander, General Calixto García, who confirmed that the Spaniards had constructed a number of blockhouses overlooking the intended landing place at Daiquirí, held by an estimated 300 men.[6]

On 22 June the warships subjected the Spanish forts to a twenty-minute bombardment. There was no response and it was later learned that the garrison had pulled out before dawn. Disembarkation commenced, using ships' boats and pontoons while the horses and mules swam ashore. Shafter and Sampson, having been unable to agree on a coordinated plan of campaign, now began to fight what amounted to separate wars. Only one road, grandly described as a 'camino real' despite being little more than a country cart track, led from Daiquirí to Santiago, following a route westwards for seven miles to the little port of Siboney and then turning inland to pass through close, rolling country. On the morning of 23 June Shafter, having learned that Siboney had also been evacuated, despatched Lawton's 2nd Division along the road with orders to defend the port until disembarkation had been completed. Hard on Lawton's heels came the dismounted Cavalry Division, the commander of which, 'Fighting Joe' Wheeler, had been informed by the Cubans that a Spanish force, 2,000 strong with two guns, was digging in across the road in the hilly country some two or three miles further on. Wheeler had no intention of being bound by the orders given to Lawton and, as Shafter had not yet left his headquarters ship, he took full advantage of his own position as being the senior officer ashore. During the night he passed Brigadier S. B. M. Young's 2nd Cavalry Brigade through Lawton's lines and ordered the rest of the division to hurry forward. The Cubans informed him that a trail ran through the bush parallel to the road, which it rejoined at Las Guásimas, where the Spaniards were now lying in wait. The Rough Riders were despatched down the trail while Young with the 1st and 10th Cavalry continued to advance along the road. At about 07:30 both columns spotted some stone breastworks on a dominant hill approximately 700 yards distant. Wheeler probed the position with Hotchkiss fire, which was immediately answered from the breastwork itself and from the tall grass, bushes and trees covering the area.

The air seemed to be so full of the crack and zip of flying bullets that Wheeler remarked he had never experienced such concentrated musketry during the entire Civil War. The Spaniards, in fact, were equipped with clip-loading 7mm Mauser magazine rifles which enabled them to maintain a much higher rate of fire than the Americans. Furthermore, they were using smokeless ammunition, making their positions difficult to spot. More often than not, the only visible indication of their presence was a briefly glimpsed straw hat or two. Casualties began to mount steadily. Colonel Leonard Wood, commanding the Rough Riders, conferred with Roosevelt, his second-in-command, and the two agreed that the only solution was to attack. Yelling as though Shafter's entire corps was behind them, the Rough Riders surged forward through the dense underbrush, firing as they went. It was the purest bluff, but it worked. The Spaniards suddenly broke and ran. On the opposite flank Young's two regiments also went over to the attack, joining the Rough Riders in chasing the enemy beyond their breastworks. Wheeler, suddenly transported back to the scenes of his youth, gave vent to a delighted yell:

'We've got the damn Yankees on the run!'

He had been sufficiently concerned about the outcome to swallow his pride and request assistance from Lawton, but before this could arrive the Spaniards had broken and, simultaneously, the 9th Cavalry from Brigadier-General S. S. Sumner's 1st Cavalry Brigade had arrived at the double.[7]

The action at Las Guásimas cost the Americans sixteen killed and 52 wounded, while Spanish casualties amounted to ten killed and 25 wounded. The skirmish raised American morale, but it was also a pointer of things to come and Shafter had little reason to feel over-confident. He was not inclined to place much reliance on his allies the Cuban rebels when it came to serious fighting since, notwithstanding their promises, they had been notable for their absence during the skirmish. Furthermore, of the 200,000 Spanish troops known to be in Cuba, some 35,000 were present in Santiago de Cuba Province, outnumbering him by two to one, and Santiago city itself was held by a 13,000-strong garrison. Luckily for him the local commander, Lieutenant-General Arsenio Linares, was not in the same league as Weyler. Linares could have made V Corps' march from Daiquirí to Santiago very difficult indeed, but he did not. He could have concentrated most of his troops east of the city and met the Americans in a pitched battle as they arrived, a possibility which would have offered a reasonable chance of success, but he chose not to do so. Instead, he opted for an entirely defensive stance, keeping a large number of his troops west of Santiago to face a wildly overestimated threat from the Cuban rebels, and prepared defensive positions to the east of the city on San Juan Ridge and at the village of El Caney, allocating a mere 1,700 men to hold them.

Even though its advance from Daiquirí and Siboney was now unopposed, V Corps soon found itself in difficulty. The camino real, never having been intended to carry so much concentrated traffic, was quickly trampled into a such a mud-wallow that, for the moment, it was decided to

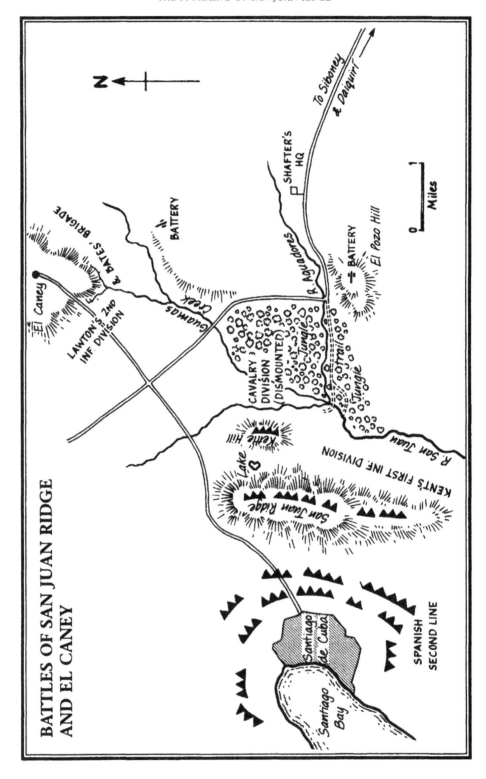

BATTLES OF SAN JUAN RIDGE AND EL CANEY

N

To Siboney & Daiquiri

SHAFTER'S HQ

Miles

El Pozo Hill

BATTERY

BATTERY

A. BATES' BRIGADE

El Caney

LAWTON'S 2ND INF. DIVISION

Guamas Creek

R. Aguadores

Jungle

CAVALRY DIVISION (DISMOUNTED)

O Trail

Jungle

R. San Juan

Kettle Hill

KENT'S FIRST INF DIVISION

Lake

San Juan Ridge

Santiago de Cuba

Santiago Bay

SPANISH SECOND LINE

bring forward only the field batteries and lighter supporting weapons and leave most of the heavy guns behind. The wagon trains bogged down regularly, requiring assistance from the heavily laden riflemen to extract them from the mire. With the temperature well above 90°F the troops, sweating into their thick uniforms as they marched or heaved guns and vehicles out of the mud, began to suffer from heat exhaustion. Packs and blanket rolls were shed regularly, to be plundered eagerly by the Cuban rebels. At length, by 30 June, Shafter's corps had reached a position from which it could strike against Santiago.

Shafter carried out a personal reconnaissance of the terrain the same day, climbing a hill named El Pozo which gave him a view across the valley of the little San Juan river, the heights beyond and, some three miles distant, of Santiago itself, with Admiral Cervera's warships lying in the harbour. On San Juan Ridge the Spaniards could be seen working on their blockhouses and trenches or stringing wire in front of them. Similar activity was taking place on a detached feature fronting the northern end of the main ridge, named Kettle Hill because of a large sugar-refining plant on the summit. In the foreground, between El Pozo Hill and the stream was a wide belt of dense jungle that his troops would have to negotiate along a single track before they could deploy for an attack on the ridge. Such an attack, however, would be taken in flank from the fortified village of El Caney to the north, and this would have to be neutralised first. After San Juan Ridge had been taken, Shafter intended isolating Santiago and cutting the city's water supply. A degree of urgency existed, in that he had been informed that Linares was expecting a column of reinforcements, several thousand strong.

Shafter assembled his orders group during the afternoon. At first light next morning El Caney was to be neutralised by Lawton's 2nd Infantry Division with one field battery in support. Two hours had been allowed for the operation, during which the Cavalry Division on the right and Kent's 1st Infantry Division on the left would debouch from the jungle track and remain along the edge of the tree line. Once El Caney had fallen, they would assault San Juan Ridge, covered by the second field battery, which had been hauled to the top of El Pozo Hill, and Lawton would re-deploy to add his weight to the attack. Curiously, Shafter did not ask Sampson to support the attack with naval gunfire; nor did Linares ask Cervera for defensive fire from his cruisers to assist in holding the position. Had either commander done so, the result would almost certainly have been decisive.

By now, tropical diseases had begun to make their first effects felt among the Americans. The following morning, 1 July, found Shafter confined to his bed, suffering from an attack of gout and the onset of malaria, although he was kept informed of developments by runner. Wheeler, too, was down with fever, as was Young, so that the Cavalry Division was commanded by Brigadier-General Sumner. Because of this, Colonel Wood assumed command of the 2nd Cavalry Brigade and Roosevelt took over the Rough Riders. With both the corps commander and his second-in-command *hors de combat*, the Americans were thus going into action effectively leaderless. The same could be said of the Spaniards, since Linares made no attempt to manoeuvre, reinforce or counter-attack during the day. In overall terms, therefore, the battle can be said to have fought itself.

Good leadership, however, was to be found in unexpected places. The 500 Spaniards holding El Caney were led by Major-General Vara del Rey, who had turned the village into a miniature fortress. It contained one major and four smaller blockhouses, a stone church and houses loopholed for defence, and a wired trench system. Lawton's division had opened its attack promptly at 07:00 when the supporting battery of 3.2-inch guns opened fire. After searching the trenches for a while they switched their fire to the blockhouses and the church, against which their light shells caused largely superficial damage. Lawton may well have overestimated the results of the bombardment, and he certainly underestimated the effects of the enemy's rapid Mauser fire, for whenever his regiments rose to rush the works they quickly sustained such heavy casualties that they were forced to seek cover. Lying prone in the long guinea grass, they returned the fire as best they could, but even this proved to be the undoing of the 2nd Massachusetts Volunteer Infantry. Every time one of its Springfield rifles was discharged the black powder left a cloud of smoke hanging over the firer's position, giving a clear aiming point to the Spanish sharpshooters. So rapidly did the regiment's casualties mount that it had to be pulled out of the line. As hour followed hour it became clear that instead of Lawton adding his weight to the main attack, he would himself require reinforcements. Having been informed of the situation, Shafter sent up his only reserve, Bates' Independent Infantry Brigade. The unbelievably stubborn defenders of El Caney, just 500 strong, were now holding off ten American infantry regiments, a total of approximately 6,000 men, plus 1,500 Cuban rebels who were firing into the village from a distant hill to the north. The dynamite gun, which Shafter had also sent up to boost the artillery support, fired only one round, springing its breech in the process, and was out of action for the rest of the day.

The battle was going equally badly for the Americans elsewhere. At 08:00 the battery on El Pozo Hill began shelling the trenches and blockhouses on San Juan Ridge, watched by an interested crowd of foreign military observers and officers who should have been with their regiments. The lack of immediate response caused the Swedish observer to enquire whether the

Spaniards had any field artillery at all. They had. It consisted of cleverly concealed, modern 77mm Krupp guns using smokeless propellant. The position of the American battery was clearly marked by a cloud of powder smoke and the Spanish gunners knew the range to a yard. Almost immediately, a complete salvo of shells burst over the guns, killing or wounding several men and dispersing the spectators. 'It was amusing to note how soon these "rubber necks" lost their curiosity', recorded Captain Brown drily in his diary, 'and how quickly they seemed to remember that their proper places were with their troops, which they then rejoined with commendable alacrity.' The fact, however, was that the American battery was practically silenced and because of this the assault on San Juan Ridge would have to be made without artillery support.

Worse was to follow. The Cavalry and 1st Infantry Divisions were now winding their way forward along the trail through the belt of jungle beneath El Pozo Hill. The Spaniards, gunners and riflemen alike, knew that they would have to use this and were suitably prepared. Shafter, however, made it much easier for them by insisting that an observation balloon was sent up from a point on the trail itself. Shells exploded among the trees and volleys of Mauser bullets clipped a steady shower of twigs and leaves from overhead. To the files trudging forward along the trail it was unnerving that men should be killed or wounded by an enemy who remained as yet unseen. The Cavalry Division passed through, forded the San Juan, turned right and took cover in the long grass at the foot of Kettle Hill. Kent's brigades came next, turning left after they had splashed through the stream, and shook out into skirmish lines. Both formations immediately drew heavy aimed fire which kept them pinned down.

At this point the observer in the balloon noticed a secondary trail through the jungle, apparently emerging near the southern end of the Spanish position. The 71st New York Volunteer Infantry, a very inexperienced unit one third of whose men had not handled a firearm until the previous month, was directed along it. As the leading battalion emerged from the tree line it attracted a storm of Mauser fire and bursting shrapnel that cut down the leading ranks. Panic-stricken, the regiment would have bolted had not Kent and his staff blocked the trail and ordered the men to lie down where they were. At about the same time the observation balloon, repeatedly punctured by bullets and shrapnel, slowly collapsed into the trees amid cheers from both armies.

Long before noon was reached and passed Shafter had become seriously alarmed. A battle which he had estimated would take two or three hours to win was still raging. From the reports he received it seemed that resistance at El Caney was as tough as ever, that his troops were pinned down everywhere and had already incurred 1,000 casualties. With nothing more to commit to the fight, defeat stared him in the face.

In the firing line, few of the regimental officers had been thoroughly briefed on the plan of battle. They had simply advanced until they were in contact with the enemy and no further orders had been received. In Kent's 1st Infantry Division Colonel C. A. Wikoff, commanding the 3rd Brigade, was shot dead and two regimental commanders were critically wounded. It was madness to hold the troops in their untenable position, yet to retire would be to invite a disastrous defeat. The remaining alternative was to advance up the 600 yards of open, bullet-swept slope to the enemy trenches, and that seemed to offer only certain death.

Fortunately, the hour produced the men. The thoughts of Lieutenant-Colonel Theodore Roosevelt, riding his horse Little Texas along the Rough Riders' firing line below Kettle Hill, were inclining towards the same sort of decisive action that had won the skirmish at Las Guásimas, notwithstanding orders that he was merely to support the attack of the Cavalry Division's 1st Brigade, consisting of the 3rd, 6th and 9th Cavalry, on Kettle Hill. Making up his mind, he told his trumpeter to sound the Charge. The men scrambled to their feet, heading steadily upwards as fast as the slope and the heat of the day permitted, passing through the 9th Cavalry in 1st Brigade's line. The attack was taken up by the 9th, then by the 6th and 3rd, and finally by the 1st and 10th until the whole division was moving steadily upwards, with individuals pausing to fire from time to time. Among the participants was a young officer of the 10th Cavalry named John J. Pershing who was to command the American Expeditionary Force in France during the First World War. Roosevelt, encountering a line of barbed wire, turned his horse loose, noting that it had been grazed twice by bullets. His elbow was nicked and at one stage his spectacles were shot off – to his fury, the latter shot came from behind, but he quickly donned a spare pair and continued. He certainly made an indelible impression on one of his tough Westerners.

'It's a sight to see him in a fight. You'd think his hide was double-chilled steel and three thicknesses, and that he known it watching him running around waving his gun to bring the boys up and taking a crack at the Spaniards now and then, just to show us how. I don't never trust no man with gold-rimmed glasses and a beaming smile no more. When I seen him at San Antonio, I figured he was raised a pet and wouldn't kick if you tickled his heels with a toothpick. I wouldn't undertake to harness him with a pitchfork.'

The Spaniards inflicted some loss but nothing like enough to stop the momentum of the attack. Most simply fled and by 13:00 the feature was firmly in the Cavalry Division's hands.

Dramatic as its capture had been, Kettle Hill was simply an outwork of the main Spanish position. Over in Kent's division Lieutenant Jules Ord, a young officer on the staff of Brigadier-General H. S. Hawkins' 1st Brigade, had asked for permission to lead an attack at about the same time. Hawkins declined either to grant or refuse formal permission, but wished him luck. Stripped to the waist, a pistol in one hand and a bayonet in the other, Ord set off up the slope, shouting at the men around him, 'Follow me! We can't stay here!' A few individuals from the 16th Infantry responded, then small groups. The Spanish fire suddenly intensified but the attackers, sustaining remarkably little loss, kept moving upwards, some aiming carefully before they fired, some hip-shooting from full magazines, others hacking their way through the strung wire with machetes. 'Very gallant, but very foolish,' murmured some among the foreign observers. 'They can't take it, you know. Never in the world. It's slaughter, absolute slaughter.'

How this forlorn hope might have ended remains a matter for speculation, for at this juncture the entire nature of the battle was changed by another junior officer. Lieutenant John Parker was a rare machine gun enthusiast at a time when the small Regular Army had little use for such weapons other than against hostile Indians on the Frontier, and he had had to lobby hard for the privilege of being allowed to accompany V Corps with a four-gun Gatling detachment. Normally, his little unit would have been regarded as corps troops, but once in Cuba it seemed to be nobody's baby, having to arrange for its own disembarkation and everything else besides. It does not seem have had a place in Shafter's plans, and if Shafter sent it forward to support the attack on San Juan Ridge the fact is not recorded in otherwise reliable published accounts of the battle. The probability is that Parker had followed his instinct, hurrying the detachment towards the sound of the guns. He had taken the secondary track through the belt of jungle, where his men had been forced to manhandle the high-wheeled carriages past the prostrate 71st New York, and emerged from the trees just as the Spaniards' attention was diverted by Ord's attack. It was the work of a moment to swing the guns round and sight them on the enemy positions lining the crest, and then the Gatlings were grinding out up to 3,600 rounds per minute, kicking up spurts of dust everywhere along the breastworks. For some of the Spaniards this was too much and they fled beyond the brow of the ridge.

For the sorely tried American riflemen, the intervention of the Gatlings provided tremendous psychological relief in that, at last, the enemy was receiving the same sort of punishment he had been handing out for several hours. Sensing that the moment had come, Hawkins took off his hat and waved the 6th, the 24th and the rest of the 16th Infantry forward to support Ord's little group.

'You felt that someone had blundered and that those few men were blindly following some madman's mad order,' wrote Richard Harding Davis later that year.[8] 'It was not heroic then; it seemed merely terribly pathetic. The pity of it, the folly of such sacrifice, was what held you. They had no glittering bayonets, they were not massed together in regular array. There were a few men in advance, bunched together, and creeping up a steep, sunny hill, the tops of which roared and flashed with flame. The men held their guns pressed across their breasts and stepped heavily as they climbed. Behind these first few, spreading out like a fan, were single lines of men, slipping and scrambling in the smooth grass, moving forward with difficulty as if they were wading waist high through water, carefully, with strenuous effort. It was much more wonderful than any swinging charge could have been. They walked to greet death at every step, many of them, as they advanced, sinking suddenly or pitching forward and disappearing in the high grass, but the others waded on stubbornly, forming a thin blue line that kept creeping higher and higher up the hill. It was a miracle of self-sacrifice, a triumph of bull-dog courage, which one watched breathless with wonder. The fire of the Spanish riflemen, who still stuck bravely to their posts, doubled and trebled in fierceness, the crests of the hills crackled and burst in amazed roars and rippled with waves of tiny flame. But the blue line crept steadily up and on, and then, near the top, the broken fragments gathered together with a sudden burst of speed. The Spaniards appeared for a moment outlined against the sky and poised for instant flight, fired a last volley and fled before the swift moving wave that leaped and sprang up after them.'

The Rough Riders had watched the progress of the infantry assault and now they charged down the reverse slope of Kettle Hill and up the slopes beyond, clearing the enemy from the northern end of the ridge. In the process Roosevelt shot and killed one of two stragglers who had fired at him from ten yards' range, using a revolver salvaged from the sunken *Maine*. Curiously, American casualties during this phase of the action were less than might have been expected. By no means all the Spaniards were marksmen, but given the output of fire available to them they did not have to be. One probable explanation for their failure to stop the attack is that, having engaged static targets at a fixed range all day, in the excitement they simply forgot to lower their sights, the result being that most of their fire went high.

San Juan Ridge had been taken, but at El Caney the struggle continued until late afternoon. By then, half the garrison was down and its ammunition supply had begun to fail. Vara del Rey, who had inspired his men throughout the day despite being hit in both legs, was killed as he was being stretchered off the field. The end of the battle is described by an eye-witness:

'Always our infantry advanced, drawing near and closing up on the village till at last they formed under the mangrove trees at the foot of the hill on which the stone fort stood. With a rush they swept up the slope and the stone fort was ours. From the blockhouses and trenches from which the Spaniards could not safely retreat, flags of truce were waved. Guns and side arms were being taken away from such Spaniards as had outlived the pitiless fire, and their dead were being dumped without ceremony into the trenches after Spanish fashion.'

Only about 40 of the entire garrison managed to escape in the direction of Santiago. What surprised, and indeed shocked, many of the Americans, was the extreme youth of their opponents. 'Many of them,' remarked one, 'seemed like little boys with men's shoes on – rope-soled, canvas shoes.'

V Corps incurred a total of 1,572 killed and wounded during the capture of San Juan Ridge and El Caney, approximately ten per cent of its strength. The Spanish losses were estimated at only 850, but for the few units involved this represented between 30 and 50 per cent of their men and this had a serious effect on morale. Linares, having been hit in the arm during the defence of the ridge, handed over command to Major General José Toral, who withdrew to an intermediate line of prepared defences between the ridge and Santiago itself.

Shafter believed that there had been 12,000 Spanish troops in the line at San Juan Ridge and El Caney. Already concerned by his own losses, he became seriously alarmed when Wheeler predicted that a minimum of 3,000 casualties would be incurred in storming the Spaniards' second line. However, when he suggested abandoning the ridge and retiring to a defensive position near Siboney the idea was voted down by his divisional commanders and vetoed by Washington. He therefore began to prepare for a siege, bringing forward his heavy guns, and awaited reinforcements.

For their part, the Spanish authorities were equally depressed. The entire point of defending Santiago was that it offered a haven for the fleet. Following the loss of San Juan Ridge it seemed probable that the city itself would fall, which would mean the simultaneous loss of Cervera's warships. On the morning of 2 July Cervera received a direct order from the Captain General of Cuba, Ramón Blanco y Erenas, to take the fleet to sea. Cervera knew that the result would be nothing more than a death ride for the honour of Spain and the service, but the following morning he complied, hoping that some of his ships would succeed in breaking through the blockade and reaching the safe anchorage of Cienfuegos, over 500 miles to the west. The Battle of Santiago Bay was little better than a massacre. Hopelessly out-gunned by Sampson's battleships, the Spanish cruisers were, one by one, set ablaze, wrecked and driven ashore with loss of 474 seamen killed and 1,750 captured. The Americans sustained some superficial damage, one man killed and one wounded.

The very public loss of their fleet caused the Spaniards' morale to plummet even further. In the eyes of many, since the reason for holding Santiago had disappeared, the army should withdraw. Such an operation, however, would be difficult because many of the troops were sick and the Cuban rebels would eagerly seize every opportunity to fall on the column. Had Toral but known it, Shafter's troops were in an even worse case, ravaged by yellow fever, malaria and dysentery to the extent that a third of them were incapacitated at any one time. Nevertheless, the arrival of heavier guns and reinforcements within the American lines suggested to Toral that V Corps was growing stronger by the day and on 17 July he surrendered uncondi-tionally. This brought hostilities to an end on the Cuban mainland, although a 5,000-strong expeditionary force under Major-General Nelson A. Miles eliminated the Spanish military presence on the island of Puerto Rico the following month.

The storming of San Juan Ridge had been the decisive event of the war since it compelled Cervera's ships to put to sea. With its fleet gone, the Madrid government, unable to supply, reinforce or communicate with its troops in Cuba, bowed to the inevitable and opened peace negotiations. Under the terms of the Treaty of Paris, concluded in December, Spain relin-quished her sovereignty over Cuba and ceded the islands of Puerto Rico and Guam to the United States, which also purchased the Philippine Islands for $20 million. It had, recalled the American Ambassador to the Court of St James, been a 'splendid little war.' Approximately 250 Americans had lost their lives as a result of enemy action, but ten times that number died because of disease; of the latter, many, the victims of badly administered camps, never even left the United States.

Shafter's battles had been won for him by the grit and raw courage of his troops, the initiative of junior commanders and the serious errors made by his opponent. Roosevelt, with his powerful connections in political and press circles, effectively destroyed his reputation. 'Not since the campaign of Crassus against the Parthians has there been so criminally incompetent a general as Shafter,' he wrote to his friend Senator Henry Cabot Lodge a day or two after the capture of San Juan Ridge, 'and not since the expedi-tion against Walcheren has there been a grosser mismanagement than this.' Roosevelt's own actions had made him the hero of the hour and he ended the war as a brigadier-general; within a year he had become Governor of New York, and two years after that he became President of the United States.

Also contained within Roosevelt's correspondence with Senator Lodge were two prescient sentences. 'We have won so far at a heavy cost; but the Spaniards fight very hard and charging these entrenchments against modern rifles is terrible. We are within measurable distance of a terrible military disaster.' The lessons of Cuba were emphasised during the Second Boer War and the Russo-Japanese War, but were ignored because in every case it was the attackers, American, British and Japanese, who had won, albeit at the heavier cost. As the powers of defence continued to increase it became clear that soon they would dominate those of the attackers, no matter how much courage the latter displayed. By the autumn of 1914 all the combatant armies of Europe had been torn apart by the very disaster which Roosevelt had predicted.

Notes

1. It is now generally accepted that the effects of the single torpedo fired at the liner *Lusitania* were greatly magnified by an explosion in a nearby coal bunker.
2. The *Kearsage* , it will be recalled, sank the Confederate raider *Alabama* off Cherbourg in 1864. Twenty-two years later the criticisms levelled at Sigsbee included failure to comply with ordnance regulations and keeping a dirty ship; the *Texas* was also found to be dirty and rusted with improperly outfitted boats.
3. Kitchener employed similar methods to bring the guerrilla phase of the Second Boer War to an end.
4. For many years after the Civil War former regular officers who had fought for the South were not allowed to serve in the United States Army, despite the issue of a general pardon in 1868. This clearly denied the Army the services of men with real ability and in due course the ban was rescinded. Wheeler was one of comparatively few such men to achieve high rank.
5. Although dynamite was the most powerful explosive of its days, dynamite-filled shells could not be fired from conventional guns because the shock of discharge would cause them to explode in the barrel. A Lieutenant Zalinski of the US Coast Artillery Corps developed a system using compressed air as the propelling agency and a number of Zalinski Dynamite Guns were installed in coastal defences. That used by V Corps in Cuba was a much smaller version employing a field carriage. The development of more stable yet equally powerful explosives quickly rendered the concept obsolete.
6. As Daiquirí was an open roadstead, Sampson was using Guantánamo Bay, 40 miles to the east, to coal his ships. His marines had already secured the environs of the bay but the difficult country between it and Daiquirí inhibited its use as a base.
7. The 9th and 10th Cavalry and the 24th and 25th Infantry were formed after the Civil War and consisted of negro soldiers with white officers. All earned an outstanding reputation on the Frontier.
8. *The Cuban and Porto Rican Campaigns*, Charles Scribner's Sons, New York, 1898

CHAPTER SEVEN

Mounted Action –
The Charges at Beersheba and Huj,
Palestine, 1917

The year was 1898 and the place Jerusalem. A young Arab and his grandfather were sitting in a coffee shop, discussing the events of the day, which included the formal entry into the city of Kaiser Wilhelm II of Germany and his glittering retinue, accompanied by the Turkish governor and the province's most important men.

'Is he the One, do you think?' asked the young man, referring to the ancient Arab prophesy that one day a leader would come from the West and deliver Palestine from the indolent, corrupt and frequently cruel rule of the Turk.

'No, he is not the One,' replied his grandfather.

'Why not? It is said that he wishes to be known to us as Hadji Mohammed Guilliamo – and has he not laid a gilded wreath upon the tomb of the great Saladin?'[1]

'Certainly he has made the Pilgrimage, but I do not understand why. His name is not Mohammed and he remains the Christian king of a Frankish country. Besides, part of the city walls had to be knocked down to admit his grand procession!'

'What has that to do with anything?'

'You forget the rest of the prophesy. The Deliverer, when he comes, will be named the Prophet of God, and, unlike this man, he will enter Jerusalem humbly and on foot. He will come, it is said, when the waters of the Nile flow into Palestine.'

'How can such things be?' replied the young man, angrily. 'That is impossible and makes nonsense of the whole prophesy!'

'If it is written it will come to pass – Inshallah! Perhaps not in my lifetime, but maybe in yours.'

If the young man was still living just nineteen years later he would have seen every detail of this uncannily accurate prophesy fulfilled.

The Kaiser's curious stance as Champion of Islam was just one element in an ultimately successful long-term diplomatic strategy that severed the ramshackle Ottoman Empire's traditional links with Great Britain and brought it within the German sphere of influence. By 1914 the process was complete and Turkey entered the Great War on the side of Germany and Austria-Hungary.

For the British, this posed a number of very serious problems. They were worried by the potential threat posed to India and their own Imperial life-line, the Suez Canal; by the possibility of disaffection among the British Empire's millions of Muslim subjects; by their inability to supply adequate military and economic assistance to the huge but under-equipped Russian armies following the closure of the only viable sea-route through the Dardanelles and the Black Sea; and, above all, by the fact that so much of the fuel oil upon which the Royal Navy increasingly relied was produced within the Turkish provinces of Mesopotamia and Arabia and the vulner-able Persian Gulf. Obviously, substantial British naval and military resources would be tied down in the Middle East, which was exactly what Germany intended.

For the first two years of the war the fortunes of the Ottoman Empire varied. An attack on the Suez Canal was repulsed and a Turkish-inspired invasion of western Egypt by the Senussi religious sect was defeated after some surprisingly hard fighting. Against this, the Royal Navy failed to force a passage of the Dardanelles and Allied landings on the Gallipoli peninsula not only proved abortive but resulted in a humiliating evacua-tion. In Arabia the Arab Revolt – in which Colonel T. E. Lawrence was later to play such a distinguished role – seriously damaged the Sultan's prestige throughout the Islamic world by capturing the holy city of Mecca, of which he was the Guardian. In Mesopotamia, however, early British advances overreached themselves and resulted in a force commanded by Major-General Townshend being needlessly surrounded and forced to sur-render at Kut-al-Amara. After this, however, Turkish lethargy reasserted itself and the British, rallied and reorganised under the command of Lieutenant-General Frederick Maude, returned to the offensive, capturing Baghdad on 11 March 1917.

It was, nevertheless, in Sinai and Palestine that the first conclusive signs appeared that, in the long term and even with generous German support, the Turkish Army was incapable of sustaining a modern war indefinitely and would ultimately be defeated. In 1916 the British and Commonwealth troops in Egypt, including many veterans of the ill-starred Gallipoli ven-ture, were formed into the Egyptian Expeditionary Force under the com-mand of Lieutenant-General Sir Archibald Murray, a former Chief of the Imperial General Staff. Murray initiated a methodical advance across Sinai, backed by a logistic infrastructure that involved thousands of local labour-ers constructing a standard-gauge railway starting at El Kantara on the Canal and moving steadily eastwards at the rate of 50 miles per month.[2]

Beyond the railhead an efficient Camel Transport Corps distributed supplies to the forward troops. In parallel, a freshwater pipeline was laid, complete with pumping stations, storage tanks, a portable reservoir holding half a million gallons and batteries of standpipes; by these means the waters of the Nile eventually entered Palestine in partial fulfilment of the ancient prophesy. In sharp contrast, the Turkish troops holding southern Palestine were at the extremities of a rickety single-track narrow-gauge railway system for the operation of which so little locomotive coal was available that felling of the sparse local timber was required. The system's limited capacity in itself therefore restricted the number of troops the Turks were able to deploy and, if put under sustained pressure, it would simply be unable to cope with the voracious demands of a modern field army.

Murray's advance across Sinai was made with his infantry divisions close to the coast and railhead and his cavalry and camel troops covering the open desert flank to the south. The cavalry was commanded by Major-General Harry Chauvel, an Australian regular officer who had served in South Africa and who, in August 1914, had been on his way to London to serve as his country's representative on the Imperial General Staff when he was diverted to the Middle East. He had commanded a brigade and later a division at Gallipoli and in due course he would emerge from the war with a reputation as the greatest horsed cavalry leader of the modern era. Curiously, he was as different from the usual idea of the 'beau sabreur' cavalry leader as it is possible to imagine, being short, wiry and quietly spoken. On the other hand, he was well versed in military history, completely familiar with every rôle mounted troops had to play, a hard-working, meticulous planner, cool in action, on good terms with his troops, careful of their lives and those of their mounts, and entirely dependable.

Most of his regiments were either Australian Light Horse or New Zealand Mounted Rifles, trained to fight a fast-moving mounted infantry battle with rifle and bayonet. The majority had lived healthy outdoor lives and they were physically more impressive than the average British infantry recruit, who had often grown up in the deprived conditions of an industrial landscape. Natural hard riders and good shots, they were mounted on big, sturdy horses known as walers, specially bred for stamina and strength in their own hot climate. Many of the men were veterans of Gallipoli or the Boer War. Their discipline, while effective, was informal. Save on the most ceremonial of parades, troop leaders and their soldiers tended to use each others' Christian names; for a junior officer to a address a man by his unadorned surname was regarded as insulting, although it was quite in order for him to prefix this with his rank if he was dressing him down. One characteristic common to both Australians and New Zealanders was a

142

tremendous sense of comradeship. In action, they would take enormous risks to maintain an unwritten law that no man, wounded or not, should be allowed to fall alive into Turkish hands. Off duty, too, their comrades came first. When, on Good Friday 1915, one of their number was rolled in the Haret el Wasser, Cairo's red light district, whole units turned out to take revenge, leaving the area all but laid waste. Their free and easy attitude could outrage British regular officers, mainly those on the Staff, but at the highest levels their worth was recognised and it was regarded as a privilege to have them under command.[3]

Also present were British yeomanry regiments, recruited on a county basis from men who, in general, also lived an outdoor life and took part in the field sports of hunting and shooting. Although armed with the sword and trained for shock action, they were more flexible in their outlook than their regular cavalry counterparts and could also perform the mounted infantry role. Indeed, in the immediate prewar years some yeomanry regiments had experimented with the concept of mechanised firepower by mounting machine guns on members' touring cars, and one at least of the richer regiments had privately acquired a purpose-built armoured car or two. All contained a number of officers and men who had seen active service during the Boer War and some regiments had already seen mounted action against the Senussi in the Western Desert.

Chauvel's cavalry divisions each consisted of three mounted brigades each containing three regiments, a mounted machine gun squadron with twelve guns, and a Territorial Royal Horse Artillery battery of three troops each equipped with four 13-pounder guns. For specific missions a light car patrol, equipped with Model T Fords mounting a Lewis light machine gun, or a light armoured motor battery (LAMB) with Rolls Royce armoured cars, might be attached.

Another formation which operated under Chauvel's command was the Camel Corps. This had a strength of 60 officers and 1,600 other ranks and was recruited mainly but by no means exclusively from the Australian Light Horse. It consisted of ten rifle companies, each of which possessed five Lewis guns, a machine gun company with eight Vickers-Maxims, and an artillery battery with six 9-pounder pack howitzers. The Camel Corps had already seen action in the Western Desert and during the advance across Sinai, its pace being slower than that of the cavalry divisions on the desert flank, it usually filled the gap between them and the marching infantry on the coast.

By the spring of 1917 Murray had cleared the Turks from Sinai, having inflicted a sharp defeat on them at Romani the previous August, taken El Arish in December and eliminated the garrison of Magruntein, their sole remaining post on Egyptian soil, in January. At this period he was the only British commander who was sending home a continuous flow of satisfactory news and there was no apparent reason why this should not continue.

The first objective of Murray's invasion of Palestine was the town of Gaza. Ostensibly, this did not present a serious obstacle since it was held by a mere 3,500 men with twenty guns and the garrison, relying on the huge and almost impenetrable cactus hedges separating the fig and olive orchards surrounding the town, had done little to fortify it. The attack, involving a frontal assault by two infantry divisions while the ANZAC Mounted Division came in from the east to secure the dominant Ali el Muntar ridge, was delivered on 26 March. The Turks, as always stubborn in defence and eager to close with the bayonet in counter-attacks, fought hard but by 18:00 their German commander, Major Tiller, having no more reserves to commit to his shrinking perimeter, despatched a radio message to his immediate superior, General Kress von Kressenstein, informing him that the situation had become desperate and that if his position came under further pressure he would be obliged to negotiate a surrender.

At that precise moment the dumbfounded British, Australians and New Zealanders were being forced to comply with specific orders to abandon all the gains they had made throughout the day and withdraw. The orders originated in the joint headquarters established by Lieutenant-Generals Sir Charles Dobell and Sir Philip Chetwode, responsible for coordinating the attack, at Ein Seiret, some fifteen miles behind the lines. There, without any knowledge of what was taking place in the town, they decided that if it had not fallen by sunset the troops should disengage rather than risk being caught between the garrison and the reinforcements that Kressenstein was known to be rushing forward. There were, too, quite groundless fears that there was insufficient water present for the ANZAC Mounted Division's horses. Needless to say, the Turks, now substantially reinforced and jubilant at having apparently beaten off the British assault, counter-attacked the following day, recovering still more ground.

The blame was not Murray's, but the responsibility was his. Understandably reluctant to report a failure after his long run of success, he compounded his difficulties by reporting that the operation 'just fell short of a complete disaster to the enemy.' Such a half-truth could not conceal forever the fact that he had been repulsed, nor that his 5,000 casualties were almost double those of the Turks. The War Cabinet, however, was prepared to back him and, having received further reports that the Turks were constructing defences in depth at Gaza, digging redoubts along the Beersheba road and fortifying Beersheba itself, hastily sent out a small detachment of obsolete tanks in the hope that these would prevent the new line lapsing into the stalemate of positional warfare.

Now that his ability to manoeuvre had been restricted, Murray could only plan a renewed assault on Gaza, using three infantry divisions. When the tanks arrived, each of the divisional commanders demanded them and Dobell, the corps commander, parcelled them out in twos and threes, ignoring the advice of the detachment's commanding officer, who emphasised in vain the Tank Corps' doctrine that the best result would be obtained if the tanks fought together.

The Second Battle of Gaza began on 17 April, lasted for three days and ended in an even bloodier reverse than the previous month's. British losses amounted to a total of 6,624 killed, wounded or missing and half the tanks destroyed or abandoned; Turkish casualties came to 402 killed, 1,364 wounded and 245 missing. Murray dismissed Dobell but was himself relieved on 11 June.

His replacement was General Sir Edmund Allenby, a former Inspector General of Cavalry who had commanded the Cavalry Corps at the First Battle of Ypres and, more recently, the Third Army during the Battle of Arras. Big and bluff, he would bellow with rage when annoyed and was referred to as The Bull. He recognised from the outset that, the recent problems with some officers in the intermediate level of command apart, he had inherited an efficient army and logistic system from Murray. He was, however, concerned by the effects that the two reverses at Gaza were having on morale and one of his first acts was to move his General Headquarters from Cairo, where staff officers worked under slowly turning fans with cool drinks within reach, to a more gritty, spartan location at Rafah, just behind the lines. Here he felt that he could exercise an efficient forward control and at the same time become a familiar figure to the troops. For the same reasons he would personally visit even the most junior formation before an operation and brief its officers on exactly what was required of them.

Allenby's relationship with his political masters was interesting. At this period the War Cabinet was sharply divided into Westerners and Easterners. The former applied the conventional military logic that victory could only be achieved by defeating the main mass of the enemy, and since that meant the German armies holding the Western Front that was where the Allies must concentrate their own efforts. The Easterners, on the other hand, took a more indirect view. They believed that if Turkey, the weakest member of the Central Powers' alliance, could be knocked out of the war, the others would fall in succession – first Bulgaria, then Austria-Hungary and finally Germany herself. Lloyd George, the Prime Minister, was an avowed Easterner and when Allenby had been appointed to his new command he had told him that he wanted Jerusalem as a Christmas present for the British nation. To that end he had provided reinforcements from the Aden garrison and the static Salonika front, as well as more modern vehicles for the Gaza Tank Detachment. Allenby therefore now possessed an army containing three corps – XX Corps with four infantry divisions, XXI Corps with three infantry divisions, and the newly-promoted Lieutenant-General Chauvel's Desert Mounted Corps, consisting of the Australian Mounted Division, the ANZAC Mounted Division, the Yeomanry Division and the Camel Corps.

Before the capture of Jerusalem could even be contemplated, however, it would be necessary to break the deadlock along the Gaza–Beersheba Line. Allenby, reluctant to launch further frontal attacks on the formidable Gaza defences, willingly accepted a suggestion put to him by Chetwode, now commanding XX Corps, that the line could be turned by the capture of Beersheba, after which it could be rolled up from the east. The entire plan hinged on water, firstly because the country to the south of the town was completely arid, and secondly because the wells in Beersheba itself would have to be captured before the Turks could destroy them if further operations on this flank were to be contemplated. In this context only Chauvel's Desert Mounted Corps possessed the speed and punch required to seize Beersheba by coup de main before the Turkish demolition teams could get to work. At best the scheme was a gamble, but in war the risk factor can rarely be eliminated and boldness often brings its own reward.

Much detailed preparation had to be done before the plan could be activated. It was calculated that during the approach march Chauvel's troopers and their mounts would consume 400,000 gallons a day, and that even then the latter would probably go thirsty. To satisfy this the Trans-Sinai railway and pipeline were extended in the direction of Beersheba. Despite this, Chauvel would be operating in virtually roadless country some twenty or more miles beyond the railhead and to keep him supplied all of the army's 30,000 baggage camels would be required during the operation itself, even if it meant temporarily stripping the infantry divisions closer to the coast of their animal transport.

It was also essential that Turkish attention should be diverted away from Beersheba by means of a deception plan that clearly indicated Gaza as being the British primary objective. Hints were dropped in quarters known to be sympathetic to the Turks that an amphibious landing was to be made north of the town, and in due course warships appeared, pointedly taking soundings off the coast. Patrol activity was intensified and apparent preparations for a renewed offensive on the Gaza sector were left improperly camouflaged and duly noted by the Turks. A notable success in the art of deception was obtained by Captain Richard Meinertzhagen of Allenby's intelligence staff. At considerable personal risk to himself, Meinertzhagen pretended to be engaged in a mounted reconnaissance into no-man's-land, knowing that he would become a target for snipers. Pretending to be hit, he dropped a satchel recently smeared with animal blood and returned to his own lines, giving all the appearance of having been seriously wounded. When the Turks retrieved the satchel they found it contained marked maps and other papers containing details of a projected attack on Gaza, which they accepted at face value.[4]

In its final form Allenby's plan for the coming offensive required Chauvel's Desert Mounted Corps, less the Yeomanry Division, to capture Beersheba before its wells could be destroyed, then exploit to the north; in the centre Chetwode's XX Corps, reinforced with the Yeomanry Division, would mount a series of holding attacks between Beersheba and Gaza, then advance in a north-westerly direction across the Turkish rear once Beersheba had fallen; and on the coast Major-General E. S. Bulfin's XXI Corps would mount a major diversionary attack on Gaza after a heavy preliminary bombardment by artillery and Allied warships. Allenby was anxious that his men should be at the peak of their fighting abilities and for this reason decided to defer the offensive until the last days of October, in the interval between the hot weather and the onset of the winter rains.

Across the lines, a number of developments had also taken place. The collapse of Imperial Russia in the spring had meant that the Turks were able to transfer troops from the now defunct Caucasus Front to the Middle East and had formed a reserve of two army corps based on Aleppo. The problem was that no agreement could be reached as to whether it could be used to best effect in southern Palestine or to recapture Baghdad. While the Turkish High Command squabbled among themselves and with their German advisers time ticked away. When, in September, General Erich von Falkenhayn, the former Chief of German General Staff now seconded to the Turkish Army, decided that Palestine held priority, it was too late to effect so major a redeployment before Allenby struck.

Nevertheless, the Palestine Front had benefited from the Russian collapse to some extent. The Gaza-Beersheba Line was now held by two armies, Kressenstein's Eighth with five divisions in the line and two in reserve covering the sector from Gaza to the Wadi el Sheria, and Fawzi Pasha's Seventh with two regiments holding the line from the Wadi eastwards towards Beersheba, in and around which two divisions had been concentrated. In strategic reserve was a further division, positioned some

25 miles north of Gaza. From this it can be seen that the Turkish centre of gravity was heavily inclined towards Gaza, just as Allenby had hoped. In total, the Turkish deployment included approximately 45,000 infantry, 1,500 cavalry and 300 guns. However, since the successes of the spring the Turks' morale had deteriorated, partly because of idleness and neglect, partly because of bad and insufficient rations, and partly because of raging epidemics which at any one time kept 25 per cent of their strength in hospital.

For his part, Allenby could deploy 75,000 infantry, 17,000 cavalry and 475 guns and a small tank detachment. This advantage was not, as has sometimes been suggested, sufficient in itself to guarantee a decisive victory. The infantry, for example, lacked the three-to-one superiority generally considered necessary for an assault on a prepared position. The preponderance of mounted troops would only become effective if the Beersheba wells could be captured intact; if they could not, the Desert Mounted Corps would find itself in some difficulty. Gun for gun, the British artillery's strength was not overwhelming, although on the coastal sector it would be supplemented by naval gunfire. The risk element, therefore, remained high.

The bombardment of Gaza began on 27 October, increasing in intensity day by day. In the meantime, the Desert Mounted Corps had been moving its units slowly but steadily eastwards so that when the time came only one night march would required to place it in position to assault Beersheba. At this period the enemy was gradually losing his air superiority, although those of his aircraft that did manage to penetrate British air space could hardly fail to notice the huge concentration of cavalry and baggage animals lying behind Allenby's right-centre, which also presented an extremely inviting target; three bombs dropped by one aircraft alone killed 40 camels and three horses and caused twenty personnel casualties. The Turkish cavalry, too, became inquisitive and displayed unusual aggression when, on 27 October, it attacked an outpost held by a detachment of the London Yeomanry. The yeomen beat off two dismounted assaults but were finally overrun by a mounted charge, only three of them surviving. The Turks were then driven off by the arrival of a larger force of British infantry. Nevertheless, despite all the indications, they remained convinced that British movements in the direction of Beersheba were simply a feint intended to draw their own reserves away from Gaza. Two days later they still believed that there were six British divisions massed in front of Gaza, but only two, including one mounted, opposite Beersheba.

Chauvel's regiments began moving east after dusk on 30 October. Those whose task was to isolate Beersheba from the east and north left first, having to cover some 30 miles before dawn. Three days' rations were carried and each trooper had two nose-bags of grain slung across his saddle, each containing a day's forage, a third day's being carried in the regimental wagons.

At 05:55 on 31 October XX Corps' artillery went into action west of Beersheba, bombarding a Turkish outpost on Hill 1070. By 08:30 this had fallen to an infantry assault and the guns were moving forward to bring the Turkish main line under fire. At 12:15 elements of the 60th and 74th Divisions launched successful attacks and by 13:30 were in possession of all their objectives, having captured three miles of trenches, taking 500 prisoners and six guns. The cost had been almost 1,200 casualties but by the standards of the Western Front the achievement was remarkable, the more so since artillery support in Palestine was approximately one gun for every 50 yards of front, one fifth of that available in France and Flanders.

The encirclement of the town to the east and north had already been completed by the ANZAC Mounted Division. The dominant features of the enemy's defences on the eastern sector were two mounds, Tel es Sakaty and Tel es Saba, rising steeply from the plain. The former fell to a dashing attack by the 2nd Light Horse Brigade (5th Queensland, 6th and 7th New South Wales Light Horse) who broke out of the wadi in which they were concealed and advanced at a gallop across the plain in open order. So unexpected was their appearance and so fast their pace that the Turkish artillery and machine guns inflicted comparatively few casualties. Riding into a hollow close to the Hebron road they dismounted, re-formed and advanced on foot towards the objective, now only 1,500 yards distant. Employing the techniques of fire and movement, they closed in on the tel by means of short rushes and by 13:00 had cleared the feature at the point of the bayonet and secured a number of neighbouring wells.

Tel es Saba, however, proved to be a much tougher nut to crack. The feature was 400 yards long, 200 yards deep and rose to a flat summit approximately 1,000 feet high, being protected on the side flanking the Wadi es Saba by almost vertical slopes. The more gradual approaches to the summit were covered by at least two tiers of trenches incorporating carefully concealed machine gun positions.

At 09:00, concurrently with the 2nd Light Horse Brigade's attack on Tel es Sakaty, the New Zealand Brigade (Auckland, Canterbury and Wellington Mounted Rifles), covered by the guns of the Somerset Battery RHA firing at 3,000 yards, was using winding wadi beds and dead ground to envelop Tel es Saba from the north and east. Its advance brought it to within 800 yards of the objective. At this point the sheer volume of rifle and machine gun fire compelled the men to dismount and, leaving their horses in good cover, they continued working their way forward on foot. Progress was slow, largely because, for a while, it proved impossible to locate the enemy machine guns and signal their whereabouts to the supporting artillery. By 11:00 the divisional commander, Major-General Sir Edward Chaytor, had

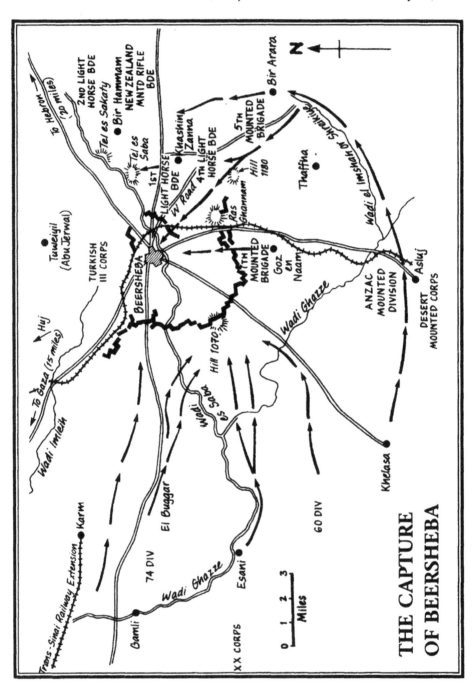

THE CAPTURE OF BEERSHEBA

become sufficiently concerned to commit first the 3rd (South Australia and Tasmania) Light Horse, followed by the 2nd (Queensland) Light Horse and the Inverness Battery RHA from his reserve brigade, in support of the New Zealanders. At about 13:30 Chauvel, worried by the delay, ordered Major-General Sir Henry Hodgson, commanding the Australian Mounted Division, to make his 3rd Light Horse Brigade available. In the event it was not used although its approach may well have contributed to the ultimate collapse of Turkish resolve. By now the converging attacks by the Australians and New Zealanders were beginning to eat into the defences. The location of the enemy's machine gun posts had also been spotted and they were being shelled by the two RHA batteries, which had closed the range to within 1,500 and 2,500 yards. At about 15:00 the summit was finally cleared in a series of rushes and the last of the Turkish defenders were fleeing in the direction of Beersheba.

There then took place one of the most incredible episodes in the entire history of mounted cavalry. Chauvel had watched the battle from the summit of a hill near Khashin Zanna, which gave him a panoramic view of the whole area around Beersheba. The capture of the vital tels and the fact that two of his light horse brigades were now trotting north to complete the isolation of the Beersheba garrison all gave grounds for satisfaction, but he had received specific instructions from Allenby that the town and its wells had to be captured by nightfall and he was deeply worried that only one or two hours of daylight remained. He had, however, spotted a route directly into the town from the south-east, and although air reconnaissance photographs revealed that the way was barred by two lines of trenches, these had not been fronted with barbed wire. Even so, the idea of pitting cavalry against unbroken infantry in trenches when the latter had the support of artillery and machine guns ran contrary to all his professional instincts. Nevertheless, it was now apparent that the town could only be secured in the time available by a full-blooded mounted charge.

With him were Hodgson, Brigadier-General William Grant, commanding 4th Light Horse Brigade, and Brigadier-General Gerald Fitzgerald, commanding the 5th Mounted Brigade, the latter a yeomanry formation which was equipped with swords and therefore better suited to the work in hand. It was for this reason that when Chauvel pointed out exactly what was required Fitzgerald requested that his men be given the task. Chauvel had always sought to remain even handed between his Australians and the yeomanry, but after a moment's thought he indicated the gap and ordered Hodgson to 'Put Grant straight at it!' Given that time at this juncture was a priceless commodity, the decision was tactically correct since Grant's brigade was much closer to Beersheba than Fitzgerald's; later, Chauvel was to comment that he had also been influenced by the wish to give Grant's regiments a chance, as they had seen very little serious fighting thus far. He also gave Hodgson instructions that when Fitzgerald's brigade arrived, it was to follow up Grant's charge without delay, as was the independent 7th Mounted Brigade when it came up.

Grant's three regiments, the 4th (Victoria), 11th (Queensland and Western Australia) and 12th (New South Wales) Light Horse, received their orders between 16:00 and 16:15 and took a little time to assemble. The 11th, in fact, were manning an outpost line to the south-west and, it being immediately apparent that it could not rejoin the brigade in time, it was ordered to follow on as quickly as possible. Because of increased enemy air activity during the day the 4th and the 12th, commanded respectively by Lieutenant-Colonels the Honourable Murray Bourchier and Donald Cameron, had been dispersed by troops to reduce possible casualties. While they were being collected by the regimental seconds-in-command, Grant, his brigade major and the two commanding officers rode forward to reconnoitre a concealed route that would bring the brigade to the point from which it would launch its charge.

At length both regiments were assembled behind a low ridge crossed by a track leading straight into Beersheba from the south-east. About four miles separated them from the town itself, but only one-and-a-half from the forward Turkish trenches. The 4th shook out to the right of the track and the 12th to the left, each regiment being deployed in column of squadrons with 300 yards between squadrons and four yards between each man. Accompanying each regiment was one sub-section of the brigade machine gun squadron, the rest of which had been detailed to cover the left flank from which, correctly, it had been anticipated that some interference with the charge would come from a feature designated Hill 1180. In position to support the attack from a range of 2,500 yards were A Battery The Honourable Artillery Company and the Nottinghamshire Battery RHA. Positioning himself on the track, Grant gave the order for bayonets to be drawn; these were useless weapons with which to fight from the saddle but, being much longer than those in use today, they would give an enemy the impression of a cavalry sword if held forward along the horse's neck.

The signal to advance was given and the brigade breasted the shallow ridgeline to find a long, gentle forward slope stretching away towards the Turkish trenches with Beersheba clearly visible in the distance. At that moment the four loneliest men in the world must have been the two ground scouts riding 75 yards ahead of each regiment. In country such as this, where an unsuspected steep-sided wadi could wreck a charge, their presence was essential to provide adequate warning, but few would care to offer odds on their chances of survival. At first the 4th were a little in advance of the 12th and Bourchier held their pace down to a trot until the latter's squadrons came up and aligned themselves. Then, for about a quarter of a mile the entire brigade maintained a steady canter until breaking into a thunderous gallop that would take it all the way to the enemy trenches and beyond. As the pace increased Grant dropped back through the ranks and finally positioned himself near the two artillery batteries where he could control subsequent events. By now, the 11th had come up and were forming a reserve line. Beyond them, a moving dust cloud indicated the approach of Fitzgerald's 5th Mounted Brigade while to the south-west the 7th Mounted Brigade could be seen coming up at a canter.

The charge of Grant's brigade was witnessed by Trooper Ion Idriess of the 5th (Queensland) Light Horse, who, in his vividly descriptive style, recorded his impressions in his book *The Desert Column*.

'There, out on the plains, came squadron after squadron, regiment after regiment, all trotting forward in clouds of dust. Guns opened up on them, but they kept moving, the thousands of flying hooves stuttering thunder, going at a rate that frightened a man; an awe-inspiring sight, galloping through the red haze – knee to knee and horse-to-horse – the dying sun glinting on their bayonet points. Machine gun and rifle fire rattled but the 4th Brigade galloped on. We saw shellbursts among them and horses crashed, but the massed squadrons thundered on. We laughed in delight when the shells burst behind them, telling that the gunners couldn't keep the range, and suddenly men ceased to fall and we knew the Turks, wild with fear and excitement, had forgotten to lower their rifle sights. The last half-mile was a berserk gallop with squadrons in magnificent line, the horses leaping the trenches, the Turkish bayonets thrusting up. One regiment leapt from the saddle and into them; the following regiment galloped on, over another redoubt, and in a roar of cheers and thundering hooves, down the half-mile slope and into the town. Then a mad rush as other troops followed in the gathering dark, mad, mad excitement – terrific explosions in the town – Beersheba had fallen!'

Idriess' description is unlikely to be bettered, yet not even his acute powers of observation could absorb all that was happening. Hill 1180 was indeed held by the enemy, who opened a heavy machine gun fire on the left flank of the 12th Regiment. The brigade machine gun squadron went into action at once but when it failed to silence this Grant galloped across to the Nottinghamshire Battery and ordered it to engage the trenches on the feature. As the failing light made it impossible to obtain a reading from the rangefinder, Major Harrison, the battery commander, estimated the

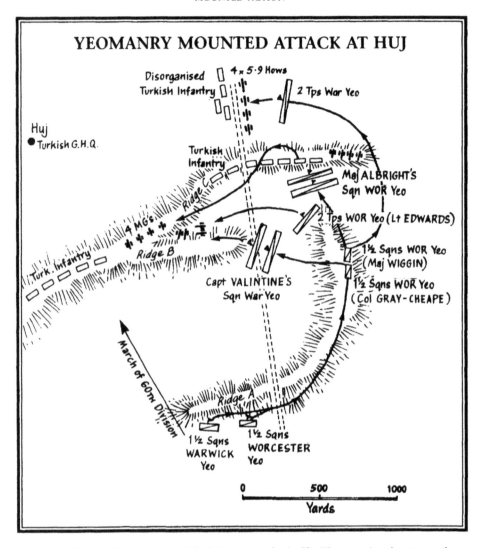

YEOMANRY MOUNTED ATTACK AT HUJ

Disorganised Turkish Infantry

4 x 5·9 Hows

2 Tps War Yeo

Huj
● Turkish G.H.Q.

Turkish Infantry

Ridge C

Maj ALBRIGHT'S
Sqn WOR Yeo

2 Tps WOR Yeo (Lt EDWARDS)

4 MGs

Turk. Infantry

Ridge B

1½ Sqns WOR Yeo
(Maj WIGGIN)

Capt VALINTINE'S
Sqn War Yeo

1½ Sqns WOR Yeo
(Col GRAY-CHEAPE)

March of 60th Division

Ridge A

1½ Sqns
WARWICK
Yeo

1½ Sqns
WORCESTER
Yeo

0   500   1000

Yards

range and hit the target with his second shell. The entire battery then opened fire, driving the Turks off the feature.

The first of the trenches covering Beersheba was found to be shallow, incomplete and held by only a handful of riflemen. The brigade sailed across this and quickly reached the main trench, which was eight to ten feet deep, four feet wide and held in strength. Having jumped the trench, the leading squadrons dismounted and waded into the enemy with their bayonets. It was in this vicious hand-to-hand fighting that the brigade incurred most of its casualties. After between 30 and 40 of the Turks had been killed the rest threw down their weapons; a few who snatched them up again to shoot unwary Australians were given short shrift. Examination of the prisoners' weapons revealed that their rifle sights had not been lowered from

800 yards and that similar incorrect ranges were set on their automatic weapons and field guns.

While the deadly struggle was taking place below ground the remaining squadrons, living walls of men and horses travelling at break-neck speed, had jumped the trench and were galloping on into Beersheba. Here took place personal adventures too numerous to detail. Trooper T. O'Leary, one of the 4th's ground scouts, successfully jumped both trench lines and was probably the first man to reach the town. There he came across a field gun team, limbered up and ready to withdraw, so intimidating the crew that they willingly drove it into a side street and waited patiently with him until the rest of his regiment arrived. Another gun, being brought out of action by a German officer, was captured by Trooper S. Bolton. Having lost his rifle but acquired a revolver, Bolton galloped after the gun, repeatedly firing at but missing the officer. Catching up with the German, he coshed him with the butt, after which the six-man Turkish gun crew meekly gave in.

As more and more troops streamed through the broken defences, the Turks in Beersheba fled in complete rout. Caught up in this were the engineers responsible for the destruction of the vital wells, who were only able to destroy two and damage two more. Darkness undoubtedly saved many from capture, but over 1,500 prisoners and fourteen guns were taken by the Desert Mounted Corps as a whole; Grant's 4th Australian Light Horse Brigade alone captured 59 officers and 1,090 other ranks, nine guns, seven ammunition limbers and four machine guns, plus uncounted transport vehicles, pack animals, stores and equipment. The Desert Mounted Corps' casualties, many of which stemmed from the enemy's increased air activity, came to 197 of whom 53 were killed; Grant's amazingly light loss of 32 killed and the same number wounded can be attributed in part to the Turks' failure to adjust their fire and partly to the sheer speed and aggression with which the charge had been delivered. The charge itself had lasted just ten minutes from start to finish and won its participants one Victoria Cross, six Distinguished Service Orders, four Military Crosses, four Distinguished Conduct Medals and eleven Military Medals.

The Turkish 27th Division had been all but wiped out. Subsequently, senior Turkish officers sought to explain their defeat by claiming that this formation, containing as it did a large Arab element, was one of the worst in their service and had fought badly. That was not the opinion of their corps commander, Ismet Bey, nor of those who has been forced to fight so hard for Tel es Saba, and in any event the regiment that had opposed Grant's charge consisted of good quality Anatolian troops with some German officers. Ismet was also criticised for his handling of the battle, despite the fact that throughout the day he had given repeated warnings of the build-up and vainly requested immediate reinforcements. In the event, he made his escape from the doomed town just ten minutes before the Australians entered it.

Falkenhayn did not reach his new headquarters in Jerusalem until 1 November. While still believing that Gaza was Allenby's real objective, his Turco-German staff had reacted strongly to the loss of Beersheba and moved two divisions, plus elements of two more, to the eastern flank with the object of recapturing the town. This never came to anything as Chauvel had already pushed troops some miles to the north and, while it meant that some of the horses went without water for 48 hours, no difficulty was experienced in holding the counter-attack. One reason for this was that he had also despatched Lieutenant-Colonel Stewart Newton, Royal Engineers, and 70 camel-mounted troopers on a wide detour deep into the Turkish rear areas with instructions to raise the local Arabs and create the impression that the Desert Mounted Corps was about to launch a cavalry raid along the axis Hebron–Jerusalem. Having brought down no less than six infantry battalions upon itself, and in the process taken the edge off the Turkish counter-attack, Newton's detachment was surrounded and forced to surrender on 2 November.

At 23:00 the previous night Allenby had further concentrated Falkenhayn's thoughts on Gaza by initiating the first phase of his diversionary attack there, on a 6,000 yard front close to the coast. Early next morning the second phase, which included the support of six tanks used in the correct manner, broke through the defences to a depth of 3,000 yards, effectively turning the flank of numerous laboriously prepared positions in the town and on the nearby ridges. XXI Corps sustained the loss of 350 killed, the same number missing and 2,000 wounded; Turkish losses amounted to 1,000 killed, an unknown number wounded, 550 prisoners, three guns and 30 machine guns. While Allenby decided to reinforce this success, Falkenhayn contributed to his own eventual defeat by rushing his reserves to the Gaza sector.

The great north-westerly wheel by XX Corps and the Desert Mounted Corps was delayed by the heavy fighting north of Beersheba, the difficulties involved in collecting sufficient water, and a strong 'khamseen' blowing off the desert. On 6 November, however, it began, steadily rolling up the Turkish line from east to west. Falkenhayn, suddenly aware of the terrible danger in which his armies stood, ordered Gaza to be abandoned during the night while elsewhere along the line the darkness was illuminated by burning Turkish supply dumps. On 7 November XX Corps captured Sheria and Hareira. There were now clear indications that Kressenstein's

Eighth Army was retreating in a northerly direction along the coast, while Fawzi Pasha's Seventh Army was diverging along a north-easterly axis, thereby opening a gap in the Turkish centre. Through this Allenby decided to launch his mounted troops against Huj, where an adequate water supply was known to exist.

Throughout the morning of 8 November Major-General Stuart Shea's 60th Division, now operating under Chauvel's command, steadily pushed the Turkish rearguard back towards Huj over open, rolling country. Shea himself, scouting ahead in a Rolls-Royce armoured car, could see enemy infantry and guns moving north-eastwards across his front. Anxious to prevent their escape, he hurried his division forward but at about 12:45 the Turkish rearguard, consisting of two infantry battalions, several artillery batteries and a machine gun unit, decided to make a stand about two miles south of Huj, which contained a large supply depot. The British infantry, advancing across ground that provided no cover at all, began to incur heavy casualties. Shea, knowing that two cavalry brigades were operating on his right, drove across with the intention of getting them to mount an attack into the flank of the enemy position.

The two brigades were Fitzgerald's 5th Mounted Brigade, of which, ironically, Fitzgerald had handed over command to Brigadier-General Philip Kelly that very morning, and the 3rd Australian Light Horse Brigade, which was still some distance away to the south-east.

Nominally, the 5th Mounted Brigade consisted of the Royal Gloucestershire Hussars, the Warwickshire Yeomanry, the Worcestershire Hussars, B Battery the Honourable Artillery Company and the brigade machine gun squadron. Unfortunately, at that precise moment the Gloucesters and all but two guns of the machine gun squadron were watering their horses some miles away, and the artillery battery had fallen far behind the advance. Thus, only the Warwicks and Worcesters were in a position to take decisive action.

The opportunity sensed by Shea had also been spotted by the Worcesters' commanding officer, Lieutenant-Colonel Henry Williams, who, recognising how thin on the ground his own brigade was, galloped off to find the headquarters of the 3rd Australian Light Horse Brigade with a view to suggesting a joint attack, adequately supported by rifle and machine gun fire.

Shortly after Williams had left, Shea arrived in his armoured car. He spoke to Lieutenant-Colonel Hugh Gray-Cheape, commanding the Warwicks, and ordered him to mount a flank attack on the enemy guns, stressing the urgency of the situation. Having few men at his disposal, Gray-Cheape rode over to the Worcesters and asked Major Edgar Wiggin, in temporary command during Williams' absence, whether he would participate in the attack, receiving an immediate assent.

By the time everyone had been assembled the Warwicks had about 86 men available and the Worcesters about the same, giving the approximate equivalent of ten troops. However, when the Hotchkiss light machine gun sections, the shoeing smiths and the led-horse holders had been fallen out, this left about 120 men for the attack itself, far too few for what was required of them. Nevertheless, Gray-Cheape, fully aware of the punishment the 60th Division was taking, could only comply with Shea's orders and, sending back a message to inform his own brigade commander what was happening, and a request that the Gloucesters, the machine gun squadron and the artillery be hurried forward, he and Wiggin prepared their plan of attack.

At that moment, approximately 13:20, the two regiments were positioned below the south-western end of a shallow, banana-shaped ridge. It was decided that they would use this feature as cover for an approach around its south-eastern end, which would then place them about 900 yards from the left flank of the enemy batteries and in position to mount a charge.

The Worcesters, being on the right, moved off first with Major M. C. Albright's A Squadron leading, followed by two troops of C Squadron; the Warwicks were led by Captain R. Valintine's B Squadron with two troops of the regiment's C Squadron bringing up the rear. The advance was made at a trot, raising an unavoidable dust cloud that alerted the enemy. Suddenly, rounding the end of the ridge, Albright's squadron came under fire from a hitherto unsuspected four-gun mounted battery and about 200 infantrymen situated on a low rise about 600 yards to the north-west. Realising at once that these troops would be able to enfilade the attack against the main enemy position, Albright did not wait for orders and, pausing only to form into a half-squadron column, immediately launched a charge. Taking place over good, open going, this quickly reached a full gallop. Unnerved, the Turkish infantry and gunners began firing wildly and then broke, running down the reverse slope of the rise. Albright's troopers were soon among them, putting many to the sword.[5] They then closed in on a 5.9-inch howitzer battery that was withdrawing to the north but at this point Wiggin arrived and ordered a halt to the pursuit, informing Albright that the principal attack against the original objective was proving to be a bloody business and that he should rally and reinforce this immediately.

As soon as Albright had launched his charge Gray-Cheape had instructed Valintine's B Squadron and the two remaining Worcester troops, the latter commanded by Second Lieutenant J. W. Edwards, to swing left, form half-squadron column and attack over the north-eastern crest of the covering ridge. This would take them down a gradual forward slope into a shallow valley and then up the other side into the gun position, with the last 150 yards becoming steadily steeper. As soon as the first ranks appeared over the crest the enemy gunners, who were Austrians, swung round the trails of their 75mm field guns and commenced a rapid fire, progressively dropping the range until their barrels were at maximum depression and their shell fuzes set at instantaneous. Likewise the four machine guns in the immediate vicinity, which were probably under German command, and the two companies of Turkish infantry that formed the escort for the guns, all engaged the approaching lines of galloping horsemen. Among the Warwicks, only one officer, Lieutenant W. B. Mercer, remained unhit, and his account of the charge is quoted from the Official History of the campaign:[6]

'Machine guns and rifles opened on us the moment we topped the rise behind which we had formed up. I remember thinking that the sound of the crackling bullets was just like a hailstorm on an iron-roofed building ... A whole heap of men and horses went down twenty or thirty yards from the guns. The squadron broke into a few scattered horsemen at the guns and then seemed to melt away completely. For a time, I at any rate, had the impression that I was the only man left alive. I was amazed to discover we were the victors.'

The Austrians had courageously fought to the muzzle, but the subsequent mêlée among the guns was brief. Those who remained upright or ran were ridden down or spitted, only those who fell flat remaining beyond reach of the thrusting swords. In return, some of the yeomen fell victim to the enemy's cruel saw-edged bayonets. At the end of it, perhaps a score of them remained mounted but, without hesitation, they spurred for the machine guns. How this might have ended there is no telling, but just then Albright's squadron came bearing down on the enemy left and overran them. Having already witnessed the determined charge against their artillery, this was too much for the Turkish infantry, who broke and fled. Some were cut down by vengeful yeomen, although the latter, being now too few in number, were unable to mount an organised pursuit. At this moment, however, the half-section of the machine gun squadron, which had followed Valintine's charge, arrived and turned its two guns, as well as the four just captured, on the fugitives, scything through the running figures. The Turkish rout was completed by Gray-Cheape, who had used the Warwicks' two reserve troops to secure the now-abandoned mountain guns and ride down the retreating battery of 5.9-inch howitzers.

As a direct result of the Warwicks' and Worcesters' charge, eleven guns, four machine guns and 70 prisoners had been taken, an unknown but substantial number of the enemy killed or wounded, and Shea's division was able to advance beyond Huj that evening.[7] The remarkable thing about the action was that, save in its concluding stages, the primary weapon used by the British had been the sword. The price, however, had been terribly high. The Warwicks had lost thirteen men killed and 23 wounded, the Worcesters nineteen killed and 35 wounded; among the officers, Albright, Valintine and Edwards were either killed or died of their wounds, and Wiggin was wounded. Well over 100 horses had been killed or had to be put down and many others were wounded, mainly by machine gun fire. Immediately after the action the area surrounding the Austrian battery presented a horrific scene of concentrated carnage. Dead troopers, Austrians, Turks and horses lay sprawled thickly together around the guns while the wounded crawled their painful way towards help. As luck would have it, an enemy field ambulance unit had been captured in a hollow behind the battery and it was thanks to the medical supplies obtained from this that many men owed their lives. There was little, however, that could be done for most of the terribly wounded horses; for many cavalrymen this was by far the most harrowing part of their ordeal, terminated only when the merciful crack of a rifle ended an animal's agony.

Astonishing as it was that the enemy's rearguard on this sector of the front had been successfully broken by so few men, Chauvel may well have doubted that Shea's problem was so urgent that its solution could not have awaited the arrival of the Gloucesters, the artillery and the rest of the machine gun squadron, which could have provided fire support and so reduced the number of casualties. Whatever subsequently passed between the generals, after Huj no further unsupported charges were made by the Desert Mounted Corps save in pursuit of already beaten troops. Yet the consequences of the charges at Beersheba and Huj, and a further charge with the sword made by the 6th Mounted Brigade (Royal Buckinghamshire Hussars, Berkshire Yeomanry and Dorset Yeomanry) at El Mughar on 13 November, were far-reaching.[8] The Turks now regarded the British and Commonwealth cavalry with awe, were convinced that they had scant regard for their own lives, and were unwilling to stand against them except in prepared positions. Analysis of these actions also confirmed that in mounted attacks the sword retained its value and the following year the Australian Mounted Division, at its own request, was trained and equipped with this weapon.

The pace of Allenby's advance following his victory at Gaza/Beersheba was partly dictated by logistic considerations and partly by the physical limitations of his mounted troops, who were sometimes forced to go without water for a day and more at a time. It was true that the rapid abandonment of Gaza had foiled his attempt to entrap Kressenstein's army, but after nine months' stalemate he had broken the enemy line beyond retrieval and was to advance 75 miles before the heaviest winter rains in living memory put an end to movement of every kind.

During the early hours of Sunday 9 December the last Turkish garrison of Jerusalem left the city. Shortly after dawn the Governor, Izzet Bey, sent out a note formally confirming his surrender and by noon the first British patrols were moving through the narrow streets. Among the Arab customers of the coffee shops there was jubilation that, save in one particular, the curious old prophesy had at last been fulfilled, for was not the British commander named Allah-en-Nebi, which could only be translated as the Prophet of God? The only unanswered question was how the latest of Jerusalem's conquerors would enter the city. Allenby, of course, was fully aware of the prophesy and may have decided to fulfill the last of its predictions; on the other hand, he may have acted from a sense of personal inclination. On Tuesday 11 December, he entered Jerusalem by the Jaffa Gate, humbly, on foot, and accompanied only by his staff. Watched in something like awe by the large crowd he walked to the base of the Tower of David. There his proclamation was read out, expressing the wish that the inhabitants should return to their daily business and guaranteeing protection for the ancient sites sacred to Christian, Jew and Moslem. Then, he left as quietly as he had come.

There is good reason to believe that Allenby could have finished off the Turkish army in Palestine during the spring of 1918. During that very period, however, he was compelled to send some of his best troops to France to assist in stemming a series of powerful German offensives that almost succeeded in breaking through the Western Front. Once the crisis had passed, two Indian cavalry divisions were sent from France to Palestine, less the statutory British regular regiments one of which formed part of each brigade, these being replaced by yeomanry regiments on arrival. This brought Chauvel's corps up to its maximum strength and enabled Allenby to plan an autumn offensive with which he intended to utterly destroy his opponents.

The battle, which was to take its name from the historic battlefield of Megiddo, some miles to the north, began on 19 September when, following a concentrated bombardment, the infantry of XXI Corps secured a breakthrough on the coast near Arsuf. Through the gap poured the entire Desert Mounted Corps, swinging right-handed across the rear of two

Turkish armies, reducing them to the lot of fugitives within days. It was Allenby's greatest triumph, and the last strategic victory to be won by mounted cavalry.

Notes

1. In 1918 this was removed by Colonel T. E. Lawrence. It now resides within the Imperial War Museum.

2. The Trans-Sinai railway remained in use until the Six Day War of 1967, after which the Israeli Army removed most of the rails for incorporation in the bunkers of the Bar Lev outpost line on the eastern bank of the Suez Canal.

3. These characteristics were equally evident during the Second World War. Rommel, doubtless with the siege of Tobruk in mind, described the Australian infantry as the toughest he had ever met. Again, it took the personal pleas of Winston Churchill and his War Cabinet for the New Zealand government to change its mind about withdrawing the 2nd New Zealand Division from the Mediterranean theatre of war after the Second Battle of Alamein.

4. Only Allenby and a few senior members of his intelligence staff were privy to the ruse. Chauvel, on whose sector the incident took place, gave Meinertzhagen a verbal flaying on his return, then reported him to Allenby for his criminal incompetence!

5. The weapon itself was the straight 1908 Pattern sword with a narrow blade 35 inches long. Highly regarded, it was designed specifically for thrusting but had only a limited cutting ability.

6. Falls, Captain Cyril, *Military Operations, Egypt & Palestine, Vol II*, HMSO 1930.

7. Kressenstein's forward headquarters had been located in Huj. During their hurried departure his staff left behind their radio code book, thereby providing Allenby's intercept operators with some interesting listening.

8. Some squadrons, on reaching their objective, dismounted and cleared it with the rifle and bayonet.

CHAPTER EIGHT

Leading the Way –
US Rangers at the Pointe Du Hoe and
Omaha Beach, D-Day, 6 June 1944

In the mist-laden, grey first light of 6 June 1944 two former cross-channel ferry steamers, the *Ben My Chree* and the *Amsterdam*, hove-to some twelve miles short of the French coast in the midst of the largest invasion fleet ever assembled. Both vessels had been converted to the rôle of infantry landing ship and in place of the lifeboats that had once hung from their davits there were now rows of assault landing craft. Hard-looking American infantry, wearing only their basic battle-order, scrambled aboard them and then they were lowered in succession into the heaving water below to circle until at a given signal they formed into loose lines and headed for the unseen shore. There was an extremely heavy, breaking swell that began to affect those prone to sea-sickness and soon everyone aboard was drenched by the clouds of flying spray that burst over the blunt bows of the LCAs. One was swamped and although its occupants were quickly picked up, smaller craft everywhere could be seen to be labouring or in difficulty. Large formations of aircraft had been passing overhead regularly, their noise smothered by the thunder of the invasion fleet's massive preparatory bombardment. Aboard the LCAs were the US Army's 2nd and 5th Ranger Battalions, commanded respectively by Lieutenant-Colonels James E. Rudder and Max F. Schneider, and the story of their mission was one of the most remarkable on a day of remarkable stories.

It had begun two years earlier, in Northern Ireland. There, Brigadier-General Lucian Truscott, having obtained the approval of the Army's Chief of Staff, General George C. Marshall, had begun to form units intended to perform the same functions as the British commandos, recruiting men of above-average physical fitness and initiative drawn from the 1st Armored and 34th Infantry Divisions, which were on the spot. They were given an unbelievably tough basic training, involving the use of live ammunition, by the Commando Training Centre at Achnacarry, near Fort William in the Western Highlands of Scotland, then sent back to pass on their newly-acquired skills. It was decided that the new units would be known as Rangers after the famous irregular unit raised by Major Robert Rogers which had so distinguished itself during the eighteenth century French

163

and Indian Wars in North America. It was also decided to follow the commando example and keep the basic unit organisation small. The ranger battalion consisted of six companies, each with three officers and 64 other ranks, and each company consisted of two platoons, each with two twelve-man assault sections and a mortar section.

Commanded by Lieutenant-Colonel William Orlando Darby, the 1st Ranger Battalion fought so well in Tunisia that by the end of the North African campaign the decision was taken to form four more battalions. The 1st Rangers therefore provided cadres for 3rd and 4th Rangers, which were raised in Algeria, and also sent personnel back to the United States to assist in training the 2nd and 5th Rangers.

Together, the 1st, 3rd and 4th Rangers made up the Ranger Force. Darby, now a full colonel, led it through the Sicilian campaign, then at Salerno and in other battles on the Italian mainland. During the bitter struggle for the Anzio beachhead, however, disaster struck when the 1st and 3rd Rangers were cut off and overrun near Cisterna, only eighteen men managing to escape. Simultaneously, the 4th Rangers sustained heavy casualties while trying to break through to their trapped comrades.

The tragedy had its roots in a basic misunderstanding of the Rangers' role. The original intention had been that the Rangers should fight short, sharp decisive actions in the commando manner and then be withdrawn to train for their next mission; they were, in fact, neither structured nor equipped to fight in any other way. But whereas the British Commandos had a powerful advocate in Lord Louis Mountbatten, Chief of Combined Operations, to ensure that this policy was strictly implemented, the Rangers lacked anyone with comparable clout to speak for them. Therefore, local American commanders, delighted to have such high quality troops at their disposal, tended to keep them in the line in the manner of conventional infantry units, thereby wasting their specialist skills as mounting casualties began to take their toll. That the Rangers had done so well prior to Cisterna was a tribute to their fighting abilities and esprit de corps.

These lessons seem to have been absorbed, for when the 2nd and 5th Battalions were committed to the D-Day landings it was in a specifically commando role. The inner flanks of the two American beachheads, Utah on the right and Omaha on the left, were some eight miles apart, physically separated by the wide sands of the Vire estuary, to the east of which was a rock shelf four miles long and up to a mile deep that formed a physical barrier to an assault landing, while east of this again were several miles of cliffs between 80 and 100 feet high, ending near Vierville-sur-Mer. Just to the east of the rock shelf was the Pointe du Hoe, on which the Germans had built a fortified coast defence battery. According to intelligence sources, this was armed with six powerful 150mm guns that were capable of enfilading both Utah and Omaha Beaches while the landings were in progress and would therefore have to be eliminated during the early stages of the operation. Neither bombing attacks from the air, nor bombardment with the 14-inch guns of the battleship USS *Texas*, could be relied upon to destroy the entire battery, and for that reason the position would have to be physically stormed by the 2nd Rangers before it could cause any damage. The actual assault would be made by the battalion's D, E and F Companies while C Company tackled the fortifications on another headland to the east, the Raz de la Percée, between the Pointe du Hoe and Vierville-sur-Mer. A and B Companies, together with the entire 5th Battalion, were to be held in reserve and come ashore at the Pointe du Hoe if the assault succeeded; if it did not, they were to land near Vierville on Omaha Beach and operate under the command of 116th Infantry on the extreme right of Major-General Leonard T. Gerow's US V Corps.

D, E and F Companies had trained very hard for their mission, climbing cliffs of similar size on the Isle of Wight and at Swanage in Dorset. The problem was that these consisted of chalk while those of the Pointe du Hoe were made of clay which, if wet, would become slimy and offer no grip. To counter this, special equipment was to be employed. Each LCA was fitted with three pairs of rocket projectors, capable of firing ropes or rope ladders to the top of the cliff, where grapnels would dig into the soil or snag the enemy's wire. In case these devices failed to work, portable rocket line throwers were also issued to platoons, as were lightweight tubular steel ladders in sixteen-foot lengths that could be hauled up and connected in succession until the necessary height had been attained. As a further precaution, four DUKWs (amphibious lorries) fitted with London Fire Brigade 100-foot extension ladders would beach immediately behind the assault craft, two light machine guns being mounted at the top of each ladder to provide covering fire. During the climb itself the leaders would be armed with pistols or carbines and grenades. Those with Browning Automatic Rifles, light mortars and demolition charges would follow. Once the assault was under way, two assault boats would touch down with the companies' 81mm mortars, ammunition, rations, more demolition equipment, personal packs and the means of hauling these up the cliff face. Every aspect of the coastline and the defences had been repeatedly studied on maps, photographs and models, and every man knew exactly what to do and where to go without the need for further orders. Almost every contingency had been thought of, the only unknown factor being the reaction of the enemy. The German formation holding this sector of the coast was, in fact, the 352nd Infantry Division, which had been formed the previous autumn and consisted of the 914th, 915th and 916th Grenadier Regiments plus supporting arms. Although the division had never been in action before, the presence of numerous Eastern Front veterans in its ranks ensured that it would give a good account of itself when the time came.

Nothing connected with this operation could be taken for granted. Indeed, so high were the risks that Colonel Rudder had been forbidden to participate in the assault. He chose to ignore the order and embarked on one of F Company's craft, quickly recognising the truth of the old saying that in war chaos is the natural state. Having already seen one of the LCAs swamped, he watched helplessly as the same fate overtook one of his supply boats while the crew of the second flung C and D Companies' packs overboard in a desperate attempt to stay afloat. For obvious reasons his assault on the Pointe du Hoe had been scheduled to begin at 06:30, some 30 minutes before the main landings. Visibility had improved very little and as that moment approached the coastline began to emerge. At first, to his horror, Rudder did not recognise any of it and then, remembering that the tide had a strong easterly set, he was able to identify the Raz de la Percée. This meant that his three companies had been carried some three miles to the east of their objective. He immediately gave his Royal Navy coxswain orders to come hard to starboard. The rest of his command conformed, the speed of the blunt-bowed LCAs falling away as they butted their way into the tide. His heart sinking, Rudder realised that he could not possibly eliminate the battery on the Pointe du Hoe before the main landings began; furthermore, his LCAs were now running parallel to the cliffs and in full view of the enemy, who opened fire from several positions, sinking one of the DUKWs.

Escorting the little flotilla were two destroyers, HMS *Talybont* and USS *Satterlee*. *Talybont's* captain had been aware that the LCAs were running off course and he had repeatedly tried to communicate the fact, in vain. Now, seeing the German defences springing to life, he began to plaster them with a rain of 4-inch and 2-pounder high explosive shells, supplemented by 20mm cannon fire, closing in steadily from a range of two-and-a-half miles. On the Pointe du Hoe the huge eruptions of earth and clay thrown up by the explosion of *Texas'* 14-inch shells ceased a little before 06:30, those aboard the battleship believing that the assault was about to commence. Lying 2,500 yards off the point, the *Satterlee's* captain saw the surface of the headland suddenly transformed into a disturbed ants' nest as troops ran from their bunkers to man defensive positions. He promptly engaged them with gunfire from his 5-inch main armament and raked the crest with the destroyer's ten .50-calibre anti-aircraft machine guns.

Further out to sea the second and larger group of Ranger LCAs, carrying the 5th Battalion and the 2nd Battalion's A and B Companies, was still not in visual contact with the shore. When 07:00 came and went without any signal from Rudder, Colonel Schneider was forced to assume that the Pointe du Hoe was not in American hands and gave orders for the craft to head for Vierville. This meant that Rudder's men were now completely alone and would remain so. The odds against them were also lengthening all the time. It was not until 07:10 that the first of their LCAs touched down on the narrow beach below the cliffs of the Pointe du Hoe. As they did so, *Satterlee's* guns ceased firing for their own safety. Rudder's original intention had been that five of the craft should come in on each side of the point so that a converging assault could be launched against the summit. In the event, all nine surviving LCAs beached on a 500-yard stretch of shore below the feature's eastern face. The cliffs had been pitted by bursting shells, as a result of which huge piles of fallen clay covered the sand below; the beach itself was also extensively cratered.

As each craft ground to a standstill the ramp dropped and the rocket launchers were fired. Although the ropes soared upwards most had been saturated with spray, doubling their weight, and they came tumbling back to earth when the rockets failed to cope with the additional burden. Aboard LCA 862, however, the crew had kept the ropes sheeted so that two of their grapnels reached the clifftop and held. The three remaining DUKWs came in, but hope of using their extending ladders vanished when they were unable to manoeuvre because of craters on the 30-yard-wide beach. Time now being of the essence, the Rangers employed their portable line-throwers, saving the sectional ladders as a last resort. German helmets now began to bob along the edge of the cliff. Potato-masher grenades rained down to explode among those below, who also began to take casualties from snipers. The BAR teams replied as best they could and *Satterlee*, observing the desperate situation ashore, went into action for a second time. Grapnels began to dig in along the cliff edge or catch in the enemy wire. Suddenly small groups of men were climbing the half-inch ropes, their boots scrabbling for support on the slippery clay. Some ropes were cut by the Germans, sending those on them plummeting to the beach below. *Satterlee*, observing the progress of the distant, tiny dots up the cliff face, again ceased firing.

First over the edge was Private First Class Harry W. Roberts. Only five minutes had elapsed since his LCA had touched down, but it seemed like a lifetime. He was joined shortly after by Lieutenant Lapres and four more men. Despite their long study of photographs, none of them could recognise a single feature, so torn up and cratered by bombing and naval gun-

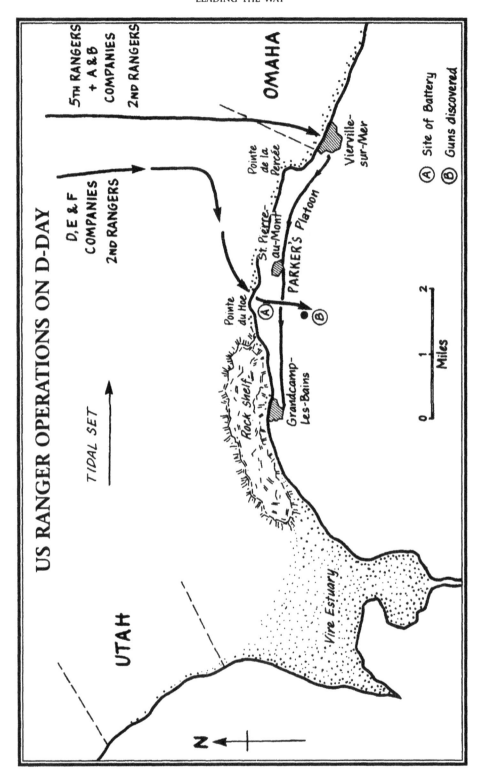

US RANGER OPERATIONS ON D-DAY

UTAH

TIDAL SET

OMAHA

5TH RANGERS + A & B COMPANIES 2ND RANGERS

D, E & F COMPANIES 2ND RANGERS

Pointe de la Percée

Vierville-sur-Mer

St Pierre-au-Mont

PARKER'S Platoon

Pointe du Hoe

Rock Shelf

Grandcamp-Les-Bains

Vire Estuary

Ⓐ Site of Battery
Ⓑ Guns discovered

N

0   1   2
Miles

fire was the terrain. Nevertheless, there being no Germans visible in the immediate vicinity, they set off for their objective. Four more men reached the top by the same route, then another five up LCA 862's lines, then a steady trickle in ones and twos.

Working in pairs, they closed in on the battery position. They had expected a hard fight but such opposition as they encountered was light and quickly overcome. The reason for this soon became apparent. The observation and command casemates were heavily damaged and the concrete gunpits had been blasted apart; furthermore, the latter were empty save for one which contained the wreckage of a 150mm gun. It began to look as though the Rangers' careful preparations and efforts had all been for nothing.

However, the situation atop the Pointe du Hoe remained fluid. The enemy gunners might have abandoned their position but plenty more Germans remained who had gone to earth among the network of battered communication trenches and other works. Now, relieved of the attentions of *Texas, Talybont* and *Satterlee*, they began to surface and engage the Americans in a series of small battles that were to last throughout the day.

The Rangers had incurred fifteen casualties on the beach but by 07:45 all of the remainder had completed their climb. When an anti-aircraft position to the west of the point began sweeping the area with its fire Rudder despatched a twelve-strong team to deal with it. This ran into an ambush from which only one man returned. A second assault was improvised but was stopped dead by artillery fire half-way to the objective, sustaining heavy casualties.

Rudder, despite having been hit in the leg by a sniper, was anxious to complete the second part of his mission, which was to cut the coastal highway between Grandcamps les Bains and Vierville-sur-Mer. Leaving a party, consisting mainly of F Company, to sit on the opposition at the headland, he struck inland. The move attracted sporadic artillery and small-arms fire which inflicted a further fifteen casualties. By 08:15, however, having established himself in a position beyond the road, he sent out patrols. At 09:00 one of these, consisting of Sergeants Lomell and Kuhn from D Company, discovered the coast defence battery's five missing 150mm guns, camouflaged on the edge of a wood beside a lane. Ammunition had been stockpiled ready for use yet, once again, there was no sign of the gunners. Lomell wrecked the recoil buffers of two of the guns with thermite charges and smashed the sights of a third, then the pair set off to obtain more explosives. While they were away an E Company patrol also came across the battery and completed its destruction. Subsequent interrogations revealed that the guns had been withdrawn from their gunpits on the point to avoid the worst effects of the naval bombardment. The intention had been that they should be moved back in time to counter the assault landings, but this idea had been abandoned when the Rangers were seen to have reached the top of the cliff. They were, in any event, able to shell Utah or Omaha Beaches from their present position; why they had not done so, and why the gun crews and prime movers had so mysteriously vanished, remained two of the day's unanswered questions.

Meanwhile, F Company had been slowly but steadily obtaining the upper hand back at the headland, enabling it to send forward reinforcements to join Rudder, who eventually managed to assemble about 60 men. Among them, quite unexpectedly, were three paratroopers from the 101st Airborne Division which, together with the 82nd Airborne Division, had been dropped the previous night into the area behind Utah Beach. The drops had been badly scattered and these men, having landed east of the Vire, had made their way towards the sound of the fighting. Shortly after noon Rudder was able to transmit the following message:

'Located Pointe du Hoe – mission accomplished – need ammunition and reinforcements – many casualties.'

Some two hours later he received a reply to the effect that no reinforcements were available. He estimated that about a third of his force were dead, wounded or missing; ammunition was running so low that captured German weapons were being taken into use; rations were also in short supply and everyone's pack now lay at the bottom of the Channel. There was also the added responsibility of about 40 German prisoners, mainly men of the 914th Grenadier Regiment who, in trying to make good their escape from the Pointe to the south, had wandered into the Rangers' position. Snipers remained a menace. During the afternoon two weak counterattacks were beaten off but towards evening it became apparent that the Germans were concentrating for a greater effort. Since no improvement in the overall situation could be expected before the morrow, the prospects for the night ahead looked dubious at best.

Rudder's predicament had its roots in the shambles that had taken place on Omaha Beach to the east. There, V Corps' assault landing, made with 29th Division on the right and 1st Division on the left, had been stopped dead at the water's edge by withering fire. It was sheer bad luck that 352 Division was engaged in an anti-invasion exercise at the time, but the launching of the assault craft so far out, the restriction of the naval bombardment to 40 minutes, the decision to assault the enemy strongpoints head-on rather than land between them, and the rejection of specialist armour with which to neutralise them, were all mistakes that had to be paid for in blood. The four-mile beach and its shallows were quickly strewn with bodies and smashed equipment while the survivors frantically scraped some cover for themselves in whatever dead ground they could find; new arrivals simply added to the carnage. At one stage Lieutenant-General Omar Bradley, commanding First US Army, seriously considered abandoning the landing and diverting the follow-up waves to the Utah beachhead, which had been secured without undue difficulty. At 07:30, the situation began to improve when eight American and three British destroyers, having observed the chaos ashore, closed to within 1000 yards and began battering the strongpoints. As the pressure eased, small groups of infantry began courageously working their way forward through the beach obstacles, wire and minefields to eliminate fire positions. By 09:00 they had secured footholds on the plateau overlooking the beach. Thirty minutes later elements of the 1st Division broke out towards Colleville-sur-Mer and thereafter the remaining beach exits were stormed in succession. By mid-afternoon the situation on Omaha had been brought sufficiently under control for reinforcements to be landed, but so stubbornly did the German 916th Grenadier Regiment contest possession of the villages beyond, that when night fell the beachhead was nowhere more than two miles in depth. This had been achieved at the horrific cost of 3,000 casualties, one-third of them killed, approximately 30 per cent of the total Allied loss on D-Day.

The experience of Colonel Schneider's Rangers was typical. Two companies landed opposite strongpoints and only half of them survived the 250-yard dash from the shallows to the nearest cover; yet only two or three hundred yards to their right the rest of the 5th Battalion landed between strongpoints and, screened by the dense smoke of a grass fire started by the preparatory bombardment, sustained just five casualties before it reached the foot of a bluff where the plateau met the beach.

Schneider was one of the original Rangers and he had obtained a great deal of experience under Darby. He had no idea what had happened to Rudder but the fact that no 150mm shells were landing on Omaha suggested that he had taken his objective. According to the overall plan, the next task for Schneider's own battalion and the two attached companies from 2nd Rangers was to join Rudder in the area he was already holding; given the present situation, however, that would be no easy matter.

It was about the time that the first cracks began to appear in the German defence that Brigadier-General Norman D. Cota, the Assistant Divisional Commander of the 29th Division, strolled into the area below the bluff. Throughout the morning's terrifying confusion and bloodshed Cota had displayed a total disregard for his own safety as he toured his division's sector of the beach, providing encouragement for individuals and suggestions as to how tactical objectives could be taken. His conduct was to earn him a Silver Star, the Distinguished Service Cross and the British Distinguished Service Order – plus a reprimand from General Bradley, who disliked the idea of senior officers with heavy responsibilities taking needless personal risks. Schneider reported to him and Cota indicated that the bluff would have to be taken. There are two versions of what was actually said. The first, recorded in David Irving's book *The War Between the Generals*, is that Cota, having noticed the distinctive orange diamond on the back of the 5th Battalion's helmets, called out: 'You men are Rangers – I know you won't let me down!' The second is that his final words to Schneider were, 'Lead the way, Rangers!' While the former seems the more probable, it was the latter which caught the imagination of the troops and the general public alike, to the extent that the phrase and the philosophy it embodies has remained the Ranger motto ever since.

Schneider wasted no time in briefing his officers; companies were to attack independently and at once, reassembling at a designated rendezvous point south of Vierville-sur-Mer. The sides of the bluff were so steep that the Rangers were forced to pull themselves up, using their bayonets in the manner of ice-axes. Having reached the top, they stormed the remaining beach defences and pressed on towards the village, where they became involved in bitter street fighting with 916th Grenadiers, who were determined to hold it to the last. By good fortune, one platoon of A Company 5th Rangers, commanded by Lieutenant Parker, walked straight through a gap in the enemy line and reached the rendezvous point unopposed. Parker, unaware that the rest of the battalion was heavily engaged in the village, reached the conclusion that it had already left for the Pointe du Hoe and set off in that direction. On the way his platoon took a number of prisoners and worked its way round an enemy position during a firefight, making contact with Rudder's perimeter to the west of St Pierre-du-Mont at about 21:00. If Rudder's men were pleasantly surprised to see Parker's, Parker himself was surprised that the rest of his battalion had not arrived and he told Rudder that he believed them to be close behind. Greatly relieved, Rudder decided to hold his ground for the night and integrated the new arrivals into his defences.

In fact, the 5th Rangers were still locked into the fight for Vierville. The village was finally cleared at about midnight, although the roads to the west, south and east of it remained firmly under German control. Rudder's position was attacked three times during the night. At about 23:30 an attack ended almost as soon as it began when charges in the abandoned battery suddenly erupted in an immense sheet of flame that silhouetted the enemy, sending them to ground. Ninety minutes later they came on again, evidently unsure where the Rangers' position was, but reached a point 50 yards from the perimeter before they were stopped. The third attack, mounted at about 03:00, was a much heavier affair, supported by sustained machine gun and mortar fire. When part of the defences were overrun, resulting in the capture of twenty men from E Company, most of them wounded, Rudder gave the order for the rest of the Rangers to retire across the coast road to the headland, where an improvised defence line was established. The order did not reach part of D Company, which found itself cut off and remained hidden in a deep drainage ditch throughout the following day.

Altogether, Rudder now had about 90 men available for the defence of the headland. With the coming of daylight, however, he was able to call on naval gunfire support and it was either because of this, or because the enemy now had more pressing matters to worry about, that no more serious attacks took place. During the afternoon supply craft reached the point with ammunition, rations and a platoon of reinforcements. By now, the strength of the German 352nd Division had been reduced to that of a single battlegroup, spread across a wide area, and its grip on the battlefield was loosening. After dark, patrols from the 116th Infantry, now in St Pierre-du-Mont, only 1,000 yards distant, worked their way through to the headland and the following morning the Rangers were relieved.

Had the battery at the Pointe du Hoe not been attacked the probability is that it would have contributed to the slaughter on Omaha Beach; equally, on Omaha itself, the Rangers had led the way. Taking place as they did only months after the disaster at Cisterna, the failure of one or both of these missions could have threatened the entire Ranger concept. As it was, their success, and that of subsequent missions, enhanced the concept to the point that in the post-Second World War army it became the responsibility of the two-battalion 75th Infantry Regiment (Rangers), which also absorbed the traditions of another famous group of men who had performed the deep penetration role in Burma, the 5307th Composite Unit (Provisional), better known to history as Merrill's Marauders.

CHAPTER NINE

Crown of Thorns – The Struggle for Hill 112, June/July 1944

Although the Allied landings in Normandy succeeded in their primary object of achieving complete strategic surprise, the price paid for this was heavy casualties and slow progress in the close bocage country beyond the beaches, which was quite unsuited to the deployment of large armoured formations. For the British, Americans and Canadians losses in men and equipment began to mount alarmingly. The Germans, however, were in little better state. The fact that they had been forbidden by the Führer himself to yield a foot of ground voluntarily meant that in addition to being exposed to overwhelming air power and a flexibly handled artillery that eclipsed in its intensity anything they might have experienced in Russia, they also remained within range of devastating naval gunfire. Consequently, the German armies in Normandy, starved of reinforcements and equipment because of the need to shore up the Eastern Front following the recent destruction of Army Group Centre, were being bled white to the point that they would be unable to fight a mobile war if the Allies broke through. Lacking the power to drive the Allies into the sea, they also knew that after a while withdrawal brought with it the risks of being swamped by the more numerous British and American armour; to Afrika Korps veterans, the situation was grimly reminiscent of the El Alamein straitjacket. For these reasons, therefore, the struggle for vital terrain in Normandy possessed a ferocity seldom equalled elsewhere during the campaign in western Europe.

To the west of Caen the little river Odon wanders through its valley and eventually joins the larger Orne south of the city. Along its southern bank is a low, rolling ridge at the eastern end of which the ground rises to a plateau forming the summit of a feature which in 1944 was marked on operational maps as Hill 112. The road from Caen to Evrecy crosses the hill from east to west, intersected to the north of the highest point by a straight track marking the course of a Roman road running from north to south, once apparently used by William the Conqueror and therefore named the Chemin du Duc Guillaume. Beside the intersection is a wayside Calvary called the Croix des Filandriers. Following the track southwards to the summit one comes across a small orchard surrounded by a tree-lined hedge with an adjoining paddock, the former bisected by a ditch running from east to west.

The hill attracts many visitors, most of whom are simply tourists, drawn to the site because it is one of the most notorious battlefields in Normandy. It is difficult for them to understand why so unimpressive a feature should have been the focus of such terrible fighting, or why Field Marshal Erwin Rommel himself should have said that he who held Hill 112 also held the key to the whole of Normandy. Once they have reached the summit, however, all becomes clear. There are commanding views of the surrounding countryside in every direction, and below the southern slopes of the hill flows the Orne, beyond which the close bocage country gives way to a relatively open landscape more suited to the operations of armoured formations than the cramped beachheads. Hill 112, therefore, was a bulwark that the Germans were prepared to defend at all costs. Montgomery, aware of this sensitivity, was determined to maintain pressure against the feature in pursuance of the Allied strategy, the essence of which was to attract the bulk of the German armour to the British sector by aggressive action while the Americans prepared for their decisive breakout to the west. His opponents, believing that the British threat was the greater, reacted exactly as he had hoped. The result was that, as the historian of the 11th Armoured Division put it, 'All the fighting for Hill 112 was cruel, and the memory of the place is bitter.'

Ever since the ending of the Second World War veterans from both sides have continued to make their way back to the hill for much the same reasons that their fathers returned to the battlefields of the Somme and Passchendaele; they wish to exorcise the sights, sounds and stench of Hill 112 from their minds and pay their respects to their many comrades who died in that place. The British veterans, with well-shone shoes and blazers bearing their regimental badges, served with the 11th Armoured, 15th (Scottish) and 43rd (Wessex) Divisions and other formations. They remember the name they gave to the whole area north of Hill 112 and especially to its northern slopes – Death Valley. Two groups make a point of visiting the summit from time to time. Both wear the Light Infantry bugle as their badge, one surmounted by a Roman 'corona muralis' and the word Jellalabad,[1] and the other by a ducal coronet and the word Cornwall. The first served with the 4th Somerset Light Infantry and they fought in the area of the crossroads near the Calvary. The second served with the 5th Duke of Cornwall's Light Infantry and they fought in and around the little wood.

Most of the German veterans belonged to the Waffen SS. They insist that they were soldiers like other soldiers but over the years they have

175

come to recognise that, because of their avowed loyalty to Hitler and Nazism and the well-documented atrocities committed by some individuals and units, neither history nor their former enemies are inclined to accept them as such. It was not simply the aggression drummed into them at SS leadership schools, for aggression is an excellent quality in a soldier and is to be respected. Rather it was that they killed and went on killing long after the need for it had ended; and because of this there were ugly incidents in Normandy when neither side took prisoners. Among themselves they preserve the memory of their elite status within the armed forces of the Third Reich when, time after time, they were thrown into the most critical battles to retrieve the situation. Those who return to Hill 112 mostly wander across its southern slopes or among the nearby villages. They refer to the hill itself as Kalvarienberg, a name which for them has a deeper significance than mere reference to the Croix des Filandriers. In the same idiom, some recall that in 1944 they had called the shell-shattered, splintered trunks of the little wood the Crown of Thorns.

Hill 112 was first fought over during Operation Epsom, by means of which Montgomery hoped to lever the enemy out of Caen, the intention being to force crossings of the Odon and Orne south-west of the city and establish a new line to the south, thus isolating the garrison and compelling its withdrawal. Operational command was delegated to Lieutenant-General Sir Richard O'Connor, commander of VIII Corps, who had won the spectacular desert victory at Beda Fomm in 1941 and only recently escaped from captivity.[2] The troops detailed included Major-General G. P. B. Roberts' 11th Armoured Division and Major-General G. H. A. MacMillan's 15th (Scottish) Division, with Major-General G. I. Thomas' 43rd (Wessex) Division in reserve. In addition to his own organic 29th Armoured Brigade, Roberts would also have the 4th Armoured Brigade under command, while the infantry received direct support from the Churchill-equipped 31st Tank Brigade. VIII Corps alone could deploy 300 guns, which were supplemented by those of the neighbouring XXX Corps on the right and I Corps on the left, giving a total of over 700. Also on call were the 15-inch guns of the monitor HMS *Roberts* and the combined fire-power of three cruisers. The operation would receive heavy air support, not simply from ground-attack squadrons but also from bombers unloading their cargoes against enemy positions on its flanks.

For much of the way VIII Corps' advance would be dominated by high ground on the right and O'Connor requested XXX Corps to clear this prior to the start of the main operation. On 25 June the 49th (West Riding) Division, supported by 8th Armoured Brigade, attacked at 04:00 and succeeded in capturing the village of Fontenay after a day-long battle. It was, however, unable to secure the feature known as the Rauray Spur, which remained a thorn in VIII Corps' side throughout the following day.

It rained heavily during the night, all but flattening the standing crops. The dawn was shrouded in ground mist and blanketed by low cloud, so that all but a fraction of the air-support programme was cancelled. Nevertheless, the flickering thunder of hundreds of guns firing in their support was comforting to the men of the 15th Division as they rose from their startlines to commence the five-mile advance to the Odon. To many, fighting their first battle, it all seemed strangely similar to the training exercises they had carried out so many times in England. The division went forward with two brigades up, the Churchills of 7th and 9th Royal Tank Regiments moving with their allotted companies just behind the leading platoons, who flushed the corn ahead for panzerfaust teams.

The terrain to be covered by the advance is described in the British Official History of the campaign.[3] 'At the start was an area of wide hedge-less fields of standing corn, falling slowly to the Mue, an insignificant stream. From there southwards the landscape is more typical of the bocage, its small farms and orchards enclosed by thick and often steeply banked hedges, its villages half hidden in hills and its outlines broken by woods and coppices. From the southwest a ridge of higher ground extends across the battlefield with spurs running northwards towards Fontenay le Pesnel and Rauray on XXX Corps' front and on VIII Corps' front towards Haut du Bosq with a final hump south-east of Cheux. The ridge conceals the ground beyond, which falls to the thickly wooded valley of the Odon and rises again to the commanding hills on the south side of the river [i.e. Hill 112] ... It is difficult country through which to attack and its broken contours and abundance of cover make it almost ideal for defence. The 12th SS Panzer Division (Hitlerjugend) and parts of the 21st and Panzer Lehr Divisions had been holding it for nearly three weeks and when the British attack opened they were familiar with its intricacies and knew every point of vantage. Infantry and machine gun positions had been chosen with skill and strengthened by wire and minefields; each was supported by two or three tanks and 88s sited in hidden positions but able to move to others if detected.'

Soon, all similarity to training vanished as return shellfire began to explode among the advancing ranks. Fire sparkled among the crops, farm-steads and woods as men began to pitch forward into the corn. Tank guns banged angrily in reply, streams of tracer from the Churchills' secondary armament slicing through the target areas while, in hundreds of small combats along the corps' front, the Scots fought their way into the outer shell of the German defences with grenade, Sten and rifle. A prisoner who had been forced to go to ground by the rolling barrage surfaced to find his unit swamped by tanks and 'furious Scotsmen hurling grenades.'

Slowly the mist dispersed and the advance continued, battalions passing through each other as objectives were secured. The German 88mm gunners began ranging with air-burst high explosive, fuzed accurately to

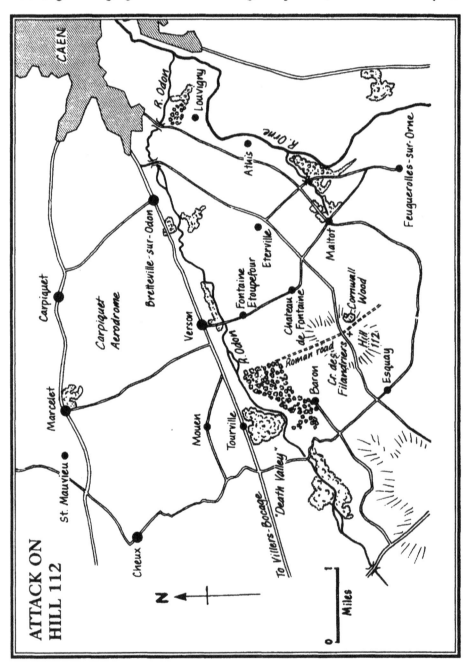

ATTACK ON HILL 112

explode directly above the Churchills' turrets with a deafening thunder-clap. It was something with which only the North African veterans were familiar, and if it did not kill the tank commander it forced him to close down and thus reduced his efficiency. The tank destroyer crews, with their open-topped turrets, were particularly vulnerable to this counter-measure.[4]

It was a confusing battle of which few participants retained any clear recollection. All that could be said was that the fighting moved slowly southwards, the British right flank being subjected the while to constant fire from the Rauray Spur and local counter-attacks. The villages of St Manvieu, Haut du Bosq and Cheux were only taken after hand-to-hand fighting with fanatical defenders. Two counter-attacks with infantry and tanks were mounted against St Manvieu, both being broken up by defen-sive fire called down by the artillery's forward observation officers. Cheux was shelled and mortared incessantly until its streets were half-choked with rubble and its new tenants, 2nd Glasgow Highlanders, had sustained over 200 casualties.

A Squadron 7 RTR was ordered to proceed through Cheux and cross the ridge separating the village from the Odon. 'The remaining tanks waddled through the streets amidst gutted and burning houses and then spread out to cross the open country beyond,' recorded Major Richard Joscelyne, the squadron's commander. 'Not until they started going up the hill was there any opposition. This came from Spandaus and snipers. The advance was nearing the crest when a well-known crack was heard – luckily a miss, but a prelude to a ghastly game of hide-and-seek, with the Churchills on one side of the crest and Panthers and PzKw IVs on the other. The only conso-lation was at that range the British 75mm could penetrate and before long brewed up a PzKw IV. Lieutenant Barrett's tank was then knocked out by a Panther. Shortly afterwards Captain Webb's tank was hit on the turret by HE, blinding both him and his gunner. The crew managed to bail out just before an armour-piercing shot followed. After another hour's snap-shoot-ing whenever a target appeared, the German tanks withdrew. The last half of the battle had not been improved by blinding rain and as dusk came tank commanders were not sorry to pull back to the forward rally.'

Meanwhile, the 43rd (Wessex) Division had been following up the Scots' advance and cleaning out the numerous pockets of resistance left behind. Roberts' 11th Armoured Division had not been called forward until noon and its 29th Armoured Brigade crossed the startline at 12:50 with 2nd Fife and Forfar Yeomanry on the right, 23rd Hussars on the left and the 3rd Royal Tank Regiment in reserve. Progress was slow. The Yeomanry were mauled by an armoured counter-attack from Rauray and 23rd Hussars, held up for a while by the congestion in Cheux, found themselves involved in 7 RTR's battle on the ridge to the south. 'As with the Churchills, so with the Shermans. As soon as the leading tank showed itself it was hit and set on fire,' recalled the regimental historian. 'Those who witnessed it will always remember the shock of seeing for the first time one of the regiment's tanks go up in flames. One moment an impregnable monster, forging irresistibly towards the enemy – the next, a terrific crack of impact, a sheet of flame, and then, where the tank had been, nothing but a helpless roaring inferno.'

At 18:00, amid torrential rain, MacMillan's reserve brigade was committed to the fighting south of Cheux but only succeeded in reaching the outskirts of Colleville. The Cromwells of 2nd Northamptonshire Yeomanry, Roberts' reconnaissance regiment, tried to seize a bridge across the Odon by coup de main but sustained casualties and were forced to abandon the attempt. Gradually, comparative silence descended upon the battlefield. VIII Corps had sustained heavy casualties but now lay within striking distance of the Odon; for their part, the Germans had also suffered severely and had only managed to contain the attack by committing the last reserves of I SS Panzer Corps.

At 05:00 on 27 June the advance was resumed in the face of repeated counter-attacks against Cheux, which had been taken over by the 43rd Division. 15th Division captured in succession Colleville, Tourville and Mondrainville, while on the XXX Corps sector 49th Division took Rauray during the afternoon. At about the same time the 2nd Argyll and Sutherland Highlanders secured a bridge over the Odon at Tourmauville, and at 18:30 the 23rd Hussars began to cross, followed by the 1st Herefordshire Regiment and the 4th Shropshire Light Infantry from 159th Brigade, 11th Armoured Division's mechanised infantry formation. A bridgehead 1,000 yards wide was consolidated, stretching from Gavrus on the right to the woods north-west of Baron on the left. As the Shermans gained the lower slopes of Hill 112 they duelled briefly with what were believed to be self-propelled guns, dimly seen near the crest; then darkness closed in.

By the morning of 28 June the weather had improved sufficiently to permit air support. The 23rd Hussars, accompanied by the 8th Battalion the Rifle Brigade, debouched from the bridgehead and began climbing the northern slopes of Hill 112, under fire from concealed tanks and anti-tank guns. Overcoming these, the Hussars and Riflemen cleared the last of the defenders from the broad summit at about noon and were able to see the nature of the prize they had taken. To the north every detail of the ground which had been fought over was clearly visible; to the north and north-east were panoramic views of Carpiquet airfield and Caen; to the south the

Orne wandered through the flat meadows of the Caen/Falaise plain; and to the west the ridge rolled away towards the towering Mont Pinçon. During the afternoon 3 RTR came up and relieved the Hussars, while 2nd Fife and Forfar Yeomanry moved onto the eastern shoulder of the hill. Following this a joint attack by 3 RTR and 8th Rifle Brigade succeeded in capturing the little wood. The German response was to plaster the hill with artillery and Minenwerfer fire. From the southern slopes the British were engaged by what were thought to be half a dozen Tigers, moving between well-concealed fire positions, although this was not confirmed.

Meanwhile, to the north of the Odon, 31st Tank Brigade and 4th Armoured Brigade, the latter consisting of the Royal Scots Greys, the 3rd County of London Yeomanry and the 44th Royal Tank Regiment, had been engaged in protecting the flanks of VIII Corps' salient. Roberts, worried that 29th Armoured Brigade's right flank seemed to be hanging in the air on Hill 112, asked the commander of 4th Armoured Brigade, Brigadier Michael (later Field Marshal Lord) Carver, to send one of his regiments south of the Odon to remedy this, and 44 RTR were detailed for the task, moving into position on 3 RTR's right rear.

During the morning of 29 June, Roberts attempted to consolidate his position within the bridgehead. 44 RTR took Hill 113, further west along the ridge, but was immediately engaged in a fierce firefight with enemy tank destroyers in which losses were sustained by both sides. Later in the day the regiment was counter-attacked and forced to abandon some of the captured ground with the loss of thirteen tanks, but succeeded in checking the enemy's progress in conjunction with the 23rd Hussars, who had been brought forward again as the pressure increased. Then, at 22:00, the British armoured units on Hill 112 received orders to abandon the feature and retire north of the Odon, leaving a smaller, infantry-held bridgehead on the south bank. Since they believed that, despite their losses, some of which had already been made good, they had it within their power to reach and cross the Orne, the orders left them shocked and bewildered, but they nevertheless complied and by dawn had completed the withdrawal.

The reasons for this apparently inexplicable development were as follows. O'Connor was already concerned that although VIII Corps had advanced five miles into enemy territory, its salient was nowhere more than two miles wide and was a natural target for the enemy to try and pinch out from the flanks. During the afternoon an officer of the 9th SS Panzer Division Hohenstaufen was captured near Haut du Bosq, and in his possession were plans for a major counter-attack towards Cheux which confirmed O'Connor's worst suspicions. Together with 10th SS Panzer

Division Frundsberg, Hohenstaufen formed SS Lieutenant-General Wilhelm Bittrich's II SS Panzer Corps. The Ultra intercept service had already warned Montgomery that this fresh, well-equipped formation was on its way south from Holland and the appearance of one of its divisions meant that the other was almost certainly in the area as well. This suited the overall Allied strategy admirably, although it simultaneously increased the tactical threat to VIII Corps' salient. Montgomery, therefore, while unable to disclose Ultra as the source of his information, was entirely sympathetic to O'Connor's misgivings and it was clearly at his urging that the salient had been shortened and VIII Corps' armour concentrated to meet the threat.

The Germans had been planning a major strategic counter-attack into the British beachhead for some time and had simply been awaiting the arrival of II SS Panzer Corps, which they believed would give it a decisive edge. Epsom, however, had caught them off balance and they were forced to bring it forward before all their formations had been fully deployed, its objective being defined as the elimination of VIII Corps by means of converging attacks on the salient. To that end, elements of no less than six armoured divisions were grouped around VIII Corps – from east to west the Hitlerjugend, 1st SS Panzer Division Leibstandarte Adolf Hitler, Frundsberg, Hohenstaufen, 2nd SS Panzer Division Das Reich, and the Panzer Lehr Division.

The counter-attack began late on 29 June and by the evening of 1 July it was over. It immediately revealed that Hitler and his cronies, working from their map tables at OKW, had not the slightest idea of what conditions in Normandy were like. Attacking in the bocage was no easier for the Germans than it had been for the British and in the close-quarter fighting the value of their tanks' superior guns and armour were seriously reduced. Tanks began to fall victim to Churchills and Shermans, to tank destroyers and anti-tank guns, and to the infantry's PIATs, fired from hedges and from among ruined buildings. Here and there, singly and in small groups, they broke into the defences only to be knocked out in the rear areas. The exact number of fighting vehicles destroyed remains unknown, but an air photograph taken a few days later showed no less than 22 burned-out hulks lying in an area of less than one square mile alone. SS Colonel-General Paul Hausser, commander of the German Seventh Army, freely admitted that 'The murderous fire from naval guns in the Channel and the terrible British artillery destroyed the bulk of our attacking force in its assembly area. The few tanks that did manage to go forward were easily stopped by the British anti-tank guns.' Hohenstaufen's report on the three days' fighting confirms what it was like to be on the receiving end:

'The division sustained extremely high casualties, mainly due to heavy enemy fire which lasted between eight to twelve hours at attrition rate. Artillery superiority forced troops to dig in. As an example, in only three hours, up to 8000 incoming shells were counted on one regimental sector alone. At one mortar battery four hundred 170cm rounds landed inside the battery position within 55 minutes.

'All attack attempts by Panzergrenadiers were foiled by well-placed enemy barrages, involving at least one artillery brigade on each objective. In the defence positions, enemy fire covered areas as far back as the Regimental command posts. The barrages included all calibres, including large naval guns from off-shore warships, with mortar batteries thickening the fire coverage in confined areas. On Panzergrenadier Regiment 19's sector, incoming shells were so dense that craters were one to two paces from each other.

'Enemy artillery fire was directed undisturbed by aerial observers in light observation aircraft, under complete enemy air superiority.'

Montgomery had every cause for satisfaction. Epsom had succeeded in its objective of concentrating the enemy's armour and writing it down. By the evening of 30 June, too, Rommel had decided to abandon Caen, only to have his decision countermanded by Hitler. The operation had cost 11th Armoured Division about 1,000 casualties, only eight per cent of the divisional strength but including one-third of the tank crews engaged. The 15th (Scottish) Division incurred 2,720 casualties, eighteen per cent of its overall strength, but among its infantry battalions the figure rose to 50 per cent. Severe as these rates of attrition were among the teeth arms, they would be eclipsed when fighting was renewed on Hill 112.

In the meantime, the German artillery and mortars had begun to bombard the Odon valley and its villages. From their vantage point on Hill 112 they were able to observe any movement as far back as Cheux and bring down accurate concentrations. Day by day casualties began to mount steadily, draining the strength of British units. Soon the once-pastoral landscape became a wilderness of ruined, gutted villages and farms, wrecked burned-out vehicles of every type, smashed trees and telegraph poles, and drifting smoke. Overlaying the constant smell of burning was the sickly stench of decomposition emanating from the bloated carcasses of dead cows. Death Valley was earning its name.

A Canadian attempt to capture Carpiquet airfield having been halted by the fanatical remnants of the Hitlerjugend, Montgomery decided that Caen could only be taken by resorting to desperate measures. On 7 July a large force of heavy bombers unloaded 2,600 tons of bombs on the ancient city, isolating the enemy holding its forward defences, which were then stormed by the British I Corps. Forty-eight hours later all of Caen had been captured save for the suburbs to the south of the Orne. It proved to be a victory without reward, for so blocked were the streets by mountains of rubble that further progress through them would be impossible for some time to come.

Simultaneously, the Allied strategy had come under renewed pressure. Lieutenant-General Omar Bradley, commanding the US First Army, told Montgomery that the Americans were only making slow progress towards the startline for their breakout; furthermore, one German armoured division, Das Reich, was known to have left the British sector for the American, and a second, Panzer Lehr, was due to follow. Determined to halt further movement, Montgomery shifted his point of attack back to the VIII Corps sector, ordering O'Connor to capture Hill 112 and several villages around its eastern slopes, then exploit to the Orne beyond.

The operation, codenamed Jupiter, was to commence on 10 July and consist of four phases. Phase I would involve the capture of the hill itself and the Château de Fontaine on its eastern slopes; Phase II required the capture of Eterville on the division's eastern flank; once this had been secured the Phase III objective would be Maltot, to the south; Phase IV would then see an exploitation south-eastwards to the Orne. Jupiter was the responsibility of Thomas's 43rd (Wessex) Division which, although it had performed a supporting role during Epsom, would be fighting its first set-piece battle. With the exception of the 1st Worcestershire Regiment, all of the division's infantry battalions were Territorial units which had spent years training for the return to the mainland of Europe. There was a leavening of experienced hands who had seen active service in North Africa and Italy, but many of the men had served together since prewar days and this, together with the local character of their units, engendered a strong sense of family. Thomas would also have the 4th Armoured and 31st Tank Brigades under command, with immediate artillery support provided by his own division's field regiments and those of the 15th (Scottish), 53rd (Welsh) and 11th Armoured Division, plus two army groups Royal Artillery, each with a number of heavy and medium regiments.[5]

Remnants of the Hitlerjugend were still holding the enemy front between Eterville and the Orne. Frundsberg held the line westwards from Eterville, including the Château de Fontaine, the summit of Hill 112 and Le Bon Repos hamlet near Esquay. To the west of Esquay, Hohenstaufen were in the process of being relieved by 277th Infantry Division, a Wehrmacht formation. The Germans' divisional artillery was still largely intact and had been supplemented by two werfer brigades, armed with the multiple projectors which were named Moaning Minnies or Sobbing Sisters by the British. During the night before Jupiter was due to commence SS-PzAbt 102, II SS Panzer Corps' heavy tank battalion, consisting of three companies each with ten Tiger Es, reached the sector and went into harbour areas near St Martin, south of Hill 112. The presence of these vehicles was to have a marked effect on the conduct of the operation, since their 88mm guns were capable of destroying any Allied tank in service at long range while their own thick frontal armour was impervious to British tank and anti-tank guns alike, although both could achieve penetration of the thinner side and rear armour at close quarters.

Phase I of Thomas's plan would be carried out by 129th Brigade (4th Battalion the Somerset Light Infantry, 4th and 5th Battalions the Wiltshire Regiment), and Phases II and III by 130th Brigade (7th Battalion the Hampshire Regiment and 4th and 5th Battalions the Dorsetshire Regiment.) H Hour was set at 05:00 on 10 July but long before that the combined British artillery had been pounding the various objectives, its effect thickened by 3-inch and 4.2-inch mortar concentrations.

On the extreme right 5th Wiltshires' two leading companies, B and D, reached their objectives near Le Bon Repos without serious difficulty and dug in. C Company passed through, its responsibility being to eliminate enemy positions beyond the crest and then fall back into an area prepared for them by A Company on the reverse slopes. On reaching the road, however, they were pinned down by fire from tanks and machine guns in Esquay. Ammunition had begun to run short when Company Sergeant Major Smith arrived with fresh supplies in a tracked carrier. Almost at once a German tank appeared on the road, shooting up the prostrate infantrymen as it ground its way slowly past. Snatching a loaded PIAT from the carrier, Smith ran forward, his progress concealed by the waist-high corn, and fired from the hip, knocking out the tank. For this achievement he was awarded the Military Medal.

A little further to the west, the battalion's Carrier Platoon, commanded by Sergeant Shorney, overran an artillery observation post that had been directing fire onto Baron, eliminating the defenders in hand-to-hand fighting. Meanwhile, C Company remained pinned down until brigade organised a diversionary attack, under cover of which it was withdrawn to Baron, being now too few in numbers to hold the position which A Company was digging. The battalion's casualties amounted 26 killed, 21 missing and 73 wounded, a heavy price to pay for an action on the flank of the main attack.

In the centre of 129th Brigade, the 4th Somersets had a 1,500-yard advance to make uphill across open country, screened only by the standing crops. Taking the old Roman road as its centreline, the battalion advanced with A and B Companies forward, each with one troop of 7 RTR's Churchills and two anti-tank guns; battalion tactical headquarters near the centreline; then C and D Companies, each again with one troop of Churchills; and finally the two remaining anti-tank guns. Following their rolling barrage closely, A and B Companies passed through many of the forward German positions without noticing them, so that when the occupants of the latter surfaced a bitterly contested action ensued. The course of this is described in the battalion history by Sergeant Hole of the Mortar Platoon:

'It is difficult to describe the attack itself, but it was more as one imagines a battle to be than any other I have seen. It was just beginning to get light and the whole scene was illuminated by burning carriers and tanks. Flamethrowers were in action. The enemy, using Nebelwerfers, was mortaring the advancing troops. Practically every weapon was in action – rifles, grenades, phosphorous, light machine guns and tanks, and the casualties were extremely heavy. Our mortars fired some 5,000 rounds.'

By the time the road had been reached the Somersets had killed over 100 of the SS Panzergrenadiers in and around their slit trenches, but their own casualties had been crippling. Three of the four rifle company commanders were down, as were most of the platoon commanders; A Company was under the temporary command of Sergeant Brewster. The commanding officer decided that the battalion was now too weak to continue to its next objective, the 100-metre contour ringing the summit, including the little wood. Instead, it dug in around the crossroads and established observation posts along the line of the road.

The supporting Churchills also suffered cruelly as Frundsberg's PzKw IVs and Panthers, reinforced by 102 Battalion's Tigers, began to intervene in the battle, and ultimately they were forced to retire into hull-down positions behind the crest. The Somersets' anti-tank gunners, however, extracted a price in return, as described by Sergeant Morgan, who commanded one of the guns:

'Two anti-tank guns were in a position guarding the flank of the left companies when a German counter-attack was put in on this front, thus catching the anti-tank guns facing the wrong way. The gun crews, quickly realising the position, swung the guns round to face the enemy. As a cornfield obscured the guns, it was not possible for sights to be laid on the tanks in the normal way. By using an unorthodox method of laying, both guns fired through the corn. So successful was this method that three tanks brewed up and a fourth retreated hurriedly with smoke pouring from its turret.'

Nearby, an Achilles tank destroyer knocked out another tank, believed to be a Tiger, which had penetrated C Company's position and was within 40 yards of battalion headquarters. In such circumstances, most tank crewmen bow to the inevitable and give themselves up. This crew, how-ever, gave every sign of wanting to continue the fight on foot and died in a burst from a Sten. Obviously, such things had to be allowed for when fighting the SS.

That was exactly what the 4th Wiltshires, on the brigade's left, were also discovering. Their objective was a track junction with the road some way to the east of the Somersets and they adopted the same formation for their advance.

'The first appearance of an easy victory was most deceptive,' wrote their historian. 'The growing corn, red with poppies, concealed numerous care-fully dug positions. These might consist of a single narrow hole contain-ing a desperate man who was quite ready to hide until several hours after the attack had passed over him, and then start sniping. Other and more elaborate positions were deep dugouts in the centre of a web of roofed-over crawl trenches leading to weapon pits ready to be manned by Spandau teams when the leading wave had passed.

'The enemy's design was clearly to cut us off from our supporting tanks and then catch us enfiladed in belts of crossfire from his Spandaus. No quarter was asked or given; no inert body could be assumed to be dead unless it bore the most easily visible wounds. Wounded SS men would throw grenades at stretcher-bearers coming up to attend them. Soon the battalion was committed to in-fighting throughout its depth. As the for-ward companies were clearing their final objectives, the reserve companies were fighting section and individual battles in the corn; flushing dugouts, verifying the deadness of corpses, and watching for the hidden sniper or by-passed Spandau teams.'

One of the worst incidents during the Wiltshires' advance occurred when 11 Platoon, commanded by Lieutenant J. P. Williams, came across an enemy position whose occupants, some of whom were wearing Red Cross brassards, raised their hands. The supporting Churchills ceased firing, but when Williams unwisely went forward to accept the surrender one of the SS men shot him at close range, inflicting a mortal wound. While Sergeant Weller went forward with the rest of the platoon to finish the business, Corporal Frank, a stretcher bearer, attended to Williams; he in turn was attacked by two wounded panzergrenadiers, both of whom he was forced to kill with his Sten in self-defence. It was just this sort of pointless, futile and ultimately counter-productive incident, repeated many times, that generated a cold, merciless fury among the British infantry.

D Company, pursuing the beaten enemy across the road, ran onto a killing ground and were forced to pull back, having sustained twenty per cent casualties. By 09:30, however, the Wiltshires were consolidating on the objective. On D Company's sector a counter-attack led by tanks was broken up by the Anti-tank Platoon and the Churchills, several enemy vehicles being knocked out. For the rest of the day the battalion was shelled and mortared constantly but further counter-attacks were stopped in their tracks by the artillery's FOOs, who took constant risks to find targets for their guns.

On the left of the divisional attack, 130th Brigade, supported by 9 RTR's Churchills, at first made excellent progress. The task of the 5th Dorsets was to capture the eastern end of the ridge of which Hill 112 formed part. Shortly after crossing the startline C Company cleared its first objective, an isolated farm named Les Daunes. D Company then fought its way through Horseshoe Wood enabling the rest of the battalion and its supporting tanks to close up to the Château de Fontaine, a large manor house which the enemy had turned into a strongpoint and which was also the headquarters of II/SS Panzergrenadier Regiment 22. The ensuing struggle for the buildings and the surrounding area was savage and during the confused fighting one of D Company's platoons became separated; its fate remained unknown and the bodies of its men were discovered a few days later. At 06:15, however, Lieutenant-Colonel B. A. Coad, commanding the 5th Dorsets, sent off a signal to the effect that the château had been taken. This proved to be a little premature, as there were still plenty of SS men willing to fight to the death among the barns and outbuildings. Snipers, too, remained active long after organised resistance had ended – when 7th Somersets from 214th Brigade moved into the château later in the day one was found 'Hidden in a junk heap in the middle of a duck pond. Another had buried himself in the mud of a wet ditch – only his head, arms and rifle were free and even these he had covered with slime and weeds. Another was burned out from a hayrick set on fire by a German shell.' Nevertheless, some 80 prisoners were captured, together with marked maps and other important documents.

The capture of the château was the signal for the 4th Dorsets to commence their attack on Eterville. As the battalion rose from its startline a junior NCO blew the Advance on his bugle. It was strange that this echo from another age should so stir men, but it did; many cheered, and one of the company commanders recalled that at that moment everyone felt glad to be present. Disregarding the shellfire directed at them, the Dorsets advanced steadily over the fields towards Eterville, close behind their rolling barrage. In support were a Churchill squadron of 9 RTR and a troop of fearsome Churchill Crocodile flamethrowing tanks from 141 Regiment RAC.

Eterville contained the headquarters of I/SS Panzergrenadier Regiment 22. Its defenders were already alarmed by the flow of fugitives from the château, bringing with them the seriously wounded commander of their IInd Battalion, and they were shaken by the intensity of the British artillery preparation. There can be little doubt, however, that it was the Crocodiles which broke their resistance and sent the survivors running from the village. The presence of these terrible weapons in Normandy had been kept a closely guarded secret. They projected powerful jets of clinging flame up to 120 yards ahead of themselves, consuming everything in their path and emitting dense clouds of black, oily smoke. Those of the Eterville garrison who saw the Crocodiles and survived were unable to form a rational evaluation. Those who were further back believed at the time that the British were using a new kind of incendiary shell.[6] Once the village had been taken, the Crocodiles were withdrawn and the 4th Dorsets consolidated the position, their own medical team working with the personnel of a captured German aid post to treat the casualties of both sides.

It was now the turn of the 7th Hampshires, commanded by Lieutenant-Colonel D. W. G. Ray. At 08:15 the battalion, supported by a Sherman squadron of 44 RTR, passed between the Château de Fontaine and Eterville, breasting the lower slopes of the spur as it advanced on Maltot with two companies from 5th Dorsets covering their right. Unknown to them, or indeed anyone else in VIII Corps, they were heading into a killing ground. Concealed in the woodland beside the Orne was a Panzergrenadier unit of Leibstandarte and harboured in a wood just east of Maltot were the remnants of Hitlerjugend's armoured regiment, with 30 tanks, including ten Panthers. These troops took a heavy toll of the advancing Hampshires and their escorting Shermans, but worse was to follow. To seal off the breakthrough at the Château de Fontaine and Eterville, SS Major General Heinz Harmel, the commander of Frundsberg, had immediately despatched the armoured battalion of SS Panzergrenadier Regiment 21, his armoured reconnaissance battalion and some of sSS PzAbt 102's Tigers to defeat the attack on Maltot.

As a result of these measures the 5th Dorsets' companies made little progress and, having sustained heavy casualties, were pulled back to the château. Some sources suggest that when the depleted Hampshires fought their way through Maltot they found themselves superimposed upon a strongly defended locality, but that is only partially correct. It was true that Leibstandarte's grenadiers were positioned in the woods to the north-east, and that Hitlerjugend's tanks, having broken harbour, had moved forward to the outskirts of the village, but the village itself had not been prepared for defence. The battalion, in fact, appears to have reached the village about the same time as Harmel's counter-attack force and it was therefore confronted with overwhelming odds from the outset. The remaining

Shermans, undergunned as they were, were quickly shot to pieces; out of four tank destroyers that courageously remained to tough it out, three were knocked out within minutes. Hit first by a mortar bomb, then by an armour-piercing round, the battalion's radio truck was wrecked, severing the rear link to brigade, with tragic results. Pushed back into Maltot, the Hampshires attempted to form a perimeter around the central crossroads, but this lacked a field of fire and they withdrew to some higher ground north of the village. Of B Company, last seen entering the woods near the river, there was no trace. Colonel Ray, though wounded twice and despite heavy shelling, continued to tour the position and offer encouragement. By 10:30 the enemy were closing in for the kill. Two of the FOOs were dead and it took some time for the call for defensive artillery fire to be answered – it was not, in fact, until the panzergrenadiers were on the point of breaking through the perimeter that an accurate barrage descended upon them, breaking up the attack. Shelling was resumed and Ray received his third wound. This time, although he was evacuated, it was to prove mortal. Because the medical officer had been killed earlier and the situation made it impossible to set up a proper aid post, many men died as a result of untended wounds. Others undoubtedly owed their lives to Captain J. L. Braithwaite of Headquarters Company who, though hit several times by flying shrapnel, continued to organise the collection and evacuation of wounded by whatever means possible, earning the subsequent award of the Military Cross. Corporal Henry also crossed a stretch of fire-swept ground to assist a group of wounded, then tackled an enemy tank crew, winning the Military Medal. The Hampshires' situation nevertheless remained hopeless and at about 15:30 they received permission to withdraw. Their losses in this, their first major action, amounted to 226 killed, wounded and missing.

At this stage a blunder of Balaclava proportions occurred, almost certainly due to a communications failure among senior officers. Even as the Hampshires were pulling out, the 4th Dorsets and one squadron of 9 RTR were ordered forward to reinforce them. For the Tigers, Panthers and PzKw IVs in and around Maltot it was like a shooting gallery. Carriers, towed anti-tank guns and tanks alike were blown apart at easy range as they moved down the forward slope; after twelve of 9 RTR's fourteen Churchills had been knocked out the two survivors retired beyond the crest to give what fire support they could from hull-down positions. As if this was not bad enough, a squadron of RAF rocket-firing Typhoons, observing movement in an area now reported clear of friendly troops, swooped down on the attackers, inflicting wounds and death. Incredibly, disorganised as they were, the Dorsets fought their way into Maltot, where they remained for the next three hours. When the order to withdraw was given it did not reach those in the village itself, the result being that many of them were taken prisoner. Of the battalion that had responded to the bugle that morning, then stormed Eterville and Maltot, all that remained were five officers and some 70 exhausted men.

For the moment, 130th Brigade was finished and of Thomas's third brigade, the 214th, the 1st Worcesters were due to relieve the 4th Wiltshires that night and the 7th Somersets were sent up to reinforce the line at the Château de Fontaine, leaving only the 5th Duke of Cornwall's Light Infantry in reserve. Fortunately, the 46th (Highland) Brigade from 15th Division had also been placed under Thomas's command and from this the 9th Cameronians moved into Eterville. As a result of these measures, when the Germans mounted counter-attacks on the Château de Fontaine-Eterville sector during the night these were defeated.

At about noon, while the Hampshires were engaged in their deadly struggle at Maltot, Rommel arrived at the headquarters of General Hans Eberbach, commanding Panzer Group West. Both were deeply worried by the situation which had arisen at Hill 112, but Eberbach was able to reassure the field marshal that a major counter-attack would be delivered during the next few hours. Hohenstaufen, having just been relieved, was to be thrown into the fight again, counter-attacking through and in conjunction with Frundsberg to recover all the lost ground. Subsequently, he telephoned Bittrich at II SS Panzer Corps emphasising that Hill 112 was the pivotal point of the whole position and must not be given up in any circumstances; the loss of Eterville might be borne, but not that of Hill 112.

At about 15:00 Thomas conferred with the commanders of 129th and 214th Brigades. There was general agreement that Maltot could not be secured until Hill 112 was in British hands. Therefore, argued Thomas, 'The hill must be taken no matter what the cost!' The only uncommitted infantry battalion left to 43rd Division was the 5th Duke of Cornwall's Light Infantry, and it was decided to bring this forward at once and launch an attack on the summit through the position held by the 4th Somersets.

The Cornishmen were commanded by Lieutenant-Colonel R. W. James, who, for all that he was only 26 years of age, possessed the gift of leadership and the ability to inspire his officers and men. James had joined a territorial battalion of the Somerset Light Infantry some years prior to the outbreak of war and progressed steadily, achieving the rank of major in September 1942. Since then he had served as a company commander with 4th Somersets until, just fourteen days earlier, he had been appointed to command 5 DCLI.

In the prevailing circumstances it was natural that he should set up his rear tactical headquarters within the perimeter of his old battalion, and there at 17:00 he met Major Richard Joscelyne, whose Churchills would support his attack, to carry out as thorough a reconnaissance of the objective as the limited time available would permit. When, two hours later, James held his orders group, few remained under any illusions as to the grim nature of the task ahead.

The battalion was to take the old Roman road as its centreline and advance with two companies forward, C Company (Captain Blackwell) on the right and B Company (Major Vawdrey) on the left, supported respectively by D Company (Major J. E. E. Fry) and A Company (Major Roberts). The attack had been timed to commence at 20:30 and in order to take full advantage of the heavy preliminary bombardment falling on the little wood, the companies moved forward promptly. This was understandable, since time was of the essence, but the tanks were still arriving and, instead of joining their designated companies they were forced to tag along behind the supporting wave. The unfortunate consequences of this were immediately apparent when concentrated machine gun fire scythed through B Company's ranks, killing Major Vawdrey and inflicting severe casualties. Major Roberts at once deployed A Company and brought it forward with some of the tanks, killing or capturing the machine gun teams. B Company then took possession of the forward edge of the wood. On the right opposition had been less severe, enabling C Company to establish itself in the south-west corner of the wood and the adjoining paddock. Both reserve companies began to dig in along the line of the ditch bisecting the wood, the work being made the more difficult by numerous tree roots. James set up his forward tactical headquarters nearby, while the battalion signallers reeled out a field telephone cable to the rear headquarters with the 4th Somersets. The DCLI's 6-pounder anti-tank guns, reinforced with four 17-pounder anti-tank guns from the divisional anti-tank regiment, came up and were emplaced on the flanks of and behind the rifle companies. Observing that only 40 survivors remained to B Company, Roberts pulled them back to cover the left flank of A Company, although this meant abandoning the forward edge of the wood.

The Germans reacted with characteristic vigour to the fall of Hill 112. The major counter-attack discussed by Eberbach and Bittrich that afternoon had been seriously delayed by traffic congestion when Hohenstaufen's vehicles, attempting to move onto Frundsberg's sector, ran into the latter's transport echelons which, having just completed their resupply tasks, were travelling in the opposite direction along the narrow lanes. Nevertheless, gathering such tanks and grenadiers as were immediately available, Harmel strove to recover the summit with an immediate counter-attack. This was defeated by the combined firepower of the supporting artillery and Churchills, and by the blaze of sustained small-arms fire along the Cornishmen's front. Like all light infantry regiments, the DCLI took a pride in their rapid-fire, accurate musketry techniques and, between the bursting of shells, Roberts could hear the section commanders ordering their men to hold their fire and mark their targets until they were certain of a kill. Somewhere in the gathering darkness a lone Panther, its supporting infantry pinned down on the slopes below, fell victim to a PIAT.

At 23:30, following standard procedure, James released the Churchills, which moved back carefully through the uncollected wounded to their forward rally area. The accepted doctrine at the time was that tanks could not fight at night, and indeed this was true in the majority of situations, but in view of what happened Joscelyne always regretted that his squadron had not remained on the hill.

No one is quite certain how many counter-attacks the DCLI threw back that night and the following day; their own history records twelve, but others give a higher figure. What is certain is that as elements of Hohenstaufen entered the battle their intensity steadily increased. For the defenders, the secret of success lay in separating the German armour from its infantry by means of artillery and mortar barrages and aimed small-arms fire, illuminated by the eerie glow of slowly descending parachute flares. For those controlling the fire of mortars and guns the difficulty lay in obtaining a clear view of the hill's eastern and southern slopes on which the German attacks were forming up.

James, whose personal presence had inspired his companies as each attack came in, solved the problem by climbing a tree at intervals and using his field telephone to signal the location of targets. It was reckless in the extreme, but he was not the sort of officer to ask anyone to do anything which he would not undertake himself.

The second counter-attack came in at about midnight. The enemy's tanks took up position on the flanks of the wood and raked it continuously with machine gun fire while their infantry attempted, unsuccessfully, to press home a frontal assault. Thereafter, further attacks came in so regularly that they seemed to merge into each other. At one point a number of 102 Battalion's Tigers broke into the wood but, their crews being almost blind and bereft of the close support of the panzergrenadiers, all they could do was wander aimlessly among the trees, firing at targets they could not properly see. Major Roberts and Sergeant Hill, seeing one halted within fifteen yards of battalion headquarters, tackled it with a PIAT at close range. The bomb failed to detonate but those within took the hint and moved on. Two more meandered into the area of the 4th Wiltshires' C Company. One overturned a priceless mug of hot tea, the furious owner of which, Private Pipe, believing the tank to be British, told its commander just what he thought of him. Suddenly discovering their real identity, the company commander, Major A. S. P. Jeans, engaged them with a PIAT and grenades, and they trundled off into the 4th Somersets's area, where one crashed through a hedge and straight over Captain Perks' slit trench without harming him, although its tracks crushed his compass and binoculars. By the light of a 2-inch mortar flare a 17-pounder anti-tank gun scored a hit on one of the pair without disabling it and they both vanished into the darkness; curiously, neither of these Tigers had taken any offensive action during their travels and the probability is that their crews, frightened, disoriented and unable to see more than a yard or two beyond their vision slits, were only too glad to be on their way home. Within the wood itself two more Tigers came close to dealing each other their death blows. One actually got off two shots at close range but missed, the gunner's nervous fingers having failed to adjust the complex optical sight, before the shaken commander of his target got off a recognition flare.

Then, quite suddenly, the Tigers were gone. The fact that they had penetrated the little wood had led to an over-optimistic report reaching Panzer Group West to the effect that Hill 112 was once more in German hands, and they were recalled. Once the truth was realised an even heavier attack was planned for the following morning.

In the meantime, James had asked for assistance. His Cornishmen, had suffered a steady toll of casualties from constant artillery and mortar fire, and from about 03:00 they were harassed by some of Hohenstaufen's machine gun teams which had established themselves in the dry stone wall at the forward edge of the wood, approximately 100 yards from the British trenches.

The response to James's request came in the form of a squadron of Royal Scots Greys, whose counter-attack bore a tragic similarity to their charge at Waterloo. At first, as then, all had gone well. Their Shermans had crossed the shallow summit and roared past both flanks of the little wood to silence or drive out the troublesome machine gunners. Unfortunately, this brought them within view of the enemy armour in the valley below and within minutes four had been set ablaze and a fifth exploded, its turret spiralling skywards before landing on its roof beside the burning hull. Wisely, the squadron commander decided to retire beyond the crest and give such support as he could from hull-down positions.

The German attacks began again at 06:15, converging from the directions of St Martin to the east and Esquay to the south. Initially they were made by the panzergrenadiers of both divisions, strongly supported by artillery, mortars and machine guns, but they were decimated by the British defensive barrages and then cut to pieces by the Cornishmen's rifle and light machine gun fire. There were times when the summit and slopes of the hill were invisible to German observers because of bursting shells. There were times, too, when the British FOOs called in their barrages to within 150 yards of their own position; one such was Lieutenant King, who, with complete disregard for his own safety, stood on an exposed bank the better to control his guns and is believed to have been killed by a splinter from a British shell.

As the morning wore on, 102 Battalion's Tigers returned to spearhead the attacks while other tanks engaged the wood with high explosive, their shells bursting among the trees and sending a shower of jagged splinters hissing downwards into the slit trenches, for which there had been no time to provide headcover. The southern thrust of the German attack ran into a particularly violent storm of artillery fire controlled by a Lysander air OP, pinning down the panzergrenadiers. The Tigers, though enjoying some protection in the sunken lane up which they were moving from Esquay, were hit repeatedly. The high explosive shells could not penetrate the thick armour, but they could cause damage to the exposed running gear and the transmitted shock of exploding medium calibre rounds could cause internal problems such as ruptured fuel, coolant and lubrication lines or unseat machinery that would ultimately render the vehicle inoperable. For the moment, however, the Tigers were still capable of fighting. They broke into the paddock, blowing apart the anti-tank guns that tried to oppose them, then, while some engaged the Greys' Shermans in a one-sided duel, others systematically destroyed the DCLI's Carrier Platoon, which had come forward to deliver supplies and evacuate as many of the wounded as possible. Yet, with their own infantry still pinned down and mindful of their experience during the night, they did not attempt to penetrate the wood. One Tiger did not return from the attack and it may well have been this which approached the Somersets and was immobilised by one of the Greys' Shermans, almost certainly a Firefly.[7] When the crew came forward to surrender a few men opened fire on them, killing three. It was the act of those who were in action for the first time and had not yet come to terms with the bestiality of war. Having, in earlier attacks, seen friends of years' standing literally blown apart in their trenches by the main armament of the enemy's tanks, they were at that moment possessed by a blinding hatred for their crews. What had occurred was uncharacteristic and it was subsequently regretted.

It was about this time that Colonel James, having again climbed a tree the better to spot for the gunners, was shot dead by a burst from a German machine gun. The news that their young and popular commanding officer had been killed deeply saddened the Cornishmen, but it remains unclear precisely what happened next. Certainly there were very few senior officers left in the battalion and, for the moment, central control seems to have lapsed. The men were terribly tired, having been three nights without sleep, and their dead lay throughout the wood. Somehow, the rumour spread that orders to withdraw had been received and the companies complied; the source of the rumour has never been identified but one theory suggests that it might have been German.

The 4th Somersets, dug in some way to the rear, had become accustomed to the trickle of Cornish walking wounded passing through their position, but at about 11:00 this suddenly expanded as groups of clearly unwounded men, some running, others supporting wounded comrades, began heading for the rear. The suggestion of panic was emphasised by a DCLI officer trying to halt them; no one could understand what he was shouting because part of his lower jaw had been shot away. One of the Somersets' platoon sergeants, noting how unsettled his own men were by the sight, threatened to 'shoot the first bastard who moved.' None of the 'bastards' did. It was Lieutenant-Colonel C. G. Lipscomb, commanding the Somersets, who recognised that the Cornishmen were not out of hand but simply confused, exhausted and near the end of their physical and mental resources. He rallied them quietly and divided them into their company groups, none of which were more than a platoon strong. Major Roberts, Major Fry, Captain Gorman, the adjutant, and the few remaining senior NCOs then led them back to the wood, where they reoccupied their positions. Half a dozen or so panzergrenadiers had moved into the trees during their absence but they had had enough and quickly surrendered. Meanwhile, anxious to reassure the Somersets that the crisis had passed, Lipscomb and Brigadier Mole seated themselves on their walking sticks and chatted amiably for a while, apparently heedless of their own safety.

For a short period the DCLI were left in comparatively undisturbed possession of the wood. At about 14:00, however, the enemy fire intensified in obvious preparation for another attack. This time it came in from the direction of Maltot, spearheaded by Hohenstaufen's assault gun battalion.[8] Some anti-tank guns remained to the Cornishmen on this flank but because of the configuration of the slope they could not be depressed sufficiently to engage the low-slung vehicles. The artillery was requested to lay smoke and under cover of this Lieutenant Bellamy had one of the 17-pounders manhandled forward until it would bear. Despite the fact that he and his crew were only able to fire a few rounds before the gun was put out of action, they seem to have scored several kills, for in his report the German commander records that three of his assault guns were knocked out and three more received direct hits, the latter probably by artillery fire. That left four to complete the task, but in the event it was to prove sufficient.

By 15:00 Roberts had been wounded and the battalion's strength had shrunk to about 100 men. Gorman had been despatched to inform the brigade commander personally that the position was becoming untenable. The assault guns were closing in, slamming high explosive shells into the wood and raking it with machine gun fire. With casualties mounting and close quarter anti-tank defence now limited to a handful of PIAT bombs, Fry, now the senior surviving officer, sent a runner to brigade with the recommendation that the remnant of the battalion should either be relieved or permitted to withdraw behind the crest. No answer was received.

He was now on the horns of a terrible dilemma. To abandon the position without orders could result in serious personal consequences; on the other hand, the Army's code would support him if, as the man on the spot, he acted with considered judgement in the light of the prevailing circumstances. Only two alternatives existed. Either he could withdrew his men, who would then form a nucleus upon which the battalion could be reconstructed; or, he could fight on in the certain knowledge that the position would be overrun in a few minutes. Whatever he decided, the wood was about to fall into German hands, anyway. In the circumstances, he decided to withdraw and, under cover of a smoke screen, the Cornishmen pulled back, carrying their wounded with them, to take up a new position behind the 4th Somersets. For the rest of his life Fry was haunted by the thought that he should have hung on and fought to the bitter end, but that would only have resulted in annihilation to no purpose. As it was, 5 DCLI had incurred 320 casualties in fifteen more or less continuous hours of battle, and of these 93 lay dead in and around the little wood; with justifiable pride, the regimental history records that only one man was taken prisoner. Incredibly, the heroism and tenacity of so many of the battalion's officers and men was not recognised by the award of a single decoration.

The withdrawal of 5 DCLI marked the virtual end of Operation Jupiter. True, the summit of Hill 112 remained a no-man's-land, but the operation had achieved its strategic objective of tying down the German armour. Fighting erupted again during the night of 15 July and continued for the next fortnight. While the summit of the hill was masked by smoke and high explosive, the 43rd, 15th and 53rd (Welsh) Divisions in succession, supported by the Churchills of 31 and 34 Tank Brigades and Crocodiles, mounted a series of heavy raids on the nearby villages – Le Bon Repos, Esquay, Evrecy and Maltot. These, as intended, provoked fierce counter-attacks which further wrote down the German armour. On 18 July

Operation Goodwood, a drive by three British armoured divisions north of Caen, was halted by a strong anti-tank defence but convinced the German High Command that the Allies intended breaking out on the British sector. On 25 July the American breakout, codenamed Cobra, began and soon the US Third Army was sweeping round the German left flank. Simultaneously, the British and Canadians were driving in the enemy's right. By the middle of August the German armies in Normandy, held fast within the jaws of a trap, had been systematically destroyed.

It would be difficult to overemphasise the part played by the sustained and costly pressure maintained on the Hill 112 sector in achieving this complete victory. Forced by events elsewhere to withdraw, II SS Panzer Corps left the area during the night of 3/4 August. A few days later some members of 5 DCLI's Assault Pioneer Platoon erected a board on the summit showing the regimental badge and the words CORNWALL HILL JULY 10th–11th 1944. Other regiments, too, felt that they had some claim on the hill but they knew what the Cornishmen had been through and not only let the board stand but also referred to the little wood as Cornwall Wood in their own histories. Later, the 43rd Division, which was to fight many battles but none so bitter as that for Hill 112, erected its own granite memorial on the same site.

The story had a postscript. In 1945, following the German surrender, Major Roberts became commandant of a prisoner of war camp and had the opportunity of interrogating two SS men who had fought at Hill 112. One had served in 102 Heavy Tank Battalion and he recalled that of the nine or ten Tigers that had attacked the wood during the night only two returned undamaged. The other was one of Frundsberg's panzergrenadiers, who stated that the regiment which had borne the brunt of the fighting had been reduced to five or six men a company. In fact, by the time of the final German collapse in Normandy Hohenstaufen and Frundsberg had each been reduced to the strength of a weak infantry battalion with only the former retaining a few of its tanks and guns. The once-mighty II SS Panzer Corps, now a skeleton of its former self, was sent to Holland to refit.

Notes

1. See *Against All Odds!* Chapter 2.
2. See *Seize and Hold* Chapter 5.
3. Ellis, Major L. F., et al, *Victory in The West* Volume 1, *The Battle of Normandy*, HMSO, London, 1962.
4. The tank destroyer was essentially an anti-tank gun housed in an open-topped turret mounted on a tank chassis. Those serving with the British and Canadian armies in Normandy were the M10, known in British service as the Wolverine, armed with a 3-inch high velocity gun, and the Achilles, which was the M10 upgunned with a British 17-pounder anti-tank gun. The Royal Artillery, responsible for anti-tank defence at the high-

er levels, was lukewarm about the concept of tank destroyers but recognised that in the close bocage country they not only possessed the ability to engage over the hedge-topped earthen banks but could also be got forward to support the infantry in a newly-captured position much more quickly than towed guns; during set-piece infantry/tank attacks, too, their powerful armament went some way to redressing the balance between the undergunned Churchills and the enemy's armour. For these reasons, therefore, the Royal Artillery's anti-tank regiments were equipped with a proportion of tank destroyers.

5. The Army Group Royal Artillery (AGRA) generally contained one heavy and three medium regiments but was flexible and could also include one or more field or anti-air-craft regiments with the latter firing on ground targets. AGRAs were usually allocated on the scale of one per corps plus one in reserve.

6. The Crocodile's flame fuel was housed in an armoured trailer. This apart, the vehicle was virtually indistinguishable from a Churchill gun tank save at very close quarters. The defenders of Eterville can hardly be blamed for failing to evaluate the purpose of the trailer.

7. A Sherman upgunned with a British 17-pounder, usually issued on the basis of one per tank troop.

8. Assault gun units were primarily intended for the close support of infantry operations and were composed of artillerymen. There were many types of assault guns, the most common being based on the PzKw III chassis, a 75mm gun with a limited-traverse mounting being housed in a low, enclosed superstructure at the front of the vehicle.

9. Both divisions were still refitting at Arnhem in September and were responsible for the isolation and defeat of the British 1st Airborne Division during Operation Market Garden. During these operations the 43rd (Wessex) Division again clashed with Frundsberg in the area between Nijmegen and Arnhem. Subsequently, although Hohenstaufen took part in the Battle of the Bulge, neither SS division achieved much and both ended their days on the Eastern Front.

CHAPTER TEN

Dak To –
Ngok Kom Leat and Hill 875,
South Vietnam, 1967

For most of its existence the American Military Assistance Command in Vietnam was haunted by the spectre of Dien Bien Phu, the battle which in 1954 had resulted in the destruction of the cream of the French strategic reserve in Indochina and led directly to the establishment of the communist regime in the north. With a vociferous anti-war lobby at home and a largely hostile media covering its conduct of the war, the one thing MACV dreaded most was the overrunning of a major American unit, the result of which would be to generate such intense political pressure in Washington that the United States' withdrawal from Indochina would take place before the South Vietnamese Army (ARVN) had been trained to a standard at which it could be expected to cope with its opponents.

In one respect, however, the approach of American commanders in the field differed radically from that of the French. They recognised from the outset that beyond the cities and towns the holding of ground for its own sake meant nothing and was therefore counter-productive; as far as warfare in the Vietnamese countryside was concerned the terms front, rear and flanks were meaningless. What mattered most was bringing the enemy to battle wherever he was encountered and killing him at a rate he found unacceptable. Fire support bases (FSBs) were established throughout the country, capable of supporting each other or infantry operations in the immediate area. Any contact would result in the communist guerrillas being shelled, attacked from the air and their retreat cut off by rapid response units airlifted into a blocking position by helicopters.

The US Army deployed two specialist airmobile formations to South Vietnam. The larger of these, the 1st Cavalry Division (Airmobile), distinguished itself during a series of hard-fought battles in the Ia Drang valley, Pleiku Province, during October and November 1965. The second was the 173rd Airborne Brigade (Separate), consisting of the 503rd Parachute Infantry Regiment,[1] which retained and sometimes used its parachute capability, and supporting arms.

The brigade had already seen action in the Iron Triangle, to the north of Saigon, and in Operation Junction City when, in early November 1967, it began moving to Dak To in the Central Highlands to reinforce Major-General William R. Peers' 4th Infantry Division, which was coming under increasing pressure from local Viet Cong and North Vietnamese Army (NVA) units. The terrain consisted of heavily forested hills up to 3,000 feet in height, separated by steep valleys containing free-flowing streams. To most of the Sky Soldiers, as the brigade's men called themselves, the move was welcome. They had served there briefly in midsummer and been grateful to be released from the energy-sapping humidity of the plains. Even so, in November the noonday temperature in the Central Highlands could reach beyond 90°F, dropping to what felt a distinctly chilly 55°F during the night.

The intelligence picture at this period indicated the arrival in the area of the NVA's regular 1st Division, consisting of four rifle regiments (the 24th, 32nd, 66th and 174th) with a total strength of between 4,500 and 6,000 men, and one artillery regiment equipped with heavy mortars. A deserter indicated that the division's objectives were the Special Forces Camps at Dak To and Ben Het, which had long been a thorn in the communists' side. After preliminary clashes between 4th Division troops and the 32nd Regiment, however, the NVA forces simply disappeared and it was concluded that, having taken note of the 173rd Airborne's arrival, they had simply abandoned their attack on the camps and gone to ground. As far as it went, this conclusion was correct, although it failed to take into account that the NVA commander might well have alternative plans. Like the Americans, he considered the holding of ground to be pointless; in fact, such a concept ran quite contrary to his army's theory of revolutionary warfare. On the other hand, he was also well aware of the American political sensitivity to heavy casualties and, knowing that his opponents would mount search and destroy operations against his troops, he decided to use these to entrap battalion-sized groups. A number of hilltops west of Dak To had already been fortified in depth. Mutually supporting bunkers protected by alternate layers of logs and earth several feet deep were linked by communication trenches and concealed by allowing the natural jungle cover to grow back over them. Aware that these hilltops were natural objectives for American search and destroy operations, the NVA commander visualised a situation in which the attackers would be pinned down in front of the defences, taken under additional fire by mortars on adjacent hills, then attacked from the rear by a manoeuvre force concealed nearby, and wiped out. This provided a reversal of the normal situation prevailing in Vietnam in that it was the communists who were seeking to bring the Americans to battle with the object of inflicting massive casualties.

To some extent they would be assisted by the 173rd Airborne's own phi-losophy, a product of rigorous training that instilled aggression from the outset, which more often than not led to attacks being delivered 'right up the middle.' There were, in fact, many officers in the brigade who felt that, whatever the value of aggression, this approach was not suited to every sit-

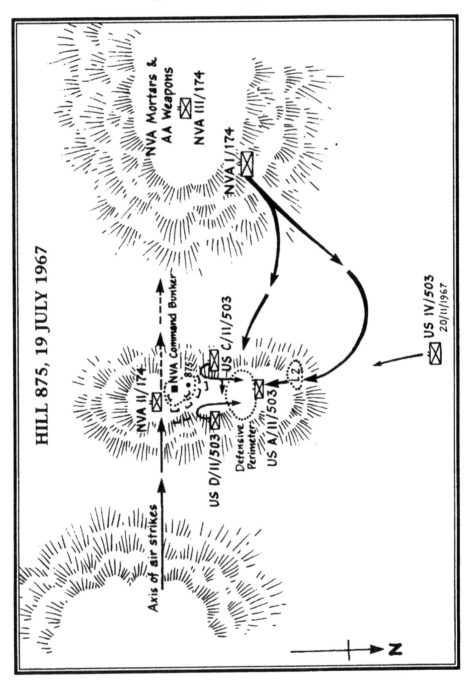

uation in Vietnam and could lead to needless casualties, contrasting it with the tactics employed by line infantry, who would execute small scale probes until the extent of an enemy position had been established, then neutralise it with sustained artillery and air strikes before going in.

The first of these battles began on 2 November when Lieutenant-Colonel James H. Johnson's IV/503rd Parachute Infantry was ordered to investigate a possible contact on a hill some four and a half miles south of Ben Het. The operation was not airmobile and the heavily laden company columns, each of which was accompanied by a Montagnard Civilian Irregular Defence Group (CIDG)[2] section which acted as guides, moved cautiously along the jungle trails behind their points. In addition to their own personal weapons – M16 rifle, M60 light machine gun or M79 grenade launcher – each rifleman carried 500 rounds of rifle ammunition, a 200-round belt for the M60, four fragmentation and two smoke grenades, and one or more directional Claymore mines; the machine gunners were further burdened by 2,000 rounds of M60 ammunition, slung around their shoulders in belts. Basic equipment, including a change of clothing, several days' rations and three full canteens of water, added another 50 pounds to the load.

While the battalion was still approaching its objective during the morning of 6 November, the brigade commander, Brigadier-General Leo Schweiter, had decided to move some of the supporting artillery forward by creating a new fire support base on a feature designated Hill 823, using air strikes and shellfire to fell the timber on the summit and create a landing zone into which the guns could be lifted by helicopter. Simultaneously, he instructed Johnson's companies to converge on the feature and secure it.

At about 11:30 Captain Thomas H. Baird's D Company came across a single strand of enemy field telephone cable and, nearby, a pith helmet, a sure sign of the presence of North Vietnamese regulars. After cutting the cable they followed it up a hill named Ngok Kom Leat, a mile to the north of Hill 823. In the lead was the company's 2nd Platoon, commanded by First Lieutenant Michael D. Burton, a graduate of the Virginia Military Academy. Moving warily up the undulating trail that wound up the spur to the summit, Burton's platoon clover-leafed at regular intervals into the jungle on either side to clear potential ambush sites. It was a slow, painstaking business but very necessary, and by now most of the older hands' instincts were warning them that the enemy were somewhere in the trees and all round them.

Overhead in his command helicopter Lieutenant-Colonel Johnson had reached the conclusion that so slow was the progress of all his companies that none of them would reach Hill 823 that day. He therefore arranged for Captain George Baldridge's B Company to be picked up and air-lifted into the embryonic landing zone, leaving A and C Companies to continue their march towards the hill while D Company completed its reconnaissance of Ngok Kom Leat.

At about 13:00 Burton's point squad came across the spoor left by several bare feet, a roll of field telephone cable and some fresh faeces. The platoon continued upwards to a point where the spur broadened out onto the summit. A few men caught fleeting glimpses of North Vietnamese soldiers in green uniforms and then the entire company went to ground as it was struck by a murderous hail of concentrated AK 47 fire that clipped leaves and branches from above and shredded stands of bamboo.

Some casualties were incurred at once. Baird was hit three times in rapid succession, one round striking the stock of his rifle, another an ammunition pouch while the third shattered his wrist. A morphine injection reduced the pain somewhat, enabling him to concentrate his platoons into a perimeter defence. At about the same time his artillery Forward Observation Officer, Lieutenant Lawrence Clewly of B Battery III/319th Artillery, was hit in the rump and incapacitated. His task was promptly taken over by his signaller, Specialist 4 Ernie Fulcher, who quickly began landing protective shells around Burton's platoon, as did Specialist 4 James Duffy with the company mortars.

Such was the noise level that Baird could hardly distinguish the sound of his own men's return fire from that of the enemy. The North Vietnamese were now pressing attacks to very close quarters and barely being contained. Baird spoke to Johnson on the radio, requesting an immediate air strike. The latter, unable to see through the jungle canopy and unaware of the scale of the enemy attack, declined on the grounds that his air priority was to continue clearing the LZ on Hill 823. Baird's reply, urgent, angry and insubordinate, made it clear that unless it received immediate air support D Company would almost certainly be overrun.

Now fully aware of the situation, Johnson took decisive action. He called in several of the F-100 Super Sabres that were strafing Hill 823, requested further air strikes and close support from helicopter gunships and, while proceeding with B Company's lift onto Hill 823, ordered A and C Companies to march to the sound of the guns on Ngok Kom Leat.

The enemy's determination was not blunted by the F-100s' first bomb run and they kept attacking Burton's platoon until their strength was whittled away by a combination of shelling, air attacks, helicopter gunships and the defenders' fire. Thereafter they engaged in periodic firefights interspersed with sniping from the treetops. The snipers were difficult to locate but the sight of one dangling head-down by a rope tied to his ankle was encouraging.

At about 15:00 the enemy began switching his attacks to the opposite end of the company perimeter, held by Lieutenant Robert Allen's platoon, which had originally formed the rear of the company column. Allen had a feeling that a large number of North Vietnamese had also followed D Company up the spur and were just waiting for the right moment to launch their attack. He had, however, used the time available to put his men in good fire positions, so that when that attack came in it was beaten off without undue difficulty. After that, air and artillery support was adjusted to cover the threat.

Meanwhile, Captain James Muldoon, commanding A Company, had received Johnson's order to go to C Company's assistance at about 14:00. A Company was then located approximately one mile to the east of Ngok Kom Leat and its route would take it down a hillside, across a stream and then uphill towards Baird's position. Muldoon ordered his CIDG guides to lead but, once within sound of the fighting, the latter used every excuse to slow down and stop. At length, losing patience, he put one of his own platoons into the lead and ordered his men to drop their rucksacks for the sake of speed. Just how great had been the delay caused by the CIDG was emphasised by the fact that Muldoon had instructed a detached rifle squad, consisting of Sergeant David Terrazas and six men, to make their own way independently to A Company's position, and that they had worked their way into Allen's sector of the perimeter by 15:30, fully an hour and a half before the rest of the company arrived.

Shortly after Terrazas' squad came in, a jet howled directly over Allen's position. Glancing up, Allen saw a napalm canister splintering its way through the branches towards him and ducked back into cover. It burst just outside the perimeter, the worst effects being masked by a large stand of bamboo. Even so, he was struck by a searing wave of heat and felt the breath being all but sucked out of his body. For the moment he was unaware of the effect it had had on the enemy, but a little later the charred bodies of fifteen NVA soldiers were found, their blackened weapons still in their hands. Clearly, his platoon would have been attacked from close quarters in strength had it not been for the providential, albeit dangerously misdirected, release of the missile.

With the arrival of A Company the enemy pressure eased. Muldoon's weapons platoon cleared a landing zone and from 18:30 until 22:00 a succession of helicopters lifted out the more seriously wounded, including Baird. During the night the enemy occasionally fired into the perimeter but was kept at bay by the presence overhead of a C-47 gunship which shredded suspected forming-up areas with its terrible fire.[3] By morning the NVA had gone, taking with them their wounded and such of their dead as they could reach. Even so, 28 bodies were left on the battlefield, together with a number of weapons, including six machine guns. Items collected from the dead indicated that they belonged to the II/66th Regiment. A Company sustained the loss of one killed and two wounded, D Company five killed and eighteen wounded.

Elsewhere, Captain William Connolly's C Company had run into an enemy bunker complex while moving towards Ngok Kom Leat. By the time this had been dealt with night had fallen and the company went into leaguer for the night, joining Muldoon at noon the following day. Captain George Baldridge's B Company had been successfully lifted onto Hill 823, later designated FSB 15. Having established a defensive perimeter on the summit, Baldridge sent out a two-man patrol to cover the enemy's most likely line of approach. Hardly had this left the perimeter than both men were shot down, as were five more who went out to rescue them. The first of several North Vietnamese attacks followed at once, the enemy using AK 47s, machine guns, mortars and rocket-propelled grenades as they pressed to within yards of the defenders. The Americans beat off every assault, using their own mortars to deadly effect, and were able to call in artillery, air and gunship support. Their casualties, however, were heavy and included Baldridge, wounded. The enemy remained in close proximity during the night but withdrew shortly before dawn, leaving over 100 dead behind. Examination of the bodies confirmed that they, too, belonged to the 66th Regiment and that they were equipped with brand new weapons.

On their own, the battles for Ngok Kom Leat and Hill 823 did not set a sufficiently recognisable pattern for the Americans to recognise that the NVA was now pursuing a deliberate policy of defensive entrapment. For the communists, foiled in their attempt to wipe out D Company, the lesson was that once the American assault had been halted it was imperative that their own attack should delivered into the enemy rear at the earliest possible moment, before he had time to organise his defences and call in supporting arms.

By the middle of the month Brigadier-General Schweiter believed, quite correctly, that in its encounters with his brigade at Ngok Kom Leat and elsewhere the NVA's 66th Regiment had been seriously mauled and was heading for the sanctuary of the Cambodian border. When, on 18 November, a Special Forces patrol reported a major contact in the area of Hill 875, situated just three miles west of the border and eight miles south of the point where South Vietnam, Laos and Cambodia meet, he reached the conclusion that the enemy were the last remnants of the 66th and decided to eliminate them by despatching his nearest battalion, Major James Steverson's

II/503rd, to secure the feature. In fact, Hill 875 was held by the newly arrived and barely blooded 174th Regiment, which had its IInd Battalion on the hill and the other battalions concealed nearby.

II/503rd was operating with only A, C and D Companies, B Company having been withdrawn because of casualties sustained in earlier actions. The previous afternoon it had stumbled, quite by chance, on an abandoned enemy base camp in deep jungle, capable of housing up to 1,000 men. In addition to the bivouacs, bunkers had been dug into a hillside and caves put to use as dressing stations, their floors cluttered with blooded bandages and medical impedimenta. All the evidence suggested the camp had been evacuated very recently and, that being the case, there was obviously a substantial NVA presence in the area.

The battalion remained on the site overnight and patrolled the surrounding area next morning without coming into contact with the enemy. Major Steverson arrived during the afternoon to brief his company commanders for the assault on Hill 875, which would take place the following day. After an air strike had softened up the objective with high explosive and cluster bombs, supplemented by artillery fire, the battalion would attack up the northern spur of the hill with C Company (Captain Harold J. Kaufman) on the right and D Company (Lieutenant Bartholomew O'Leary) on the left. A Company (Captain Michael Kiley) would protect the rear, using two platoons to maintain a physical link with the assault companies while his weapons platoon prepared a landing zone. C and D Companies would each be deployed with two platoons forward and one back, each platoon moving uphill in two parallel columns. When the assault went in, it was envisaged that the NVA would attempt to escape down the southern slopes of the hill, where their retreat would be blocked by the same Special Forces unit that had established the enemy's presence in the area. Steverson was not one of those who favoured the Airborne's traditional 'straight up the middle' approach in these circumstances and he ordered his company commanders to pull back if they encountered heavy opposition, which would be eliminated by further air strikes. During the afternoon the battalion saddled up and moved to an overnight leaguer area approximately 800 yards north of Hill 875.

On the morning of 19 July, while the F-100s pounded the face of the hill and the sound of their fading jet engines was replaced by the crump of artillery shells bursting on the slopes, the II/503rd's Roman Catholic chaplain, Father Charles Watters, provided Communion for those who wanted it. At 09:00 the companies moved off, climbing slowly but steadily upwards through the trees, underbrush and bamboo while the jets delivered a final strike.

At about 10:30 the two assault companies reached the edge of a bomb- and shell-torn clearing some 400 yards wide, beyond which they could see the crest of the hill. Apart from the cratered earth and tangled trees nothing was visible, but as soon the first man entered the clearing he was shot down, as was a medic who went to his assistance. Suddenly the Americans were struck by a wild firestorm of AK 47 rounds, grenades, and RPG-7 anti-tank rockets. Pinned down, they were unable to locate more than a few of the enemy's bunker fire slits but returned fire as best they could.

Kaufman reported the contact to Steverson, now hovering above the hill in his command helicopter, and was told to continue the advance. O'Leary, breaking into the net, reminded Steverson of his earlier instructions and was sharply rebuked for his trouble. The renewed assault gained only a few yards before it, too, was shot flat. Steverson laid on artillery support, some of which fell short before it began landing on the enemy bunkers. As the shelling lifted, the paratroopers attacked again, but succeeded in covering just 30 yards before they were compelled to seek cover. From 13:00 four F-100s bombed and strafed the summit for an hour. Once more, C and D Companies rose to the attack but now found themselves under fire from behind as well as in front as the enemy made use of his crawl tunnels to reoccupy bunkers the Americans believed they had suppressed.

Meanwhile, at the base of the hill Kiley's A Company was deployed in the shape of an elongated U with two platoons stretching upwards to provide flank protection for C and D Companies while the rest of the company covered the rear. A steady stream of wounded were making their way down the hill and at 13:00 Kiley, worried by the slow progress his weapons platoon was making in clearing sufficient trees for the medevac helicopters to get in, requested an LZ kit, consisting of chainsaws, lumber axes and a quantity of explosive. This arrived shortly after 13:00 and almost immediately the enemy launched attacks in overwhelming strength on the thinly-stretched A Company from the west and south. Those at the foot of the hill stood little or no chance. The wounded, waiting patiently for evacuation near the incomplete LZ, were butchered at once. The two flanking platoons received a frantic radio message from Kiley: 'Get everyone you can down here! I need help – now!' Then there was silence.

Lieutenant Thomas Remington's 2nd Platoon was ambushed as it approached the command post. Several men were killed and others, including Remington, were wounded, although they also took a toll of their attackers. This may have cleared the way for Lieutenant Joseph Sheridan's 3rd Platoon, which reached the command post hollow shortly after, only to find Kiley and five others lying dead. Both officers then concentrated on getting their survivors up the hill and into C and D Companies' positions, where they dug in using knives, helmets and anything to hand.

It is probable that very few of those on the hill's lower slopes would have survived had it not been for the self-sacrificial action of Private First Class Carlos Lozada. Many people considered that Lozada, a 21-year-old from a tough background in the Bronx area of New York, was a no-hoper. Those who knew him best thought otherwise and were proved right when, blazing away with his M60 machine gun at close quarters, he cut a swathe through the attacking North Vietnamese. Then, pausing to clear a jam, he moved slowly backwards up the spur's central trail, firing his weapon from the hip as he covered his comrades' withdrawal. It was inevitable, given the volume of fire directed at him, that he would be killed and at length he fell, shot through the head. His action was to earn him a posthumous Medal of Honor.

Kaufman, the senior officer on the hill, decided to tighten his perimeter, although this meant abandoning most of the hard-won gains. By 15:00 it was apparent that II/503rd was fighting for its life. After nearly five hours' continuous fighting, ammunition was beginning to run short. Every helicopter which attempted to drop in fresh supplies ran into a curtain of automatic fire, until six of them had either been seriously damaged or shot down. Such ammunition as was dropped fell just outside the perimeter and cost casualties to bring in.

Schweiter was now aware of the situation. He gave the trapped battalion priority on air strikes and ordered Lieutenant-Colonel Johnson's IV/503rd to march to its relief, realising that this could not be effected until the following morning. The artillery laid a girdle of bursting shells around Kaufman's two companies, the sweating gunners pausing only when jets howled in to drop high explosive and napalm. Overhead, a C-47 gunship spewed out long jets of tracer at the enemy's probable forming-up points, tearing apart everything they touched. What most survivors recalled of this period of their long nightmare pinned down among the shattered timbers was the sudden appearance of Chaplain Watters wherever he was needed most, always with a little precious water for the sorely wounded and words of comfort and hope for the dying.

Despite the fact that the situation was far from promising, Captain Harold Kaufman, the senior officer present, still believed that it would be possible to complete the capture of the objective with an attack the following morning, and by 18:30 he had managed to assemble his platoon commanders and sergeants at his command post. Shortly after, a Marine Corps pilot entered the Forward Air Controller's radio net, asking whether the latter had any use for two surplus 500-pound bombs. The answer was affirmative and the pilot was told to bomb into a napalm fire burning near the top of the hill. Unfortunately, he seems to have misunderstood the direction his bomb-run was to take and came in over the embattled II/503rd, with results that came close to ending the battle there and then.

His first bomb produced good results. It burst among an NVA platoon preparing to attack, killing an estimated 25 of them. The second bomb, however, sailed into the crowded interior of the perimeter and exploded in C Company's command post. Altogether, it killed 42 Americans, including Kaufman and Watters, and wounded 45 more. Severed limbs, heads, flesh and blood were blown everywhere; a naked torso hung grotesquely in the branches of a tree. Sights such as these, and the sound of prolonged, agonised screams following hard on the bomb's impact, would never leave the minds of those who survived.

Almost immediately, another NVA attack closed in on the perimeter. After fifteen minutes' hard fighting it faded away, leaving the Americans to reorganise themselves amid the carnage. Of the sixteen company officers present, eight were now dead and the rest wounded. Lieutenant O'Leary, blown into unconsciousness by the bomb, regained his senses to discover that he was now in command and turned over D Company to Lieutenant Bryan McDonough, the survivors of A and C Companies being led respectively by Lieutenant Sheridan and Sergeant Peter Krawtzow. A quick headcount revealed that the already under-strength II/503rd had sustained about 80 killed as a result of the fighting and the bomb blast, and that of the numerous wounded 48 were serious cases requiring immediate evacuation, which was clearly impossible. After checking that the perimeter was secure, O'Leary's first task was to re-establish radio links with Major Steverson and the supporting artillery. This involved heaving aside bodies in the shambles that had been Kaufman's orders group until a couple of sets in working order could be found. At O'Leary's urgent request Steverson terminated all further air strikes and then, obviously shaken by what had befallen his battalion, communicated the news to Schweiter. O'Leary also arranged for the artillery to fire a box barrage around the perimeter, adjusting this outwards when a shell landed short, killing one man and wounding four more.

Just why the NVA did not press their advantage and overrun the stricken battalion during the night remains an unanswered question. One possible explanation is that they had absorbed far greater punishment than they allowed for; another is that they now regarded the trapped paratroopers simply as the bait with which to lure an even larger relief force into ambush. Whatever the truth, they contented themselves with isolated probes towards the perimeter and the Americans, anxious to avoid betraying their positions with muzzle flashes, responded with grenades until all sounds of movement had ceased. Throughout the hours of uneasy darkness the cratered hillside and its splintered trees, now still save for the stealthy movements of individual soldiers, remained bathed in the eerie light provided by a Spooky flareship.[4]

Meanwhile Schweiter, as concerned as Steverson for the safety of the trapped battalion, had been making arrangements for its relief. At 19:15, now fully aware of the terrible casualties inflicted by the stray bomb, he stressed the urgency of the situation to Lieutenant-Colonel Johnson of IV/503rd: 'Jim, you've got to get your people to that hill. Get them there as fast as you can.'

Johnson made arrangements for his companies to be concentrated in succession at FSB 16, whence they would advance on Hill 875 indirectly and off the established trails to avoid ambush, and behind a rolling barrage. As the remnants of II/503rd would need resupplying, each rifleman would carry a double load, including no less than 600 rounds of ammunition, ten grenades, one 60mm mortar round and several spare canteens. Leonard's B Company led off at about 09:30 on 20 November, followed at intervals by Muldoon's A Company and Connolly's C Company. Progress was slow but sustained and by 13:00 B Company was within a mile of the hill and moving along its final compass bearing. On the way it had come across a number of abandoned NVA camps, one containing several recently dead enemy soldiers, severed limbs and a pile of bloodied bandages. Ahead, the sound of sniping and enemy mortars confirmed that there were still Americans alive on Hill 875. At 14:20 Leonard made radio contact with O'Leary and told him that he anticipated arriving within two hours. To the latter's men, dispirited by the inability of the casualty evacuation and supply helicopters to penetrate the enemy's storm of fire, their food, water and pain-killing morphine now exhausted, the news re-ignited a spark of hope that, sooner or later, their ordeal would end. At about 16:00 Leonard's point section reached the base of the hill and began climbing warily. The first body they came across was that of a young paratrooper sprawled across his M60 machine gun with spent cases scattered all around; it was Private First Class Carlos Lozada. Beyond were the intermingled bodies of Americans and North Vietnamese, then, higher still, more and more trees shattered by the sustained impact of bombs and shells. Of the enemy there was no immediate sign, but there was a real danger that any further unheralded movement would attract fire from the II/503rd. Halting, the point shouted their arrival and in response several heads appeared among the tangle. The rest of the company came in and took up positions, distributing food and water as they did so, while their medics at once went to work among the wounded.

A Company came in at 21:00 and C Company 90 minutes later. None of the new arrivals had ever seen such destruction and carnage concentrated in so small an area, with bodies and parts of bodies lying everywhere amid the deep piles of splintered timber, broken weapons and discarded equipment. Over everything, too, hung a sickly, all pervading stench combining the odours of decomposition, blood, human waste and high explosive. Together, the sights and smells caused stomachs to rebel.

Even while the relief force was on its way, O'Leary had set some of his men to work clearing a small landing zone in dead ground. Once Leonard's company had arrived Steverson sent in a command group, consisting of his executive officer, Major William Kelly, and two more officers, to take over the remnants of II/503rd. A similar attempt earlier in the day had failed when their helicopter had been driven off by anti-aircraft fire, but on this occasion the craft got in and held its position long enough for its passengers to jump into the primitive LZ.

The fact that IV/503rd had not had to fight their way into the perimeter suggested the enemy's hold on Hill 875 was beginning to relax; the truth, however, was that while the North Vietnamese commander had loosened his grip on II/503rd, almost certainly because of the heavy losses, he had no intention of giving up the hill, which would be used to inflict further casualties on the Americans. His II/174th Regiment would continue to hold the bunkers at the summit for as long as his opponents wished to capture them. The I/174th, which had attacked into the rear of II/503rd's A Company on the first day of the battle, had been withdrawn onto features west of Hill 875 where, with III/174th, it continued to put up such heavy anti-aircraft fire that the American helicopters were forced to keep their distance.

Schweiter was equally determined that, once the II/503rd had been relieved, Hill 875 *would* be captured, even if it was abandoned when the last of the defenders had been eliminated. For both sides, therefore, the struggle had become a fight to the death. Once the sources of the anti-aircraft fire had been identified, these were suppressed by the American artillery. This proved to be the key to the problem, for during the morning of 21 November helicopters were able to drop in flamethrowers and 66mm Light Anti-tank Weapons (LAWs) for use against the NVA bunkers when IV/503rd attacked the hilltop that afternoon, as well as additional ammunition and rubber water containers. At 14:30 more helicopters arrived at the LZ and began lifting out the wounded.

The summit had already been hit by artillery and air strikes for several hours when, at 15:05, the IV/503rd's companies rose to attack. The flamethrowers had to be left behind as they had been dropped without their igniters and were therefore useless; again, as comparatively few men had been trained in the use of the LAW, their issue had to be restricted to officers and NCOs. The fallen tree trunks and tangle of broken branches served as a natural abatis, forcing the paratroopers into vulnerable upright positions as they strove to force their way forward. Worst of all, the volume of fire from the enemy bunkers – machine guns, AK 47s, rockets, mortar rounds and grenades – was undiminished. Nevertheless, the attack was pressed home with grim determination. In some places men came close enough to pitch a grenade into a narrow fireslit and a bunker would fall temporarily silent. Elsewhere, LAWs made no impact whatever on the stout log and earth constructions. At length, after almost three hours' fierce close-quarter fighting the IV/503rd's companies retired within their perimeter; all three had sustained severe losses.

At this point Schweiter decided that he would employ massive firepower to eliminate the defenders before another assault went in. The night remained comparatively quiet but throughout 22 November the bunker complex was battered not only by 173rd Airborne Brigade's own organic 105mm field artillery, but also by the 8-inch, 155mm and 175mm guns and howitzers of heavy batteries made available specifically for the purpose. When the now-balding hilltop was not shuddering under the impact of shells it was being battered by flights of screaming jets with high explosive bombs and drenched with tons of blazing napalm. An additional battalion, Major Long's I/12th Infantry, had been made available to Schweiter by 4th Division and during the afternoon this was airlifted onto the southern slopes of the hill. Simultaneously, the evacuation of wounded continued from a freshly cut LZ below IV/503rd's position.

Schweiter's plan for the 23rd involved further artillery and air preparation followed up with converging attacks on the summit by IV/503rd and I/12th. Among the former, some remembered that at home it was Thanksgiving Day, but the thoughts of many were concentrated on the fact that, once again, they would be going up the tangled, shell-torn slopes into a blizzard of flying steel. A goodly number, of all faiths, took Communion from the battalion's Roman Catholic chaplain, Father Roy Peters.

The NVA, sensing what was taking place, combed the two battalions' forming-up areas with their mortars but caused little damage. In IV/503rd, Leonard, Muldoon and Connolly gave the order for their companies to advance at 11:00. They did so behind a creeping barrage fired by their own 81mm mortars. Behind came the few unwounded survivors of II/503rd. The plan did not require their presence but they had asked to be included and there was general agreement that if anyone had earned the right to be present at the final capture of the hill, they had.

Overhead in his command helicopter, Johnson watched his battalion's attack develop. At first the paratroopers moved warily in short, rapid rushes, using the tactics of fire and movement. Then, the tiny figures below seemed to be moving much faster. Reports from the company commanders indicated that, light mortaring apart, resistance was negligible. Suddenly the figures were among the bunkers, hurling grenades and satchel charges through the fireslits and shooting up communication trenches, moving steadily upwards. There were some casualties, five men being killed by a single mortar round. Leonard, shot clean through the leg by an enemy rifleman, refused assistance and hobbled on.

Twenty-two minutes after crossing the start line, the first of the Sky Soldiers reached the bare, scorched earth of the summit, giving vent to the American paratrooper's triumphant yell of 'Geronimo!!' Minutes later, they were shaking hands with the infantrymen of the I/12th, who had climbed the southern slopes without encountering opposition. The celebration was cut short by the company commanders who, worried by the possibility of a counter-attack, deployed their men into defensive positions. This did not materialise and at length the complete absence of enemy activity confirmed that the NVA had finally accepted defeat on Hill 875.

Johnson landed and, after touring his battalion to congratulate the men on their success, he examined the enemy bunkers. They were marvels of construction and concealment, some having head cover no less than six feet deep, and many had survived the fearful punishment to which they had been subjected. There was evidence that they had been in existence since July. Schweiter dropped in briefly to add his congratulations and then Johnson gave orders that the traditional Thanksgiving Day turkey dinner should be flown out to the hill. It arrived at dusk, being thoroughly enjoyed by most, although a few found they had no appetite.

The cost of Hill 875 had been high. II/503rd's casualties included 87 killed, 130 wounded and three missing; IV/503rd's 28 killed, 123 wounded and four missing. It was never possible to establish the full extent of the NVA's losses. Although several dozen bodies were found in and around the bunkers, it is clear that, with the exception of a small stay-behind party, II/174th Regiment had slipped away, taking with them as many of their dead and wounded as they could carry, in accordance with their usual custom. That a comparatively large number of bodies had to be left behind suggests in itself that the battalion had suffered severely. American patrols on the lower slopes and in the surrounding area discovered perhaps a hundred more bodies. In addition, nine prisoners were taken. The only certainties were that the 174th Regiment as a whole had been severely mauled and that it, together with the other units forming the NVA's 1st Division, were crawling their painful way to the safety of the Cambodian border. Many of the Sky Soldiers wanted to pursue and finish them off, but that would have been politically unacceptable.

General Giap, the North Vietnamese commander-in-chief, had hoped that by committing a large body of regular troops to the Central Highlands he would divert American attention away from the preparations for his Tet Offensive, due to start at the end of January. In the event, the NVA 1st Division sustained crippling casualties and the foray had little bearing on the disastrous outcome of Tet, which underlined the fallacies inherent in some aspects of his philosophy of revolutionary warfare. He was disappointed, too, that operations in the Central Highlands had failed to entrap and destroy a major American unit. On the other hand, while callously indifferent to his own losses, he was well aware of the effect continued casualties were having on American public opinion, and those incurred in the battles around Dak To had been undeniably heavy. Giap, having no timescale in which to produce ultimate victory, could afford any number of battles such as that for Hill 875; conversely, the American public would only tolerate them for as long as it seemed they would produce decisive victory.

Nevertheless, the fight for Hill 875 would rank alongside that for Pork Chop Hill in the annals of the US Army; it had been a very bloody contest of wills in which neither side had sought quarter, and in the end the Americans had prevailed.[5]

Notes

1. During its Second World War incarnation the 503rd Parachute Infantry had been responsible for the capture of Corregidor Island in Manila Bay, making an incredibly dangerous low-altitude drop in a strong cross wind onto tiny, enemy-held drop zones bordered by cliffs that dropped vertically to the sea.

2. Opinion regarding the Montagnard tribesmen varied, although their dislike of the communists was genuine enough. Some American officers thought highly of their fighting abilities, but others saw them as mercenaries who were inclined to disappear when they ran into serious trouble.

3. A Douglas C-47 armed with three multibarrel 7.62mm machine guns capable of a total output of 18,000 rounds per minute, firing from the door and two windows of the port side of the passenger compartment. Because of the great belch of flame whenever the guns fired the aircraft was nicknamed Puff the Magic Dragon.

4. Another version of the C-47 capable of producing intense illumination by dropping one million candlepower flares.

5. Pork Chop Hill, an isolated outpost held by the US 7th Division, was used by the Chinese to test American resolve during the negotiations that ended the Korean War in 1953. After being almost overrun during heavy fighting, the hill was recaptured by an American counter-attack.

Bibliography

Anglesey, The Marquis of, *A History of the British Cavalry, Vol 5: 1914–1919 Egypt, Palestine & Syria*, Leo Cooper, London, 1994.

Archibald, E. H. H., *The Fighting Ship in the Royal Navy 897–1984*, Blandford, Poole, 1984.

Baker, Anthony, *Battle Honours of the British and Commonwealth Armies*, Ian Allan, Shepperton, 1986.

Barthorp, Michael, *The North–West Frontier*, Blandford, Poole, 1982.

Berry, F. Clifton, *Sky Soldiers*, Bantam Books Inc, New York, 1987.

Birdwood, Lieutenant-Colonel Lord, *The Worcestershire Regiment 1922–1950*, Gale & Polden, Aldershot, 1952.

Brown, Captain W. C., *The Diary of a Captain, Campaign of Santiago de Cuba 1898*, Society of the Army of Santiago de Cuba, Richmond, Virginia, 1927.

Buchan, John, *A History of the Great War Vols III & IV*, Thomas Nelson & Sons Ltd, London, 1922.

Cary, A. D. L. and McCance, Stouppe, *Regimental Records of the Royal Welch Fusiliers Vol I 1689–1815*, Forster Groom & Co Ltd, London 1921.

Cosmas, Graham A., *An Army for Empire*, University of Missouri Press, 1971.

Daniell, David Scott, *Regimental History The Royal Hampshire Regiment Vol 3 1918–1954*, Gale & Polden Ltd, Aldershot, 1955.

Darby, William O. and Baumer, William H., *We Led The Way – Darby's Rangers*, Presidio Press, San Rafael, California, 1980.

Dierks, John Cameron, *A Leap to Arms – The Cuban Campaign of 1898*, J. B. Lippincott Company, Philadelphia and New York, 1970.

Duncan, John and Walton, John, *Heroes for Victoria*, Spellmount, Tunbridge Wells, 1991.

Edwardes, Michael, *Battles of the Indian Mutiny*, Batsford, London, 1963.

— , *Red Year – The Indian Rebellion of 1857*, Hamish Hamilton Ltd, London, 1973.

Ellis, Major L. F., et al, *Victory in the West Volume 1 – The Battle of Normandy*, HMSO, London, 1962.

Featherstone, Donald, *Victorian Colonial Warfare – India*, Cassell, London, 1992.

Fletcher, Ian, *Wellington's Regiments – The Men and Their Battles 1808–1815*, Spellmount, London, 1994.

Forbes, Archibald, et al, *Battles of the Nineteenth Century*, Cassell & Company, London, 1896.

Glover, Michael, *That Astonishing Infantry – Three Hundred Years of the History of The Royal Welch Fusiliers*, Leo Cooper, 1989.

Graves, Donald E., *The Battle of Lundy's Lane on the Niagara 1814*, The Nautical & Aviation Publishing Company of America, Baltimore, 1993.

— , *Red Coats & Grey Jackets – The Battle of Chippewa 5 July 1814*, Dundurn Press Ltd, Toronto and Oxford, 1994.

Groves, Lieutenant-Colonel Percy, *Historical Records of the 7th or Royal Regiment of Fusiliers*, Frederick B. Guerin, Guernsey, 1903.

Harris, John, *Without Trace – The Last Voyages of Eight Ships*, Eyre Methuen, London, 1981.

Haythornthwaite, Philip J., *The Napoleonic Source Book*, Arms & Armour Press, London, 1990.

— , *The World War One Source Book*, Arms & Armour Press, London, 1992.

— , *The Armies of Wellington*, Arms & Armour Press, London, 1994.

— , *The Colonial Wars Source Book*, Arms & Armour Press, London, 1995.

Hogg, Ian V., *The Illustrated Encyclopedia of Artillery,* Quarto Publishing plc, London, 1987.

Hogg, Ian V. and Weeks, John, *Military Small Arms of the 20th Century,* Arms & Armour Press, London, 1991.

How, Major J. J., *Hill 112 – Cornerstone of the Normandy Campaign,* William Kimber & Co Ltd, London 1984.

Jones, Virgil Carrington, *Roosevelt's Rough Riders*, Doubleday & Company Inc, New York, 1971.

Knight, C. R. B., *The Historical Records of the Buffs 1704–1814*, The Medici Society, 1935.

Knight, David C., *Shock Troops – The History of Elite Corps and Special Forces,* Bison Books, Greenwich, Connecticut, 1983.

Lloyd, Alan, *The Scorching of Washington – The War of 1812*, David & Charles, Newton Abbot.

McElwee, William, *The Art of War Waterloo to Mons*, Weidenfeld and Nicolson, London, 1974.

McKee, Alexander, *Caen – Anvil of Victory*, Souvenir Press, London, 1964.

Mileham, P. J. R., *Fighting Highlanders! The History of the Argyll & Sutherland Highlanders*, Arms & Armour Press, London, 1993.

Murphy, Edward F., *Dak To – The 173rd Airborne Brigade in South Vietnam's Central Highlands, June–November 1967*, Presidio Press, Novato, California.

Napier, W. F. P., *History of the War in the Peninsula and in the South of France 1807–1814, Vol III*, Constable & Company Ltd, London, 1993.

Nevill, Captain H. L., *North West Frontier*, Tom Donovan Publishing Ltd, London, 1992.

Ott, Major-General David Ewing, *Vietnam Studies – Field Artillery 1954–1973*, Department of the Army, Washington DC, 1975.

Padden, Ian, *U.S. Rangers – From Boot Camp to the Battle Zones*, Bantam, New York, 1985.

Pearse, Colonel Hugh W., *History of the 1st & 2nd Battalions The East Surrey Regiment Vol I 1702–1914*, Spottiswoode, Ballantyne & Co Ltd, London, 1916.

Rogers, Colonel H. C. B., *Napoleon's Army*, Ian Allan, Shepperton, 1974.

— , *Wellington's Army,* Ian Allan, Shepperton, 1979.

Sherer, Captain Moyle, *Recollections of The Peninsula*, Longman, London, 1825.

Steward, T. G., *The Colored Regulars in the United States Army*, Arno Press and The New York Times, New York, 1969.

Swinson, Arthur, *North West Frontier*, Hutchinson, London, 1967.

Turner, John Frayn, *Invasion '44 – The Full Story of D Day*, George G. Harrap, London, 1959.

Watson, Major D. Y., *The First Battalion The Worcestershire Regiment in North West Europe*, Ebenezer Bayliss & Son Ltd, Worcester.

Wilkinson-Latham, R. J., *Discovering Famous Battles – The Peninsular War*, Shire Publications Ltd, Aylesbury, 1973.

Wilmot, Chester, *The Struggle for Europe*, William Collins, London 1954.

Woollright, H. H., *History of the Fifty–Seventh (West Middlesex) Regiment of Foot 1755–1881*, Richard Bentley & Son, London, 1893.

Index